84-8889-2

D1222213

HARVARD ECONOMIC STUDIES

Volume 152

The studies in this series are published under
the direction of the Department of Economics of
Harvard University. The department does not
assume responsibility for the views expressed.

Vertical Integration and Joint Ventures in the Aluminum Industry

John A. Stuckey

HARVARD UNIVERSITY PRESS

Cambridge, Massachusetts, and London, England   1983

Library of Congress Cataloging in Publication Data

Stuckey, John A. (John Alan), 1949–
    Vertical integration and joint ventures in the
aluminum industry.

    (Harvard economic studies; v. 152)
    Includes bibliographical references and index.
    1. Aluminum industry and trade—Consolidation.
2. Joint ventures. I. Title. II. Series.
HD9539.A62S89 1983   338.8'042   82-23294
ISBN 0-674-93490-3

Acknowledgments

Without the contributions of a number of individuals and institutions, this book would never have evolved. The inspiration and knowledge required came from my association with the Industrial Organization group at Harvard University and, in particular, Richard Caves and Michael Porter. I owe a great deal to Richard Caves for his advice and encouragement. Also of great intellectual importance was my exposure to modern ideas in both economics and business management through John Lintner's Business Economics program at Harvard. Exposure to the two rather different views of the world taught by the Business and Economics Schools was stimulating and, in my now biased opinion, brought me closer to the "truth" than either of the pure approaches would have done.

I am also grateful to several Australian institutions for financial and other assistance. The Australian government helped fund my postgraduate study through the Overseas Fellowships in Management program. During the preparation of the book, I was funded and encouraged through a Visiting Fellowship provided by the Australia-Japan Research Center at the Australian National University. Finally, I am indebted to the Department of Economics at the University of Sydney for allocating to me a teaching schedule conducive to research.

Contents

VERTICAL INTEGRATION AND JOINT VENTURES
IN THE ALUMINUM INDUSTRY

1 Introduction

Conventional economics performs poorly as a descriptor and predictor of the way in which the activities undertaken within the economic system are divided among firms and other economic institutions. Economic theory typically specifies an institutional setting at the outset, including firms, markets, consumers, government and so on, and then proceeds to describe how these institutions interact. Given their existence and scope of activities, the economic agents involved pursue their interests in a rational fashion, but theorists pay little attention to if and how the overall system *determines* their existence and scope. In the opinion of R. H. Coase, an economist well known for his criticism of the vacuum concerning institutions that is present in much of modern economics, "we are, in fact, appallingly ignorant about the forces which determine the organization of industry." [1] My aim here is to begin to redress this imbalance.

The contribution of this book is to analyze why the activities constituting the international aluminum industry are divided among firms the way that they are. Coase's statement is this book's raison d'être, and it is consistent with his hope that "what one would expect to learn from a study of industrial organization would be how industry is organized now, and how this differs from what it was in earlier periods; what forces were operative in bringing about this organization of industry, and how these forces have been changing over time; what the effects would be of proposals to change, through legal actions of various kinds, the forms of industrial organization."[2] In the aluminum industry, and in more familiar terms, this amounts to a study of vertical integration, joint ventures, and market-mediated interfirm transactions. Together, these three forms of vertical organization provide the machinery for coordinating the flows of material and information along the vertical stream extending from the bauxite mine down to the final-product user. The main reason for selecting the aluminum industry as a case study is that vertical integration and, more recently, joint ventures play a much greater role in this industry than in most others. The arm's-length markets that conventional economics presumes are noticeably thin.

My main concern is with the question of *why* the industry is organized in the way that it is, but the research also yields normative results, or at least normative implications. I spend less time on these issues, partly because the link between the industry's vertical structure and its performance is forged relatively well in existing studies. Apart from normative results pertaining to the industry's performance this book also has prescriptive implications for the individual firm in the management of its vertical organization.

To illustrate that both firms and public authorities perceive a link between the vertical organization and the economic performance of an industry, consider vertical integration itself. The conventional wisdom within the aluminum industry is that complete integration is almost a necessary condition for good performance of a firm. As the management of the de novo Harvey Aluminum assured stockholders in 1962 as it battled to finance a vertical structure in an industry dominated by vertically integrated giants, "A completely integrated operation is far more important in the aluminum industry than in most other industries. Both for competitive reasons and because of the basic need for reliable sources of supply, it is highly desirable to maintain control over all materials from the raw bauxite to the finished product. This is the company's long-range program . . . As the corporation further integrates, profitability may increase without a corresponding increase in sales volume."[3]

Of course, what is optimal for the individual firm may not be optimal for society. Already the policies of public authorities have had major impacts upon vertical integration patterns within the aluminum industry. For example, in the United States after World War II the U.S. government's Surplus Property Board decided to allocate government-constructed wartime aluminum capacity to two more or less new firms, the Reynolds Metals Company and Kaiser Aluminum and Chemical Corporation. The decision to "create" only two new firms to compete with the prewar monopolist, the Aluminum Company of America (Alcoa), was in large part due to the existence of only two government-owned alumina plants and to the opinion of the board that the new entrants into the industry should be as vertically integrated as Alcoa. The board believed that the new entrants could then effectively compete with Alcoa. In contrast to this decision fostering vertical integration, the Justice Department in 1963 forced Alcoa to dissolve its recent acquisition of the Rome Cable Corporation because it ruled that the acquisition would substantially lessen competition. Similarly, in 1962 the Federal Trade Commission ordered that Reynolds dissolve its downstream merger with a small firm specializing in florists' foil.

Although public authorities have been interested in vertical integration in the aluminum industry for some time, they have recently begun to show signs of interest in the role of joint ventures, not surprising, given the industry's joint venture "explosion." By 1979, approximately 35 percent of the non-Communist world's capacity to produce primary aluminum metal, 66 percent of its capacity to produce bauxite, and 51 percent of its capacity to produce alumina were in jointly owned plants. These proportions are significantly higher than in, say, 1965 when they were 16 percent for primary and 13 percent for both bauxite and alumina. Of the capacity added between 1965 and 1979, over 80 percent of new capacity for bauxite production was in jointly owned plants, about 60 percent of new capacity for alumina, and 45 percent of new capacity for primary. With an eye on these quite dramatic changes, the U.S. Council on Wage and Price Stability concluded, in its report on the industry in 1976, that "the extensive use of joint ventures by the world's major aluminum producers presents the potential of lessening competition

among these firms in a concentrated oligopoly such as aluminum."[4] In the body of the report, the council wrote:

Direct evidence concerning the competition-reducing impact
of partnerships among the six leading firms does not exist.
However, it seems unlikely that the cooperative management
and control of major production facilities would not include
discussion of market conditions and pricing policy in the
major world markets, including the U.S. economy. Similarly
cooperative decision making with respect to expansion of
capacity and changes in production levels for jointly owned
facilities could hardly proceed rationally without examination
and evaluation of each partner's plans for production and
growth in other, independently owned facilities elsewhere in
the world.[5]

The conclusion of this report is typical of the few comments on
joint ventures that are scattered throughout the published research into the industry, all based on extremely limited analysis.
The inference usually is that joint ventures foster collusion and
reduce competition. If this is the case, then aluminum firms are
motivated to form joint ventures to reap the benefits of collusion. Naturally the firms would deny this and argue that the
private benefits accruing from joint ventures are simultaneously
social benefits, because joint ventures facilitate new entry by
reducing the capital requirements and the technological barriers
to entry, because they encourage the achievement of economies
of scale and well-designed plants, and because they allow rationalization of capacity additions over both time and space and
hence help keep prices more stable. Another private benefit,
with more dubious social advantages, is the spreading of an
individual firm's risks. Opinions suggest, therefore, that joint
ventures have both benefits and costs from society's point of
view. One of the aims of Chapter 4 is to assess the net effect of
aluminum's joint ventures on overall economic efficiency.

The increasing use of jointly owned facilities in the aluminum
industry indicates that their net private benefits are positive.
They do, however, present their partners with a number of
management problems. For example, partners must come to
agreement on issues such as rates of production, input and
output transfer prices, the timing and size of capacity expansions, the distribution of earnings, and the financing of losses. At

the planning stage, potential partners must identify each other, decide who should and should not be allowed into the partnership, and then decide on equity shares and the type of joint venture contract to be adopted. There is an unfortunate paucity of public information on how joint ventures in this industry cope with these problems or, indeed, how big the problems actually are. In Chapter 4 I have combined the little that is available with information gleaned from my discussions with aluminum managers. The results may be useful to practicing managers and to academics in business management interested in improving the design and operation of joint ventures.

The aluminum industry is not totally void of markets for intermediate products, though they tend to be thin and are sometimes unreliable. This means that there is no such thing as a free-market world price for bauxite or alumina, the industry's two upstream commodities. These circumstances recently prompted the Australian government to attempt to introduce a radical and controversial policy to control bauxite and alumina exports. Australia is the world's largest national producer of both bauxite and alumina. The great bulk of the country's "upstream" production, that is, production prior to primary aluminum smelting, is exported as either bauxite or alumina, about half via intracorporate transfers and half via third-party sales. Australia's Minister for Trade and Resources, Douglas Anthony, believes that the exports resulting from intracorporate transfers could be leaving the country at "unfair" prices, and that "the problems of establishing a 'fair and reasonable' price for bauxite and alumina is [sic] because of the vertically integrated nature of the aluminium industry." [6] On the other hand, Anthony claims that the exports from arm's-length sales are liable to unattractive terms of sale because "individual Australian companies face buyers who are co-ordinated or who have a high degree of consultation and who, as a result, can and do successfully play one seller off against another." [7]

Anthony's response to this interpretation of the situation has been the introduction of a policy of extensive governmental intervention.

I will determine the parameters within which a company or companies will be authorised to negotiate.

Such parameters might include, as circumstances require it,

pricing provisions, tonnage, duration or other usual provisions of commercial commodity contracts.

If during the negotiations a company wishes to change the parameters it will be necessary to seek an approval to the variation.[8]

It has been suggested that Mr. Anthony's strong language was chosen to assert his own preeminence in future negotiations so that the Australian affiliates of U.S. companies could formally collude to achieve better deals for Australia, under the aegis of the Australian government's authority, and hence to avoid U.S. antitrust laws! Speculation aside, Anthony's concern with bauxite and alumina exports stems from the vertical organizational characteristics of the industry: prices and other terms of transfers within vertically integrated firms, and prices and other terms of arm's-length transactions determined on markets with a small number of traders.

The study of vertical integration, joint ventures, and long-term contracts in the aluminum industry necessitates an international perspective. Nature and history have combined to spatially separate major bauxite deposits from major aluminum consumption points; consequently, upstream vertical integration for most aluminum firms has meant direct investment in foreign countries. International horizontal integration has also been common, though such firms have been motivated more by commercial strategy than by physical necessity. The result is that almost every independently owned aluminum firm has equity in important overseas operations, the only significant exceptions being several Japanese firms. In this study, furthermore, the partners in fifty-seven of the sixty-four joint ventures I examine come from at least two different countries.

An international perspective is not strictly consistent with the traditional approach taken in industrial economics, in which the familiar structure-conduct-performance model of industrial economics has been applied to national markets. In recent years a considerable amount of work has been done in an attempt to make the national market model account for international influences, but many researchers still consider the individual national market or industry the most useful unit for analysis. In contrast, my approach has been to take the worldwide industry as the unit of analysis. Accordingly, I classify aluminum firms on the basis of their status worldwide, with factors such as their home country or their participation in the aluminum industry of a particular country being of secondary importance. I assume that firms have global strategies, and I consider the markets for aluminum products (to the extent that they exist) to be world markets. These one-world assumptions are not completely realistic, as will become quite evident, but they are operationally efficient.

The international approach is not without its problems, however. The limits of my own travels and knowledge of foreign languages have unfortunately restricted the treatment of some firms and countries, and this book is biased toward English-speaking countries, particularly the United States and Australia, and their aluminum firms, a bias partially justified by the dominant role these two countries play across the stages of the industry. This book, for obvious reasons, is also restricted to the non-Communist world; consequently, expressions using *international* or *world* actually refer only to the non-Communist countries (excluding, incidentally, Yugoslavia).

Within the context of the "world" industry, I focus on the individual firm. This focus is consistent with the industrial economics research methodology developed by Edward Mason and his followers in the 1930s but is in some contrast with the bulk of the work on industrial organization done over the last two decades, in which the role of the individual firm is played down. The two approaches differ basically in their emphasis on the effect of differences between individual firms' strategies on an industry's long-run performance. My choice of which approach was best was determined by practicality rather than theory: that this study is restricted to a single industry with relatively few independent firms allows for closer analysis of the different strategies of individual firms. Indeed, much of the analysis of vertical integration and joint-venture behavior relies upon these differences, or often on those of groups of firms having a similar vertical integration or similar joint-venture strategies. More important, though, the structure of the overall industry at any point in time is crucial, because it sets the "rules of game" in which the individual firms play. In terms of the traditional structure-conduct-performance model, vertical integration and joint ventures are seen as elements of either structure or conduct depending upon the time frame in which they are considered.

Several practical matters on my presentation are best mentioned now to avoid confusion. First, throughout this book I frequently use data on plant capacities, sales, ownership structures, and other information concerning both separate firms and individual countries, but to avoid having distracting footnotes on sources and methods in the text, I have included a separate section on data: any of these sorts of data for which a source is not given in the text can be found in Appendix A. Second, I often give tonnages of bauxite, aluminum, and so on. All of these are metric tons, equal to 2,204.6 pounds and approximately 10 percent larger than short tons. Finally, dollar amounts mean 1979 U.S. dollars, unless otherwise indicated.

It is useful at this stage of the book to describe the technology and cost structure of aluminum production, essential information for understanding the vertical organization behavior of aluminum firms. The production of aluminum products involves a series of distinct technical processes that can be thought of as a vertical chain stretching from "upstream" mining to "downstream" finished products. Throughout the industry's large-scale commercial history, available technology and relative prices have been relatively invariant, allowing the chain of processes to be broken down into a set of well recognized and technically independent stages of production, at least "upstream." Throughout, this study conforms with the tradition of describing the stages prior to primary aluminum smelting as "upstream" and the stages after smelting as "downstream," the smelting stage itself falling into both categories. The stages are depicted in Figure 1.1.

Each stage of production usually combines the output of the previous stage with an array of other goods and services to produce a relatively homogeneous output. Bauxite mines produce a mineral called bauxite and alumina refineries produce a semiprocessed mineral called alumina. Primary smelters produce a metal called primary aluminum (or just primary), which includes a variety of alloys and shapes such as sheet ingot, casting

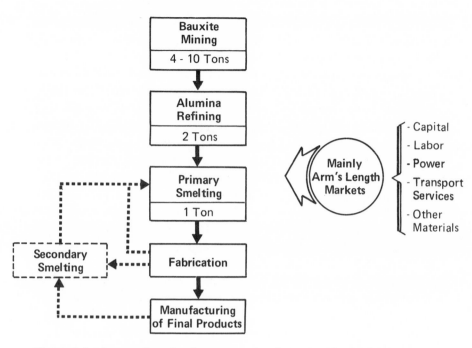

Figure 1.1 Stages of production, conversion factors, and other inputs.

ingot, and extrusion billet. Fabrication mills produce a wide range of products such as plates, tubes, and cables, which are shaped from primary aluminum.

The claim of discrete stages of production is easily established upstream, because many of the world's bauxite mines, alumina refineries, and primary smelters are spatially separated. Alcoa and its subsidiaries provide a good example of this. At least 40 percent of the bauxite that Alcoa has the capacity to produce must be shipped considerable distances to alumina refineries. In turn, less than 20 percent of the output of its alumina refineries could be absorbed by nearby primary smelters. This sort of pattern is typical of the industry. There has been a trend toward building alumina refineries adjacent to bauxite mines in undeveloped areas, but this is a reflection of economies in infrastructure development and increased distances from final markets (largely in the Northern Hemisphere), rather than of the advent of new technical economies resulting from linked operations. The point is that if there are any savings in operating costs resulting from physically linking any of the upstream stages, they must be small, or at least overwhelmed by other factors.

The downstream stages of production are not as clearly defined or so often physically separate. While a number of primary smelters have semifabrication plants (producing rolled and shaped products) attached to them, smelting and fabricating are really quite distinct processes. In the case of Alcoa, only six of its forty fabrication plants are attached to primary smelters. The distinction between semifabrication and final fabrication is not clear-cut, for it varies by product; consequently, I often lump the two stages together.

The first step in the production of finished aluminum products is, of course, the mining of bauxite, an ore occurring naturally in the earth's crust, composed of a mixture of minerals that is at least 30 percent hydrated aluminum oxide ($Al_2O_3 \cdot nH_2O$). It is not a homogeneous ore, differing in composition across deposits and sometimes within the one deposit. Aluminum oxide content is the most important variable, but there are other variables that also have important implications for the technology and costs of processing the ore. Most bauxite is mined by open-pit methods, where mining costs largely depend upon the depth of the overlay. The commercial prospects for a given bauxite deposit thus depend principally upon the aluminum oxide content, the depth of the overlay, the availability of a local economic infrastructure, the distance from major markets, and the "market price" of bauxite.

Given these constraints, the number of known and commercially feasible deposits of bauxite is quite limited. The major deposits are in Jamaica, Surinam, Guyana, Australia, Guinea, and Brazil. Collectively, these six countries account for about 80 percent of bauxite production. Australia, Guinea, and Brazil produce over 50 percent of the total, and it is probable that their share will become even more dominant over the next decade or two. The existing and potential mines in these countries are extremely large and have usually involved the formation of major infrastructures.

The cost structure of bauxite mining varies widely from mine to mine and has varied over time with the shift to distant, undeveloped areas. The evidence suggests that mines in developed areas (such as in France, Greece, and the United States) have fairly flat long-run average costs, when costs are expressed as a function of output rate, and hence do not offer significant economies of scale. This claim is based on the observation that these mines are small on an industry scale, and even though they have been mined for many years (indicating substantial reserves), the scale of their operations has not varied significantly. In these mines the majority of costs are variable in the short to medium run, and the rate of the mining can be varied readily without much affecting average costs. However costs do rise somewhat as a function of cumulative output, owing to depletion of the deposit, especially in underground mines.

Cost structures in Carribbean mines are somewhat different. These mines were developed in the 1950s and early 1960s, principally by the major North American aluminum companies and generally have shown a steady but slow increase in production capacity over the years. There were probably some economies of scale possible in these mines when they were developed, most likely, economies from infrastructure indivisibilities, such as the rail links and port facilities often financed by the mining firms. Judging by the initial capacities of the Caribbean mines, economies of scale were (on average) exhausted when an annual production capacity of roughly one million tons was reached. In the late 1950s and early 1960s, when a number of new companies in the aluminum industry were contemplating bauxite mining, and when the Caribbean was the prime potential site, a new mine of the (assumed) minimum efficient scale of 1 million tons would have added approximately 5 percent to the non-Communist world's capacity. The capital cost for such a plant, including costs for the infrastructure, would have been only about $20 million.[9] In the late 1950s and early 1960s, then, economies of scale and capital costs were not great barriers to entry into bauxite mining.

Today, the fourteen Caribbean mines have an average annual capacity of about 2.3 million tons, which means they are quite large. But their average cost functions are probably fairly flat, at least below capacity, because their capital costs in current dollars are likely to be low, and because the variable costs that are due to revised royalty and production levy schemes in the Caribbean countries have been recently increased substantially. Even before these increases, variable costs in a sample of four Caribbean mines were estimated to be about 60 to 80 percent of total costs.[10] This means that average costs are not heavily dependent upon mining rates. Nor, as yet, are they very sensitive to cumulative output, because most deposits are far from depleted.

Since the mid-1960s most of the new bauxite capacity has been added in large chunks by way of five mines in Australia and one mine in Guinea. By 1979 these mines had an average capacity of 6.6 million tons per year. Four of the mines are adjacent to alumina refineries, but Comalco Limited's Weipa, Queensland, mine and the Boke Consortium mine in Guinea are separate bauxite mines. Comalco's complex cost about $200 million in 1976 dollars, or about $18 for each of the 11 million tons of capacity.[11] The Boke project cost about $400 million in 1976 dollars, including over $100 million for rail and port infrastructure.[12] This amounts to $44 for each of the 9 million tons of targeted capacity. The wide discrepancy in costs per ton is largely explained by the need for a much greater infrastructure in Guinea. The enormous capacities of these two mines were due, at least up to a point, to economies of scale. The Boke project was initially (in 1965) planned to have a capacity to produce 1 million tons, but an independent study undertaken by the World Bank recommended a capacity of at least 6 million tons, because of the lumpy infrastructure. The initial capacity of the Weipa project was 7 million tons, but when the complex had reached that capacity and was in full operation after several years, the complex was expanded to a capacity of 10 million tons. That such magnitudes of production are necessary to achieve minimum efficient scale in bauxite mines in undeveloped areas is further indicated by the new and massive Tombetas project in the Amazon Basin of Brazil. The mine's opening has been delayed because of the depressed state of final markets for aluminum, but the plan is for an initial capacity of 3.35 million tons, with staged expansion to 8 and 10 million tons. The cost for the 3.35 million tons was estimated at $300 million (1978 dollars), but this includes an elaborate infrastructure (rail, port, and town).[13]

The evidence suggests, then, that new bauxite-mining projects in the recent past and in the future lie on an L-shaped long-run average cost curve that dictates a minimum efficient scale of at least 5 million tons and a project cost of about $500 million, in 1979 dollars. A mine of 8 million tons would add about 10 percent to the world's capacity, while a project costing $500 million would have absorbed, say, Alcoa's 1979 consolidated cash flow from operations.

Bauxite is refined into alumina (Al_2O_3) by the Bayer process, in which from 2 to 5 tons of bauxite are needed to produce 1 ton of alumina. All refineries use basically the same process, but it must be modified to suit the different types of ore. As a result, there are basically two different types of alumina refineries. Thus, the bauxite from any given mine can be processed only by some of the refineries, and similarly, each refinery can use ores from only some of the bauxite mines.

Substantial economies of scale exist in alumina refineries. Table 1.1 shows how one source estimated the average costs of production in American refineries in the mid-1960s. Other data, discussed in a study by the Charles River Associates indicate that costs may continue to fall up to a capacity of 500,000 tons, but this is not inconsistent with the observation that in 1979 the average capacity of North America's ten refineries was over 800,000 tons, only two being under 500 million tons. The minimum efficient scale of new alumina plants constructed in other highly developed industrial locations during the 1970s

Table 1.1 Estimated average costs of production in American alumina refineries in the mid-1960s.

Plant capacity (tons)	Index of average costs (equals 100 at 300,000 tons)
55,000	139
90,000	124
150,000	114
300,000	100

Source: United Nations, *Pre-Investment Data for the Aluminum Industry,* Studies in Economics of Industry, 2, ST/CID/9 (New York: United Nations, 1966), p. 6.

appears to have been of a similar magnitude: Aluminium Oxide Stade GmbH, West Germany, 517,000 tons; Mitsui Aluminium Company, Limited, Japan, 400,000 tons; and Nippon Light Metal Company, Limited, Japan, 333,000 tons. The economies of scale in plants located in these highly industrialized countries apparently result from technological or process economies. However, it seems that diseconomies owing to transport costs appear when capacity is about 1.3 million tons, because the biggest plants are about this size, and they are well located on major sea routes to eastern North America (Point Comfort and Corpus Christi, Texas, and Arvida, Quebec).

Bauxite mining accounts for approximately 28 percent, other materials and power 20 percent, labor 13 percent, and capital (depreciation, interest, and maintenance) 33 percent of the costs of running efficient plants at near capacity in the industrial countries.[14] Once a plant is constructed, the elasticity of substitution between the various inputs is virtually zero.

The alumina plants in highly industrial locations represent about 50 percent of the world's current capacity. The other major share, 34 percent, is in ten plants located near the bauxite mines of the principal bauxite-producing countries. These refineries tend to be larger than those in the industrial countries, having an average capacity of over 900,000 tons. Undoubtedly such sizes reflect higher minimum efficient scales resulting from the addition of infrastructure indivisibilities to the basic technological economies in alumina refining. All of the refineries in this group are located near bauxite mines, and the mine (or mines) and the refinery invariably have common ownership. Some of the refineries, generally the smaller ones, have been tacked on to a mining complex after the mine has been operating for years. The relative smallness of these refineries may reflect the consideration that the infrastructure costs were already sunk in the mine before the alumina plant was planned — hence the size of the alumina plant was bounded from below by technological economies alone.

The more important alumina refineries in the bauxite-producing countries were planned and constructed simultaneously with bauxite mines, the two usually having balanced capacities. The costs of the infrastructure in these projects are spread across the two production stages. The projects are also able to cut their total transport costs, a substantial saving, given that the volume of bauxite drops by at least 50 percent after it is refined to alumina. The six alumina plants in this category have an average capacity of 930,000 tons, but if Revere Copper and Brass's unusually small complex in Jamaica (200,000 tons capacity) is omitted, the average lifts to 1.1 million tons. The Revere complex closed in 1975, probably because it was too inefficient.

There are two other categories of alumina refineries. First, a number of small, largely domestic firms have vertically integrated aluminum operations that are generally below minimum efficient scale. These occur in Brazil, India, Greece, Italy, the United Kingdom, Taiwan, and Turkey, and are often of the "national champion" type. Alumina plants in this category number fourteen, but they have an average capacity of only 150,000 tons and account for only 5 percent of world capacity. Second, there are two large alumina refineries that do not fit into any category. One of these is a consortium refinery at Gladstone, Queensland; it is distant from both bauxite supplies and primary smelters, but it is the largest refinery in the world (its capacity is 2.4 million tons, more than 8 percent of the world's capacity). The other one is also a consortium refinery, located on the island of Sardinia, and has a 1-million-ton capacity. It also is separated from bauxite supplies and primary smelters. The anomalous character of these two refineries is explained by factors other than economies of scale and transport costs and will receive considerable attention in later chapters.

The capital costs of alumina refineries vary considerably according to the size of the plant and the infrastructure required, and comparisons are complicated by inflation and fluctuations in exchange rates. Reported costs for several refineries built during the 1970s, expressed in 1976 dollars after adjustments for exchange rates and inflation, are: $62 million for Nippon Light Metal's 333,000-ton plant (Japan, 1970); $60 million for Mitsui's 200,000-ton plant (Japan, 1970); and $250 million for Aluminum Oxide Stade's 600,000-ton plant (West Germany, 1973).[15] The capital costs in 1976 dollars of several of the combined bauxite-alumina projects are: the Gove project, $480 million (Australia, 1970–1975); the Alumina Partners of Jamaica (Alpart) project, $420 million (Jamaica, 1969–1973); and Revere's Jamaica project, $140 million (1970–1975). The Queensland Alumina plant cost $730 million (in 1976 dollars) between 1967–1973 to reach its capacity of 2 million tons.[16]

In summary, alumina refineries experience substantial economies of scale resulting from technological economies and infrastructure costs. Technological economies seem to require that a plant have a minimum efficient scale of 300,000–500,000 tons per year, while infrastructure costs require it to add another 500,000 tons to its capacity. In 1979 an efficient-scale plant of 1 million tons would have added 3 or 4 percent to world capacity and cost over half a billion dollars if the plant were combined with a bauxite mine. The penalty average cost for plants of inefficient scale is significant. Average costs at capacity consist mainly of capital costs and the costs of bauxite, with capital costs overwhelming at low rates of capacity utilization.

Primary aluminum metal is produced from alumina at a ratio of 1 to 1.95 by the Hall-Heroult electrolytic process. Several variations of the process exist, but their economics are very similar. The output of the process is either 99.5 or 99.9 percent pure aluminum metal. Smelters consist of many individual pots arranged in one or more potlines. Individual pots, or entire lines, can be switched on or off to vary the rate of output, but significant fixed costs are associated with doing so.

Economies of scale in smelters are significant, but generally the minimum efficient scale is not as large as the efficient scale (measured in primary equivalent units) in alumina refining, nor are the penalty costs of inefficient size as great. The scale economies come from the technology of the potline. The minimum efficient scale is at least a capacity of 100,000 tons per year, but average costs apparently fall slightly, up to 130,000 tons.[17] This concurs with the observation that the forty-one smelters less than ten years old in 1979 had an average capacity of exactly 100,000 tons, though their capacities varied considerably, from 18,000–200,000 tons. The large number of smelters of less-than-efficient scale reflects the fact that the penalty cost is slight, estimated at less than 5 percent of the minimum long-run average cost for a plant of only half minimum efficient scale.[18] The smaller plants (in Brazil, Venezuela, South Africa, Iran, Korea, and a number of other places) are often designed to serve small local markets. Such plants are probably quite efficient when transport costs are taken into account. Even in the large industrial countries, smelters rarely have a capacity of over 250,000 tons, indicating diseconomies of one type or another (transport costs, power supply, and so forth).

Additions to primary capacity are often made in relatively small amounts by adding a potline to an existing smelter, or even just additional pots to an existing line. This means capacity additions do not have to expand the overall capacity significantly, nor are they necessarily very expensive. In fact, *per ton*, capacity added to existing smelters may be up to 50 percent cheaper than building a new plant, and it is quite common for a new smelter to begin with a single potline and have one or two lines added over a number of years.[19] According to recent announcements of plans for new smelters, capital costs are running at about $2,000 per ton of annual capacity. This means a smelter of 100,000 tons would cost $200 million, but a smelter with one potline might cost only half this amount. Adding capacity to existing smelters seems to cost only about $1,300 per ton.

The average total costs of operating an efficiently sized U.S. smelter at near capacity during the mid-1960s were estimated to consist of the following costs: alumina, 28 percent; electrical power, 14 percent; other material inputs, 16 percent; labor, 10 percent; and capital costs (depreciation and interest), 24 percent.[20] Considerable variations occur according mainly to variations in power costs and alumina costs. It has been estimated recently that 30 to 40 percent of total costs at capacity are effectively fixed, depending on how electrical power costs are classified.[21] The proportion of fixed costs has declined gradually over the years, largely because the relative prices for alumina, power, and labor have tended to rise. Average total costs obviously vary markedly with capacity utilization, but average variable costs are virtually constant up to capacity. This means marginal costs are also constant up to capacity.

The remaining stages of production depicted in Figure 1.1 require only brief mention, because the technologies and cost structures in these stages do not have particularly important implications for vertical integration and joint-venture behavior. The differences between semifabrication, final fabrication, and end-product manufacture are best described diagramatically (see Figure 1.2). Some products require only one fabricating step, while others require two steps. Each of the eleven different fabricating processes shown in the boxes under the fabricated stage are often performed in separate plants, although there are numerous plants that combine more than one process under one roof. The end-product stage involves the manufacture of many products, some consisting largely of aluminum (such as windows, awnings, and mobile homes) and some with small quantities of aluminum (such as motor vehicles and refrigerators). Obviously, the manufacture of most of these aluminum-containing end-

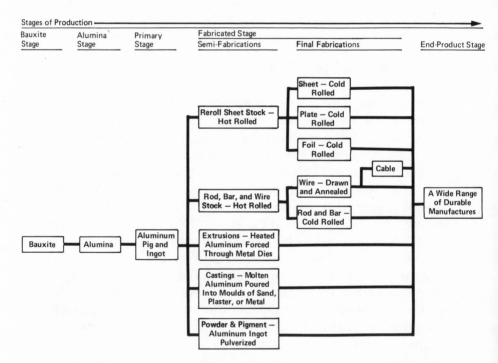

Figure 1.2 Details of the downstream stages of production. Source: M. J. Peck, *Competition in the Aluminum Industry: 1945–1958* (Cambridge, Mass.: Harvard University Press, 1961), p. 6.

products is really a part of another industry, such as the automobile industry or the refrigerator industry.

Semifabrication and fabrication operations are small scale, relative to the earlier stages of production, and their economies of scale are usually not significant. However, there are significant economies in some fabricating operations, particularly in sheet, plate, and foil mills. U.S. plants for these products had average shipments of 48,000 tons each in 1972.[22] More specific evidence that there may be some scale economies in sheet and plate mills comes from the capacities of several U.S. plants: Consolidated Aluminum Corporation's (Conalco's), Jackson, Michigan, plant has a capacity of 150,000 tons; Martin Marietta Corporation's Lewisport, Kentucky, plant, 180,000 tons; and Reynolds's Listerhill, Alabama, and McCook, Illinois, plants have capacities of 375,000 and 295,000 tons, respectively. However, many sheet and plate mills are much smaller, which indicates that average costs in small plants are not prohibitive. The capital costs of fabricating plants vary according to the plant's size, and while a large sheet and plate mill might have cost $100 million in 1979, most other fabrication plants cost between $5 million and $20 million.

The average costs of most fabricating plants are largely variable. According to the 1972 census of manufactures, 75 percent of the value of shipments from sheet, plate, and foil mills (Standard Industrial Classification [SIC] number 3353) was absorbed by the cost of materials, and an additional 14 percent by payroll costs; capital costs therefore absorbed only 11 percent. For extruded aluminum products (SIC 3354), materials absorbed 61 percent, and labor 22 percent, of the value of shipments, and for rolled and drawn aluminum products (SIC 3355), 79 percent and 14 percent.

Production of secondary (or recycled) aluminum involves remelting old and new scrap, often with the addition of small amounts of other metals, and formation of secondary ingots. About 70 percent of the total scrap is new, coming from the clippings and so on produced in the course of fabricating primary aluminum products. On average, 20 percent of all aluminum consumed is secondary aluminum, a close but generally inferior substitute for primary aluminum. The process in which secondary aluminum is reduced is relatively simple and well known; its economies of scale are of minor importance, and its capital costs are low by the aluminum industry's standards. The United States, West Germany, Japan, Italy, and the United Kingdom collectively are responsible for producing over 80 percent of the world's secondary aluminum. In 1976 these countries had, respectively, 128, 27, 28, 21, and 36 secondary reduction plants, producing, on average, 10,200; 11,900; 10,600; 9,800; and 5,300 tons.

The processes used in the various stages of production have undergone very few fundamental changes since the commercialization of the industry in the late nineteenth century, and Figures 1.1 and 1.2 depict essentially the same processes in use then. Within each stage, particularly downstream, there have been major technological advances, and improved machines, automation, new alloys, welding techniques, and new end-product applications have all been developed. While the processes have remained constant, so too has the practice of most of the companies to integrate vertically across the processes. This has been particularly the case in the upstream stages of production.

2 Upstream Vertical Integration

The integration of bauxite mining, alumina refining, and primary smelting into one firm has always been the predominant form of vertical organization in the upstream aluminum industry. The aim of this chapter is to explain why the industry is organized in this vertical way, rather than in a system of intermediate-product markets and interfirm transactions. I do not attempt to develop an all-embracing theory or model to explain vertical integration, because the complexity and multiplicity of forces favoring or opposing alternative forms of internal organization for a given firm make a general theory of vertical integration intractable. Instead, I resort to a partial approach in which each of the most important explanations for vertical integration is examined separately and an effort is made to determine the magnitude of that explanation's causal role.

For the most part, this chapter assumes two types of vertical organization: vertical integration with intrafirm transfers, and intermediate-product spot-markets with arm's-length interfirm transactions. A firm is defined as being vertically integrated upstream when it has ownership interests, direct or indirect, in the facilities of any two or all three upstream stages of production. This means that other fairly permanent vertical relationships, such as long-term contracts, are of the second type of vertical organization. On the other hand, a firm having a 5 percent interest in a joint venture operating at another stage of production is classified as being of the first type.

These distinctions are obviously somewhat arbitrary, but they serve only as a way to organize the available quantitative data and not as theoretical distinctions. Theoretically, I regard vertical integration, long-term contracts, and so on as alternative means of coordinating the flows of commodities and information between the various stages of production, alternatives that fall on a continuum between vertical integration via a wholly owned plant (the standard concept of vertical integration) at one end and by spot-market purchases or sales (the transaction mechanism traditionally presumed in economics) at the other. When I ignore in this chapter intermediate forms of vertical organization, such as long-term contracts and joint ventures, I do not mean that they are insignificantly different from integration and spot markets; indeed, I devote separate chapters to discuss how contracts and joint ventures do differ.

Measurement and Data

Empirical research into vertical integration generally has been severely limited because of the problems involved in making quantitative measurements of the phenomenon. Fortunately, in the case of the upstream aluminum industry, a relatively good measurement is possible. The first step is to define the intermediate markets that integration supplants, or alternatively, to identify the stages of production; as I have pointed out, mining, refining, and smelting are well defined and distinct stages of aluminum production. The next step is to find some variable that measures the size or extent of a firm's involvement in each stage of production. The measure, including the units of measurement, must be applicable to all production stages, to different firms, and to different periods of time. These are demanding criteria. In the aluminum industry, the relevant measure is annual production capacity for bauxite, alumina, and primary, denominated in (metric) tons of primary aluminum equivalent.

This measure is justified on the following grounds: first, because the upstream technologies are very similar from firm to firm and do not change much over time, and because the tech-

nologies combine the factors of production in almost fixed proportions, the capacity of a plant is a meaningful and comparable
measure of the plant's economic size over time. Significant
changes in a plant's capacity take a year or more to implement, so
they are a medium- to long-run decision and signal throughout
the industry the firm's intentions. Capacity figures are not subject to biases resulting from short-term business conditions, as
are figures for sales, inventories, and so forth. By adjusting the
capacities of bauxite mines and alumina refineries to reflect the
aluminum content of these commodites, capacities across the
stages are then in equivalent units. Finally, it is the industry's
practice to publish information on plant capacities, particularly
of alumina and primary plants, and hence the data are available.

Not surprisingly, there are also some problems with using
capacity data. Estimated capacities for bauxite mines are only
approximations, and the capacity of some mines can be altered
quite easily. However, capacity figures for the large new mines in
remote areas are more reliable, because they are often set by the
capacity of lumpy pieces of capital such as rail links or loading
facilities at a port. Another difficulty is that public information
on the capacity of bauxite mines is not easy to find. A bigger
problem, though, is the derivation of factors to convert figures
on bauxite to their primary aluminum equivalents. The aluminum content of bauxite varies markedly across mines and, over
time, even within a single mine. Very limited public information
is available to overcome this problem, and the conversion factors
used here can only be described as best guesses in some cases.
This is particularly true of some of the older and smaller mines,
but fortunately, quite reliable conversion factors are available
for the large, new mines.

Another problem with using capacities to measure vertical
integration is that some bauxite and alumina is diverted from the
straight vertical chain. In aggregate, approximately 7 percent of
bauxite production is diverted to other industries, particularly
abrasives and refractories, while approximately 8 percent of
alumina production is for nonmetallurgical uses. I have been
able to deduct some of these leakages from capacity figures by
communicating directly with firms supplying these outside industries, but the capacity data for bauxite and alumina remain

slightly overstated. The final problem with the capacity data is that additions to capacity are very lumpy, which makes capacity time-series rather steplike and can make comparisons of the existing capacities of two or more adjacent plans unreliable. It would be preferable to compare potential capacities (the sum of existing, planned, and under-construction capacities), as potential capacity is most relevant for assessing firms' vertical strategies.

Subject to these limitations, I collected data giving the annual capacity at the beginning of each year from 1955 through 1979 for each significant bauxite mine, alumina refinery, and primary smelter in the non-Communist world. The sources and methods of data collection are presented in Appendix A, but the major sources were the companies' annual reports and industry periodicals. The capacity of each plant was then distributed across aluminum firms, and aggregate capacities for each firm over production stages and years were computed. This was not as clear-cut as it might first appear, owing to the large number of joint-venture plants with complicated ownership structures. The capacity of a wholly owned plant went in total to the owning firm (or to the parent, in the case of subsidiaries), while the capacity of a jointly owned plant was distributed across its owners by a method that attempted to account for intraindustry management and control. The method is detailed in Appendix A, but the basic principles should be spelled out here, because they have major implications for the meaning of the final numbers I have used.

First, I made a list of "basic aluminum firms," which included only those with widely held equities or those owned by interests not otherwise significantly involved in the aluminum industry. The list obviously includes firms like Alcoa, Reynolds, Kaiser, and so on, but it does not, for example, include firms like Volta Aluminium Company, Limited. Kaiser owns 90 percent, and Reynolds, 10 percent, of Volta, and these two firms are "basic aluminum firms" in their own right. However, several important joint-venture firms owned by other aluminum firms *are* treated as "basic aluminum firms." The main ones are Comalco, British Aluminium Company Limited, and Alumax and are so treated because they are managed independently and have their own corporate identities.

I next distributed plant capacities across the firms on the list. The capacities of plants owned jointly by firms on the list were distributed according to how many shares they owned. The capacities of plants owned jointly by firms on the list and by firms from outside the industry were distributed only to the listed firms, in proportion to the listed firms' equity ratios. The capacities of plants owned jointly by one listed firm and by one or more outside firms were distributed totally to the listed firm, unless that firm's share was small and it gave no indication of its management input. The reader familiar with some of the intricate interconnections of ownership in the industry will realize that these principles do not cover all possibilities (although Appendix A attempts to).

The logic of these rules for distributing capacity was based on the use to which the data would be put. The theory developed below suggests that firms involved operationally in the upstream aluminum industry have strong incentives to avoid reliance upon arm's-length markets, and, by definition, such avoidance can be achieved by ownership of plants in all stages of production. Intermediate-product exchanges then become intracorporate transfers, and the market is circumvented. The basic aluminum firms on the list are the firms that are involved operationally in upstream aluminum, and the capacity-distribution rules calculate for each of these firms its effective in-house capacity. Nonbasic firms are excluded because they are not involved in the industry's operations and management but rather are involved for such purposes as simple portfolio investment, in the case of organizations like life insurance offices and investment houses, or for protecting national sovereignty, in the case of state-owned firms.

There could well be some debate over the implementation of these principles in particular cases, or even over the principles themselves, but because the methods were devised to allow a neat and meaningful summarization of the large volume of data, the results are useful to this extent. In any case, the analysis of vertical integration does not rely upon the numbers alone, because I often analyze the details of individual plants and firms and scrutinize the differences between wholly owned plants and joint-venture plants.

For each basic aluminum firm, then, there are twenty-five observations from 1955 through 1979 on each of the following: total controlled annual bauxite capacity in primary equivalent tons at the beginning of the year; total controlled annual alumina capacity in units of primary equivalent tons at the beginning of the year; and, total controlled annual primary capacity in tons at the beginning of the year.

Integration and the Life-Cycle Theory

The life-cycle theory of vertical integration was suggested by George Stigler in 1951, when he used Adam Smith's famous theorem that the division of labor is limited by the extent of the market to help predict the pattern of vertical integration within an industry over a long period of time.[1] Examining this theory is appropriate because it is the only theory of vertical integration that offers a direct explanation of historical trends, rather than concentrating upon an equilibrium at one point in time. While it proves to be an inadequate theory in the case of the aluminum industry, over its ninety years of large-scale production, testing it has the benefit of providing an empirical picture of the absolute levels of vertical integration across the production stages and their changes over time. One can then look for better explanations of the levels and trends.

The idea of the theory is that when the industry's market is large, numerous firms will specialize in each stage of production so as to achieve economies of specialization, but when the market is small (during the industry's infancy and old age) the fewer firms will have to be integrated through the stages because volume is too low and future prospects too uncertain or too bleak to support specialists.

Young industries are often strangers to the established economic system. They require new kinds or qualities of materials [such as bauxite or alumina] and hence make their own; they must overcome technical problems in the use of their products and cannot wait for potential users to overcome them [such as rolling foil and welding]; they must persuade customers to abandon other commodities and find no specialized merchants to undertake this task. These young industries must design their specialized equipment and often manufacture it . . . When the industry has attained a *certain size and prospects,* many of these tasks are sufficiently important to be turned over to specialists. It becomes profitable for other firms to supply equipment and raw materials, [and] to undertake the marketing of the product . . . And, finally, when the industry begins to decline, these subsidiary, auxiliary, and complementary industries begin also to decline, and eventually the surviving firms must begin to reappropriate functions

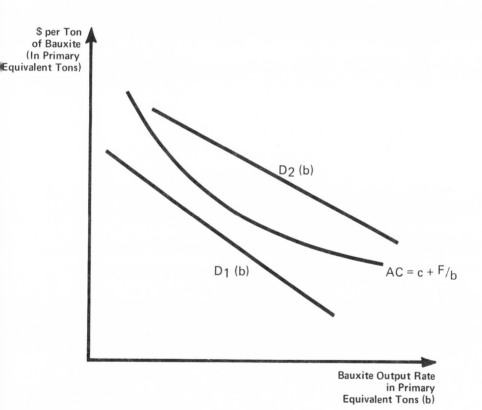

Figure 2.1   An illustration of the conditions under which the life-cycle theory of integration occurs. When derived demand is $D_1(b)$, independent miners cannot operate profitably (unless they are subsidized by the downstream producer).

which are no longer carried on at a sufficient rate to support independent firms [emphasis mine].[2]

The theory can be stated formally using the following simple and specific model, illustrated graphically in Figure 2.1. Let there be two stages of production, bauxite mining and aluminum production (embracing refining, smelting, and fabrication all "under one roof"). Bauxite mining has a constant marginal cost of c and a fixed cost of F, and the quantity of bauxite mined and sold is denoted by b. There is one downstream producer that, when maximizing profit subject to its production function, has an inverse derived demand function for bauxite denoted by $D(b)$. The existence of fixed costs in mining means that the average cost of bauxite production, $c + F / b$, is a declining function of b.

Stigler's life-cycle theory is based on changes over time in the relationship between $D(b)$ and $c + F/b$. In the early years of the industry, the final demand that the downstream producer confronts is small, and hence its $D(b)$ curve is close to the origin, say, $D_1(b)$ in Figure 2.1. $D_1(b)$ lies below $c + F / b$ for all b, and hence an independent miner's profits, given by

$$\Pi(b) = b \, D_1(b) - cb - F,$$

are negative no matter what the level of output. Under these circumstances bauxite will not be produced by specialist miners (unless they are subsidized in some way). But it is possible that it is worthwhile for the downstream producer to integrate backward into bauxite: the condition is that the integrated firm's net benefits be positive. The integrated firm's net benefits on bauxite are equal to the surplus under $D_1(b)$, namely

$$\text{Net Benefits} = \int_0^b D_1(b)db - cb - F$$

$$= \left[\int_0^b D_1(b)db - b \, D_1(b) \right] + [b \, D_1(b) - cb - F]$$

$$= \left[\int_0^b D_1(b)db - b \, D_1(b) \right] + \Pi(b).$$

So long as $D_1'(b) > -\infty$, a likely condition, the first term is positive. Even though $\Pi(b)$ is negative, it is therefore possible that net benefits are positive, and if so, the downstream producer will integrate backward into mining. The model as presented here assumes certainty, but intuitively it appears that the addition of uncertainty and risk aversion would (if anything) strengthen the results.

According to Stigler, growth in the industry's final demand pulls the $D(b)$ curve along with it, say, to $D_2(b)$, and then it is profitable for specialist miners to arise. If there are no other reasons for integration, the integrated producer might just as well dispose of its mines and rely upon independents. Disintegration occurs so long as $D(b)$ continues to shift out, although eventually, if the industry is replaced by other industries and the derived demand curve shifts back toward $D_1(b)$, the downstream firm will then be forced to reintegrate. Combining the era of industry growth with the era of decline, we end up with a negative relationship between absolute market-size and degree of integration, or a U-shaped relationship between time and degree of integration.

These relationships are testable empirically, but they are based on too simplistic a version of the life-cycle theory. Several important complications need to be recognized. One is that Stigler implicitly assumes that the averge cost curve for bauxite mining, $c + F / b$, is stable over time. It is obvious in Figure 2.1 that if $c + F / b$ also shifts around while $D(b)$ shifts around, the profitability of specialist mining depends upon the relationship between the two curves at any point in time. Then trends in the degree of vertical integration depend upon trends in both demand and costs. A convenient way of simultaneously capturing demand and cost trends in one variable is to consider the ratio of the absolute size of the market to the minimum efficient scale (MES) of operation in bauxite mining. The absolute size of the market tracks the movements in the industry's $D(b)$ curve, while the MES of bauxite mining captures the horizontal movements in the typical miner's $c + F / b$ curve. An increase in the ratio probably means that the $D(b)$ curve is moving out faster than the $c + F / b$ curve, and, according to the life-cycle theory, this should be associated with a decline in the degree of integration. Conversely, a decline in the ratio should be associated with an increase in integration. Of course this negative relationship between the ratio and integration is very much long run in nature. In an industry like aluminum where there is more than one input and more than two stages of production, the theory predicts that this negative relationship will exist for the level of integration between one stage of production and every other adjacent stage that has a separable technology and its own (declining) long-run average cost function.

Another complication that needs to be recognized is that the disintegration process in a growing industry is likely to be influenced by the number of firms involved in the industry. Stigler's analysis glosses over the likelihood that an industry with declining average cost curves will be highly concentrated, at least in the early years and in some of the stages of production. Consider in more detail, then, an industry that has just reached the point where its total market is just large enough to support an independent input-plant. Before this point there were presumably several integrated producers, though probably not very many. Now the *sum* of their final-product outputs are large enough so that the *sum* of their requirements for the input product can allow an independent producer of the input product to achieve normal profits. Stigler argues that the several integrated producers will hand over the input stage of production to an independent. They will not be concerned about the new firm's monopoly status, because "it will be confronted by elastic demands: it cannot charge a price for the process higher than the average cost of the process to the firms which are abandoning it. With the continued expansion of the industry, the number of firms supplying process Y_1 [the input stage] will increase, so that the new industry becomes competitive." [3] This is certainly a story of the "lived happily ever after" variety, but even allowing the considerable number of years that Stigler probably had in mind for the transition to occur, one sees that he ignores several factors that may make the going integrated firms disinclined to hand over the input process to a new entrant-monopolist. I will not dwell on these factors here, but keep in mind the following points.

First, a new entrant-monopolist is not the only means of achieving low-cost input production: one of the going firms could take over the input stage on behalf of the industry, or the going firms could form a joint-venture plant. Second, whichever of these means is adopted, a small-numbers exchange relationship is going to exist until the industry has expanded quite substantially beyond the point where only a single plant can achieve profits in the input process. Third, if the technology of the input process is such that average costs fall with the cumulative volume (the learning curve) as well as with the output rate, or if the technology is likely to advance over time, or both, the ability of the previously integrated firms to restrain the monopolistic tendencies of the new entrant will weaken over time.

Following Stigler, I ignore these complications and compare the integration of the major stages of production in the aluminum industry over time with the trends predicted by the theory. The comparison is organized both by time period and pairs of vertically adjacent stages of production. It is worth noting that vertical integration motivated by the mechanism of Stigler's model is generally beneficial from society's point of view. Integration occurs only if the integrated producer's net benefits are positive, and in most circumstances this means that society as well as the producer is better off with the industry than without it.[4]

Integration from 1888 to the Mid-1950s

An ideal test of the life-cycle theory would involve the construction of vertical-integration indices over the life of the industry. This has been possible only for the last several decades, but the history of the industry before World War II indicates that the few significant firms operating during that fifty- or sixty-year period behaved quite consistently with the life-cycle theory. That is, they became highly vertically integrated in virtually every stage of aluminum production. Copious evidence supporting this claim was presented by Donald Wallace in his famous study of the international aluminum industry from 1888, when the Hall-Heroult process was invented, through 1935.[5] In the first decade or so after 1888, the infant aluminum industry was not highly integrated vertically; a number of small producers of bauxite, alumina, and fabricated products supported the few primary-aluminum producers. This structure did not last long in the United States, however, and not too much longer in Europe.

Wallace explained that in the United States, attempts were first made by Alcoa to interest foundries, rolling mills, and wire-drawing plants in the use of aluminum, but inertia and ignorance proved more powerful than curiosity. Moreover, as subsequent experience demonstrated, the working of aluminum required methods different from those developed for the casting and rolling of brass, copper, and steel. A few years were sufficient to persuade Alcoa that the campaign of demonstration and education must include fabrication.

Forward integration by Alcoa was soon followed by vertical integration of almost every significant aspect of the aluminum business. Wallace recorded that the ore produced at Alcoa's mines was converted into aluminum oxide for its reduction furnaces. Most of the electricity fed into the reduction cells was generated by the company, which also owned a substantial part of the rights to the waterpower that turned its dynamos. Carbon anodes and furnace linings were manufactured internally. A substantial portion of the aluminum run into ingots at the reduction plants was later rolled into sheets or rods; fabricated into tubes, cooking utensils, or other manufactured shapes or articles; or pulled out in the form of wire. Vertical integration by the European producers was similarly pervasive.

> Right from the beginning, the oldest established groups (Pechiney or Alusuisse in Europe, Alcoa in the USA) have been obliged to make direct provision for their supplies of bauxite and electrical energy necessary for their manufacturing activities . . . The number of producers was very small and, aluminum being a novelty, they were obliged from the beginning to develop every element in the basis of their production . . . This led to the early prospecting activity and purchases of open pits in the South of France. Alongside the companies which were later to become Groupe Pechiney now Pechiney Ugine Kuhlmann [PUK] purchases of French deposits were also made by Alusuisse, Alcoa and subsequently the British.[6]

The major aluminum producers continued to be highly integrated vertically during the remaining period of Wallace's study (up to 1935). While the world-market growth rate declined from the compound annual rate of 25 percent from 1895 through

1910 to around 10 percent between 1910 and 1925, the producers continued to expand into all facets of the business. Wallace did not indicate whether or not the degree of vertical integration rose or fell, just that it was high throughout. In any case, the history of the industry to this point is certainly consistent with the life-cycle theory.

One might expect that during the 1930s the aluminum industry would have passed the hump in its life cycle, and that the divestiture of most vertically connected stages of production would have begun, but during the thirty years between say, 1925 and 1955, developments in the aluminum industry were influenced more by exogenous factors (the Great Depression, World War II, the rise of state aluminum producers, and interference by antitrust authorities) and by the anticompetitive behavior of the incumbent firms (national monopolies and international cartels) than by the rational, competitive economic forces presumed to predominate in Stigler's model. There are insufficient data on vertical integration during these years to make any sort of assessment of trends, and in any case, the organization of the industry went through too many major disturbances for any kind of sequence of equilibrium states to have emerged. There is no point, therefore, in attempting to compare vertical-integration behavior in this period with the predictions of the life-cycle model. The best approach to overcome this discontinuity of information on the industry's life cycle is to take the level of vertical integration in the industry in, say, 1955 as if the industry were instantly created in that form, and then to trace the changes in vertical-integration patterns since then.

Before proceeding, some justification for choosing 1955 as the "year of creation" is necessary. By 1955 the aluminum companies of the major producing countries had experienced their first sequence of several years of relatively free and unfettered operation for over twenty years. In North America, Kaiser and Reynolds had been "created" in 1945, Alcoa and Alcan were finally severed completely in 1950, the Korean War price controls and purchase guarantees were terminated in 1955, and the twenty-year-old monopolization case of *United States* v. *Aluminum Company of America* was dismissed in 1957.[7] In Japan, the occupying allies permitted revival of primary aluminum production in

1948, the boom caused by Korean War demands ended abruptly in 1951, and in 1952, 50 percent of the nation's major producer, Nippon Light Metal, came to be owned by Alcan. In West Germany, the state-owned Vereinigte Aluminium-Werke (VAW) was given free rein by the Allies in 1951, while the industries of the other important producing countries in Europe were operating smoothly by 1955. Furthermore, since the mid-1950s, the aluminum industry has once again become international, in the sense that the producers are cognizant of their international setting and act accordingly. This was not so much the case in the post–World War II years, as shown by Merton Peck's conclusion: "for the years 1946 to 1957, market behavior in the American aluminum industry can be examined with little reference to developments abroad." [8] So, by about 1955 aluminum firms may not have been in positions of entirely their own choosing, but they were largely free to adopt strategies, including vertical-integration strategies, as they wished.

Recent Upstream Integration: 1955–1979

How integrated were the producers in 1955? What have been the changes since then? Have the changes been consistent with the life-cycle theory? To answer the first two questions, two indices of vertical integration were calculated for each pair of adjacent stages, bauxite-alumina and alumina-primary. The two indices for bauxite-alumina integration are denoted by AVIB (alumina vertically integrated with bauxite) and BVIA (bauxite vertically integrated with alumina). To avoid confusion, the precise definition of AVIB is as follows, where t denotes the year and i and j denote individual basic aluminum firms (as defined previously).

$$\text{AVIB}_t = \left[\left(\sum_i AC_{it} + \sum_j BC_{jt} \right) \Big/ \left(\sum_i AC_{it} + \sum_j AC_{jt} \right) \right] \cdot 100$$

where

$AC_{i\,or\,j,\,t}$ = the alumina capacity in primary equivalent tons of firm i or j in year t;

BC_{jt} = the bauxite capacity in primary equivalent tons of firm j in year t;

i = the summation index for firms with $BC \geqslant AC$ in year t;

j = the summation index for firms with $AC > BC$ in year t.

AVIB is a percentage, and it measures the percentage of world alumina capacity that could *potentially* be supplied by *intracorporate* transfers of bauxite.

For example, AVIB in 1979 is calculated at 79 percent, which means that if all bauxite mines and alumina refineries were operated at equivalent rates, and if all possible intracorporate bauxite transfers were affected, then only 21 percent of bauxite transfers to alumina refineries would have been at arm's length. PVIA (primary vertically integrated with alumina) is the exact analogy and measures the percentage of the world's primary capacity that could potentially be supplied by intracorporate transfers of alumina.

Both AVIB and PVIA look at the downstream side of their respective commodity markets; the analogous variables on the upstream side are denoted by BVIA (bauxite vertically integrated with alumina) and AVIP (alumina vertically integrated with primary), respectively. BVIA measures the percentage of potential bauxite output that could be absorbed via intracorporate transfers to alumina refineries, while AVIP measures the percentage of potential alumina output that could be absorbed via intracorporate transfers to primary aluminum smelters. To grasp the differences, consider AVIB and BVIA. AVIB is always greater than BVIA, because the world's bauxite capacity was greater than the world's alumina capacity between 1955 and 1979. Furthermore, the extent of "excess" bauxite capacity has increased slightly over time, and its distribution among firms has also varied somewhat. These factors explain why AVIB and BVIA are not perfectly correlated. The main reason BVIA is less than AVIB is that approximately 7 percent of bauxite production goes to other industries (which is consistent with the average annual differential between AVIB and BVIA of 10 percent, the remaining 3 percent being true excess capacity, measurement error, or both). For measurement of the absolute level of inte-

gration within the *aluminum* industry, AVIB is therefore the
relevant statistic (and PVIA for primary-alumina integration).
The analysis concentrates accordingly on AVIB and PVIA.

Time series for the four vertical integration statistics from
1955 through 1979 are plotted as three-year moving averages in
Figure 2.2. The moving averages flatten out the bumps in the
raw series caused by the start-up of large plants; three-year
averages are used because the typical mine or plant takes about
three years to construct. Looking first at integration across the
alumina market, the data clearly indicate that integration has
been extremely high throughout the twenty-five year period,
with PVIA averaging over 90 percent. This means that if each

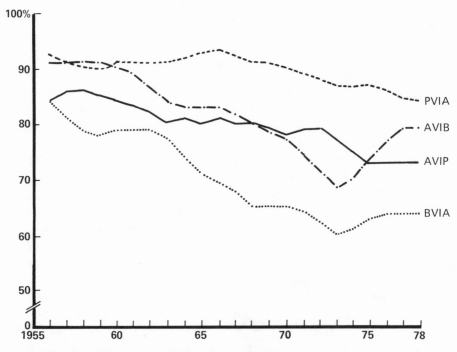

Figure 2.2 Upstream vertical-integration trends—three-year centered moving averages, 1956–1978 (in percentages). *Source:* Data described in Appendix A. See J. A. Stuckey, "Vertical Integration and Joint Ventures in the International Aluminum Industry" (Ph.D. diss., Harvard University, 1981), p. 56, for details.

producer of primary aluminum exploited all available in-house sources of alumina, only 10 percent of alumina transfers into smelters would be at arm's length. Remember, though, that these data are based on potential, not actual, transfers although, to the extent that information on actual transfers is available, not much difference between the two is apparent. For example, my estimate of PVIA for 1972 is 88 percent, while a totally independent and authoritative source, M. R. Rayner, has estimated from actual 1972 transfers that about 90 percent of the installed smelter capacity received alumina supplies from integrated alumina production sources.[9]

The plot of PVIA in Figure 2.2 shows an irregular but slight downward trend. Integration over the five years of 1955 through 1959 averaged 92 percent, while the most recent five-year period averaged 85 percent. Admittedly, this difference could be due to measurement biases, but assuming they do not exist, it can be quite significant in terms of the life-cycle theory. The alternate-series AVIP has a more distinct downward trend, but its greater slope is due to the relative increase in "excess" alumina capacity.

The plot of the three-year moving average of the AVIB series indicates that integration between bauxite and alumina has also been high throughout the twenty-five-year period, averaging 81 percent for potential transfers. Actual transfers were not markedly different, at least for 1972: Rayner estimated that approximately 75 percent of the world's alumina capacity was supplied in 1972 with bauxite from integrated bauxite-supply sources, while my estimate for potential transfers is 68 percent.

The AVIB series shows a distinct downward trend until 1973, when it moves upward. This irregular behavior is explained partially by the sudden nationalization of Alcan's wholly owned Demerara Bauxite Company in Guyana in 1972, which caused the noticeable 1972–1974 trough in AVIB. But the reversal in the trend indicates a systematic change during the early 1970s in some firms' attitudes toward long-term bauxite contracts. Chapter 3 explores this subject in depth and comes to the conclusion that the rapid downward trend in AVIB during the 1960s was due to special circumstances occurring at the time, and that the recent upward trend indicates a move by firms to reestablish preferred bauxite-alumina integration strategies. Future bauxite-alumina integration levels will in all likelihood have no significant long-term trend one way or the other. Here, it is best to assume that AVIB has had a slight downward trend, similar to that of PVIA.

It seems impossible to test rigorously whether or not the observed trends in PVIA and AVIB are consistent with the life-cycle theory. Recall that the theory predicts that the degree of integration between two vertically connected stages of production depends upon the ratios of the size of the market to the minimum efficient scale of operation in the two stages. The problem with estimating these ratios is to define, and then to measure, the appropriate minimum efficient scales. For example, the minimum efficient scale of a smelter varies with time, countries, and technologies, and it varies according to which costs it includes (operating, nonoperating, transport, tariffs, and so forth).

There are, however, some data that shed light on how the life-cycle theory fits the upstream aluminum industry. If one assumes that the minimum efficient scale of operation at a stage of production can be proxied by the average size of plants actually operating at that stage of production, then the life-cycle-theory ratio for, say, alumina can be estimated as follows:

life-cycle-theory ratio for alumina

$$= \frac{\text{size of the world's alumina market}}{\text{MES for alumina refining}}$$

$$= \frac{\text{size of the world's alumina market}}{\text{size of the world's alumina market} / \text{number of alumina plants}}$$

$= $ number of alumina plants.

As an absolute measure this is obviously a very crude estimate, but all that we require is a reliable estimate of the trend in the ratio. As long as any biases are consistent over time, then the trend in the number of plants is a plausible proxy for the trend in the life-cycle-theory ratio. It is quite consistent with the spirit of Stigler's theory to argue that a significant increase in the number of spatially separate plants in either or both stages of production should lead to a decline in vertical integration.

Over the twenty-five-year period of 1955 to 1979, the number of each type of plant (bauxite, alumina, and primary) has approximately doubled. At the same time, the total market (as measured by primary capacity) has increased fivefold. Even admitting the limitations of using the number of plants as a proxy for the life-cycle-theory ratio, it seems quite clear that the ratio has declined consistently and strongly. Stigler's theory therefore predicts a decline in vertical integration across both markets, and this is what PVIA and AVIB indicate. In terms of trends, the data are consistent with the theory. Furthermore, if multiplant firms did not exist, the two markets would presumably be competitive and thick.

But, if the life-cycle theory is the full explanation of vertical integration, it might reasonably be expected that disintegration should have been greater between 1955 and 1979, given the doubling of the life-cycle-theory ratios. After all, PVIA and AVIB decline very modestly. Support for this suspicion that the life-cycle theory does not tell the whole story is found in an examination of the vertical-integration strategies of firms that entered the industry between 1955 and 1979. Entry was quite common, with about twenty significant new firms, a large increase, given that only eleven significant firms existed in 1955. With this sort of increase in the number of firms, concurrent with the strong growth in the market, there was ample opportunity for the forces of the life-cycle-theory to exert their influence. That is, it cannot be argued that the life-cycle theory's forces did not work because of general inertia within the industry.

Contrary to the predictions of the life-cycle theory, most of the new firms in the industry have either become more integrated as time has passed or have indicated an intention to do so. Table 2.1 lists the significant privately owned independent firms that entered the industry between 1955 and 1979 and gives their bauxite, alumina, and primary capacities on entry and at the end of each relevant five-year interval since entry. Nine of the fifteen firms have become more integrated, most of them entering at one or two stages and then integrating at a later date. Of the remaining six, two, Alumax and National Steel Corporation, have clearly indicated plans to integrate in the future. Another

Table 2.1 Integration strategies of significant private entrants between 1955 and 1979[a] (capacities in thousand of tons of primary equivalent).

Firm and date of entry	Stage of production	Year after entry				
		0	5	10	15	20
Anaconda	B	0	0	0	124	163
1956 (U.S.)	A	0	0	0	124	163
	P	54	54	59	159	272
Comalco	B	0	0	250	1,778	2,500
1956 (Australia)	A	15	15	31	83	231
	P	7	13	54	93	149
Martin Marietta	B	0	0	0	0	385
1958 (U.S.)	A	0	0	163	168	210
	P	49	79	157	317	191
Revere	B	0	0	0	102	102
1959 (U.S.)	A	54	54	97	197	197
	P	55	55	83	179	258
Olin Mathieson	B	0	96	140	160	exit
1959, exit 1973 (U.S.)	A	106	201	267	138	exit
	P	108	108	135	exit	
Billiton	B	104	521	625	625	
1964 (Netherlands)	A	0	0	0	0	
	P	0	48	96	0	
Hindustan	B	22	77	85	130	
1964 (India)	A	22	77	85	93	
	P	20	60	95	100	
Mitsubishi	B	0	0	0		
1965 (Japan)	A	0	0	0		
	P	30	108	345		
Alumax	B	0	0	0		
1967 (U.S.)	A	0	0	0		
	P	79	119	199		
Guilina	B	0	0	0		
1969 (West Germany)	A	62	67	77		
	P	32	54	54		
National Steel	B	0	0			
1970 (U.S.)	A	0	0			
	P	163	163			

Table 2.1 (*continued*)

Firm and date of entry	Stage of production	Year after entry				
		0	5	10	15	20
Phelps Dodge	B	0	0			
1971 (U.S.)	A	0	74			
	P	64	126			
Mitsui	B	0	0			
1971 (Japan)	A	77	205			
	P	38	119			
Noranda	B	0	160			
1972 (Canada)	A	0	138			
	P	64	127			
Gove Alumina	B	478	649			
1972 (Australia)	A	77	190			
	P	0	0			

Source: Data described in Appendix A.
a. Omits several small entrants, state-controlled firms, and firms connected with other going firms.

two, Mitsui and Gove Alumina Limited, have an ownership connection that amounts to a form of integration for both (in 1973 Gove Alumina became a 10-percent owner of Mitsui's alumina subsidiary). And recently Gove Alumina has announced plans to enter smelting.

The data also indicate a strong positive correlation between length of time in the industry and degree of vertical integration. At entry, the firms in Table 2.1 operated in an average of 1.53 stages of production; after five years the average rises to 1.87; after ten years, to 2.0; after fifteen years, to 2.4; and after twenty years it reaches the maximum of 3.0. Furthermore, the tendency to integrate is not just a characteristic of the 1950s and 1960s. Of the five entrants in the 1970s, only National Steel shows no sign of integration, but since 1974 it has been engaged in an alumina-from-alunite (a substitute for bauxite) test project in Utah. Besides, ever since National Steel first started to enter aluminum in 1968, the company has been quite explicit and certain about its plans to integrate upstream.[10]

> The broad plan was to provide primary aluminum capacity, while working forward and backward from the smelter . . . Upstream the objective was to acquire raw material positions in bauxite and alumina. (1969)

> During the past four years, many bauxite-alumina projects around the world have been investigated in an effort to implement our policy of integrating backwards through raw materials. The most promising solution to backward integration at present is an alunite development program based on a 700,000,000 ton alunite ore body located in southwestern Utah. (1973)

National Steel's unquestioning attitude about the desirability, or even necessity, of vertical integration in the aluminum industry is typical of the great majority of aluminum firms, as revealed in numerous statements in annual reports, press releases, and so on. For example, when Alumax (then a division of Amax, Incorporated) entered the industry in the mid-1960s, the company's objective was "to seek further growth in metals and minerals and where possible to integrate our operations from mine to market." [11] To this end, the company has had mining rights on a large bauxite deposit in Western Australia since 1968 and has made frequent statements over the past decade about planning a consortium bauxite-alumina project.

Similarly, the Anaconda Company, originally a copper producer like Amax, reported in 1968 after twelve years in aluminum that

> especially notable was the progress in aluminum, where Anaconda made great strides toward its goal of becoming a major, fully-integrated producer of aluminum products . . . Since 1955, when Anaconda began producing aluminum, we have purchased alumina for reduction to metal and fabrication. That will no longer be necessary as Anaconda holds a 36.8 percent interest in bauxite reserves and a new alumina plant in Jamaica, West Indies . . . Thus the traditional Anaconda role of integrated production and manufacturing, "from mine to consumer," will apply in our aluminum operations as well as in copper and other metals. [12]

Similar examples could be presented for most other aluminum firms, but the point seems clear: even though the aluminum market has for many years been growing much faster than minimum efficient scales of operation have been increasing, aluminum producers, particularly the unintegrated new entrants, believe that vertical integration is a necessary condition for success in the upstream aluminum industry. And furthermore, they have been allocating capital resources accordingly. So even though integration trends in the upstream aluminum industry (PVIA and AVIB) are consistent with the life-cycle theory, there are other forces that work in the opposite direction and keep upstream integration higher than would be the case if the life-cycle theory was the full explanation of integration trends.

Recent Downstream Integration: 1955–1979

The life-cycle theory and Wallace's work indicate that the founding aluminum firms integrated downstream into fabrication to facilitate the growth of the aluminum market through new-product development and buyer education. While there probably has continued to be some need for this, the acceptance of aluminum as a standard metal during the last several decades has obviated the importance of large-scale user educational programs. Metal merchants and metal users are now familiar with the properties and uses of aluminum. Furthermore, economies of scale in fabrication are generally small, relative to the market, allowing numerous fabricators to operate efficiently as specialists. The life-cycle theory for the entire industry therefore predicts that downstream vertical integration should not be high, which means it should have declined since the period of Wallace's study, when it was most probably about 80 to 90 percent.

Data across countries and time are not readily available to test this prediction, but by looking at one country and at several major producers, one can get a better idea of its validity. The obvious country to look at is the United States: its market is sufficiently large to eliminate the effects of any downstream scale economies, and reliable data on primary–fabricated products integration are available for a thirty-year period. The data are the primary producers' shares of U.S. wrought products shipments for various years between 1946 and 1979 and are pre-

sented in Table 5.1 as part of the chapter that examines downstream integration specifically. Primary–fabricated products'
integration in the United States has been high throughout the
entire post–World War II period, but it has followed two distinct and opposite trends. Up to the early 1960s it declined
significantly, from something like 90 percent in 1946 to 65
percent in 1965, a trend totally consistent with the life-cycle
theory. But since the mid-1960s there has been a definite reversal, with the degree of integration climbing steadily to about 76
percent. This reversal contradicts the prediction of the life-cycle
theory, because the U.S. market, the number of plants, and the
number of separate producers have all increased significantly
since the mid-1960s. The significance of these facts is analyzed in
depth in Chapter 5, but it is obvious that the life-cycle theory and
actual integration of primary and fabricated products in the
United States are not fully consistent.

The same conclusion is reached when the downstream integration behavior of several major producers is examined over
time. Figure 2.3 plots the percentage of third-party fabricated-
products shipments against the total third-party shipments of
fabricated products and primary aluminum, both measured in
dollars, for five major aluminum firms. The percentage is a
measure of the proportion of consolidated primary-aluminum
production that is fabricated within the firm's network of plants.
It is biased upward by the value added in fabrication, but because
this bias can be assumed to be a fairly constant proportion, the
trends in the percentages should not be affected.

Figure 2.3 indicates that in each case downstream vertical
integration has increased. The trend has been quite pronounced
for Alcan, but is also evident for Alcoa, Alusuisse, Reynolds, and
Kaiser. The instability of the series for Alusuisse over 1971 to
1973 is at least in part due to Alusuisse's exclusion of Conalco (its
U.S. subsidiary) from its consolidated accounts during that interval. The series for Reynolds and Kaiser are short, because
data is unavailable, but the upward trends are sufficiently persist-
ent to be considered significant.

In summary, the evidence over recent decades in the United
States and in five major producers indicates that there has been
an upward trend toward greater downstream vertical integra-

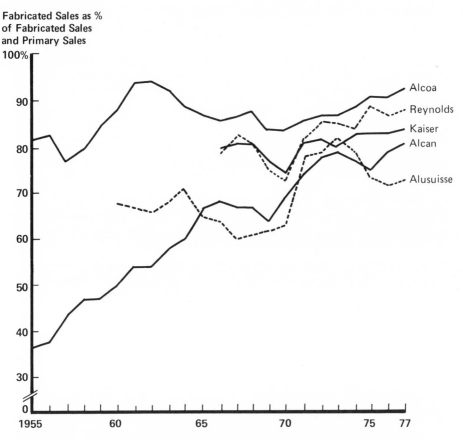

Figure 2.3 Downstream integration trends for five major firms. *Source:* Annual reports and the U.S. Securities and Exchange Commission's 10-K forms. See Stuckey, "Vertical Integration and Joint Ventures in the International Aluminum Industry," p. 70, for details.

tion. This is in contrast to the prediction of the life-cycle model. It appears that factors encouraging vertical integration have swamped the factors encouraging disintegration that the life-cycle theory suggests. (The search for these other factors is the subject of Chapter 5.) But the inconsistency between the life-cycle theory and the experience in the downstream aluminum industry does not mean that the life-cycle theory should be rejected as unreliable: as Stigler himself pointed out, "this [the life-cycle theory] is not the whole story of vertical integration." [13]

Integration into Other Activities

So far, no mention has been made of integration into other activities, such as electrical-power generation, shipping, carbon-anode production, and so on. Integration into these activities is not covered by this book, partly because they produce less important factor inputs, but more because integration into these activities seems to have closely followed the life-cycle model. Prior to the rapid growth of the industry in the 1950s and 1960s, the major aluminum firms were integrated heavily into some of these activities, particularly electrical-power generation for primary smelting. The rapid growth in primary-aluminum capacity during the 1950s was accompanied by comparable growth in intracorporate power-generation plants, but more recently, most new smelters have been built upon the security of long-term power contracts with public utilities. This is particularly true of smelters in the highly developed countries. So while the older aluminum firms still own and operate power plants, most of their newer smelters, and the smelters of the second-tier producers, do not rely upon intracorporate power transfers. Integration into other activities, such as materials supply and transporting, has also been less important.

In summary, the life-cycle model of vertical integration in the industry offers a sound explanation of vertical integration trends throughout the industry during its first half-century or so of large-scale commercial operation. At the end of that period, integration from mine to fabricated products, and into subsidiary activities such as power generation, was pervasive. However in the last twenty or thirty years, when the life-cycle theory would predict general disintegration, the evidence suggests that levels of vertical integration continue to be high, particularly throughout the main vertical chain. In some cases, integration even seems to have increased. It is fitting to echo a conclusion reached by Timothy Greening in his recent study of vertical integration in the oil industry: "It is much easier to explain how vertical integration became the dominant strategy of firms engaged in the production or refining of crude than to explain why it remains such a common feature of firm structure in this industry."[14] Much the same can be said about the aluminum industry.

Market Failure Due to Bauxite and Alumina Heterogeneity

Evidence has been presented that the upstream aluminum industry has been and still is highly integrated vertically. One of the major explanations of why this continues to be the case derives from the fact that bauxites and aluminas are both heterogeneous minerals. The bauxite in any deposit has unique chemical and physical characteristics and is often sufficiently different from other bauxites to require special refining facilities. In the extreme, a mine for a unique type of bauxite and its associated alumina refinery represent a bilateral monopoly across the market; the bauxite mine has only one possible outlet, while the alumina refinery has only one source of supply. The bargaining problems that inevitably arise under bilateral monopoly can be attentuated by common ownership of the mine and refinery, or by vertical integration. Such an extreme case of pure bilateral monopoly is not common in the industry, but bilateral oligopolies occur throughout. Similarly, the alumina used for smelting into primary metal is not homogeneous either, and although it is less varied than bauxite, one type may not be substituted for another without modifying the smelter. So, bilateral oligopoly also prevails in the alumina market. It should be noted that bilateral oligopoly in bauxite and alumina is also caused by factors of the industry's structure, which I discuss below, that are independent of problems resulting from the commodity's heterogeneity.

Bauxite Heterogeneity and Bilateral Monopoly

Because bauxite is chemically and physically heterogeneous, a number of its properties have major implications for the optimal design of alumina refineries. A refinery's design—technology for handling materials, processing chemicals, and disposing of waste—is typically selected to match the properties of the bauxite it is intended to process, and such matching often results in substantial differences among refineries. To some extent, then, a bauxite mine and an alumina refinery are locked into each other vertically. Measuring the strength of this complementarity between pairs of mines and refineries or, put another way, to what degree one kind of bauxite can be substituted for another, is worthwhile because, first, the empirical results become an important building block in my theory, and second, because "one of the common mistakes outsiders make about the aluminum industry is that the alumina refining process is homogeneous — far from it! There are as many versions of the process as there are refineries — each one is 'tailor-made' for the bauxite it is going to process." [15]

The mineralogical features of bauxite of prime interest to refinery design are: its total alumina content, the type of alumina it contains, the total silica content, reactive silica content, and, of lesser importance, content of iron and organic impurities. Total alumina content is important in refinery design because it largely determines the volume of bauxite required to produce each ton of alumina, and the ratio of ore to yield of alumina has obvious implications for the plant's capacities to handle materials and dispose of waste. The type of alumina is important because different types require different processing technologies. Alumina always occurs in bauxite as hydrated alumina, but it can be either alumina trihydrate ($Al_2O_3 \cdot 3H_2O$) or alumina monohydrate ($Al_2O_3 \cdot H_2O$). The basic step in refining is the separation of the alumina (Al_2O_3) from the water (H_2O), achieved by mixing a caustic soda liquor of the proper concentration with bauxite at a suitable temperature. Bauxites containing monohydrate aluminas require temperatures of 170–190 degrees centigrade and concentrations of caustic soda of about 350 grains per liter; bauxites containing trihydrate aluminas require temperatures of only about 130 degrees centigrade and concentrations of caustic soda of only 150–190 grains per liter. The digestion chamber and its associated components must be designed accordingly, and apparently the differences are substantial. It is possible to run trihydrates through monohydrate digestion facilities because of the trihydrates' more moderate digestor requirements, but inefficiencies often arise. It is also technically possible to run monohydrates through trihydrate facilities, but the yield of captured alumina is reduced drastically.

In addition to the dissolution of hydrates of alumina during the digestion stage, several other important reactions affect the quality of the alumina and the efficiency of processing the ore. Most important, a portion of the silica in the bauxite, known as reactive silica, combines with caustic soda and alumina to form sodium aluminum silicate (approximately $3Na_2O \cdot 3Al_2O_3 \cdot 5SiO_2 \cdot 2H_2O$). Although removing the silicate from the process-ing liquor rids the liquor of the unwanted reactive silica, it also means a loss of both caustic soda and alumina. The temperature of the digestion process and the proportion of the silica that is reactive are most important. If a trihydrate bauxite is run through a refinery designed for monohydrate bauxites, the un-necessarily high temperatures used will activate previously inac-tive silica (largely quartz) and lead to caustic soda and alumina losses, which can be substantial; for example, in the Darling Range bauxites, each additional kilogram of reactive silica causes a loss of about 0.8 kilogram of caustic soda and 1.0 kilogram of alumina.[16]

The other properties of bauxite do not have such important implications for refinery design, but they can be significant. Unwanted substances such as nonreactive silica and iron oxide must be removed to assure alumina purity, and their varying amounts in bauxites make different demands on the technology and capacity to remove them. Organic impurities, such as humus and cellulose, produce carbon dioxide, which converts caustic soda to sodium carbonate during digestion. Converting the car-bonate back to caustic soda requires the addition of lime, which causes precipitation of calcium carbonate and also causes the formation of insoluble calcium aluminate, which is lost as resi-due, taking some alumina with it.

Variations in the physical structure of bauxite have implica-tions for the ore's storage qualities. Some bauxites can be stored in uncovered stockpiles, while others must be protected from precipitation to prevent moisture absorption. For example, Weipa bauxite is in the form of small, round pebbles (known as pisolitic); it is free-flowing and free-draining, and can hence be stored in the open. Conversely, Jamaican bauxite becomes muddy if wet and must be stored under cover and transported on covered conveyors. This difference is not trivial, given the size of typical stockpiles and the length of some conveyor systems. An engineer associated with Queensland Alumina's Gladstone re-finery, a plant supplied solely with Weipa bauxite, estimated the cost of modifying the refinery to take bauxites requiring cover at "a substantial number of millions of dollars."[17]

The importance of the relationship between bauxite type and

refinery design becomes clearer when one realizes how much variety there is in currently mined bauxites. Table 2.2 presents a basic description of the bauxites coming from the world's major mining areas, which constitute about 75 percent of the world's bauxite capacity. The data indicate considerable variations, and each bauxite is unique in one way or another. This means that each bauxite has its own specific refinery-design requirements.

A good illustration of how the basic refining process is tailored to the characteristics of a particular bauxite is found in Alcoa of Australia Limited's bauxite-alumina complex in Western Australia. Alcoa currently mines over 10 million tons of bauxite annually from the Darling Ranges in southwestern Australia and transports the ore by rail and conveyor to two coastal refineries capable of handling about 1.25 million tons each, the largest single upstream complex in the world. Both refineries, and a third one now under construction, have unique designs to cope with the peculiar features of Darling Range bauxite (refer to Table 2.2).

The most striking feature of Darling Range bauxite is its low alumina content. This immediately dictated major modification of the typical refinery design to account for the low yield of the ore (3 to 4 tons of bauxite to 1 ton of alumina, almost twice the average). The refineries' capacities to handle the feed materials must be almost twice as large per ton of alumina as the capacities of most refineries. The treatment and disposal of residue are likewise massive operations by comparison with those of other refineries. For each ton of alumina, approximately 2–3 tons of residue are produced; the usual ratio is one to one. The low alumina content of the bauxite also meant that the standard Bayer process for thickening the liquor had to be modified to prevent premature precipitation of alumina, and specially designed washing equipment was required to remove the large volume of quartz. Equipment for separating residue and washing represents about 10 percent of the total capital investment in the refinery, compared to approximately 5 percent for most refineries. The highly erosive effects and large volume of the unwanted quartz and iron also presented problems in designing the lining of pipes, valves, and vessels.

One of the major advantages of Darling Range bauxite is its

Table 2.2 Composition of bauxite in several major developed deposits (average percentages).

Bauxite	Available alumina	Trihydrate content	Monohydrate content	Total silica content	Reactive silica content	Iron content
Boke (11)[a]	60	major	small	2.0	0.8	24
Gove (7)	50	major	small	4.5	4.0	15
Weipa (16)	55	40	10	6.0	3.0	7
Darling Range (7)	33	major	0	22.0	1.5	17
Jamaica (21)	48	major	small	2.5	2.5	20
Surinam (9)	48	major	—	6.0	4.5	10
Dominican Republic (2)	47	major	small	3.0	—	20
Var, France (2)	51	—	major	8.0	—	—

Source: E. A. Kirke, "Alumina from Darling Range Bauxite" (Paper presented to the Australian Institute of Mining and Metals Conference, Perth, Western Australia, May 1973), p. 557; and various company publications.
a. Numbers in parentheses are percentages of world capacity in primary equivalent tons.

total trihydrate composition and the absence of monohydrates, combined with a low content of reactive silica. This makes possible a digestion process that uses relatively low temperatures and concentrations of caustic soda, lower than would be possible for efficient digestion of most bauxites. But as noted earlier, caustic soda consumption and alumina yield rates are very sensitive to small variations in reactive silica content, dictating accurate grading of the bauxite before it is refined. Indeed, in Alcoa of Australia's second alumina refinery at Pinjarra, better control over quality was achieved by constantly monitoring the grade of bauxite with an automatic sampling plant and by blending the bauxites in 200,000-ton stockpiles to obtain a feed with a more uniform grade for refining.

The substantial modification of the standard Bayer process required in Alcoa's Western Australian refineries indicates that Darling Range bauxite could not be processed economically in any other existing refinery. Analogously, the vast majority of bauxite from other deposits could not be processed economically in Alcoa's refineries. When Alcoa's third refinery in the same complex is completed, something like 20 percent of the world's bauxite and alumina capacity will be locked in to that one complex. Although the peculiar features of this bauxite-alumina complex probably make its relationship more locked in than is usual, it indicates the kind of one-to-one relationships that tend to exist between bauxite mines and alumina refineries.

It is important to point out that technically, any bauxite can be run through any refinery. The problem is, however, efficiency, particularly in regard to alumina yield, caustic soda usage, and effective capacity. The sensitivity of efficiency to switching bauxites from one refinery to another is the crucial parameter in measuring substitutability and is very difficult to quantify, because it probably varies for each possible bauxite-refinery pair, and because switching occurs so rarely that even experts in the industry can only guess at the degree of substitutability for any given pairing. A better estimate can be made, though, by comparing the costs of alumina production from a given bauxite in a tailor-made refinery with those from the same bauxite but in a different type of refinery.

Two such comparisons have been made possible by information supplied by a chemical engineer employed in a major aluminum firm. The examples are hypothetical, but the data are quite realistic. Table 2.3 compares the average costs for bauxite and caustic soda per ton of alumina produced that would be incurred by running a bauxite with significant monohydrate content through a high-temperature refinery, designed to separate monohydrate aluminas, and through a low-temperature refinery, designed to separate only trihydrate aluminas. In this example the costs of bauxite and caustic soda per ton of alumina produced increase by a drastic 77 percent, owing to the decline in yield resulting from the loss of the monohydrate alumina in the low-temperature refinery. This problem of reduced bauxite and caustic soda yields alone implies that average total costs increase about 30 percent, but the reduction of capacity by half and the dramatic increase in residue would cause an overall increase in average total costs (including capital costs) on the order of 100 percent. Inefficiencies of this magnitude and for these reasons could be expected if, for example, Weipa bauxite were fed into any one of five of the seven Caribbean refineries. Even worse inefficiencies would occur if the largely monohydrate bauxites of Europe were fed into low-temperature refineries.

Table 2.4 presents equivalent information for a trihydrate bauxite processed in a suitable low-temperature refinery, and in a refinery where temperatures are unnecessarily high. Here the inefficiencies are more subtle, but still significant. The total of the major cost components goes up by 20 percent, owing largely to the increased caustic soda consumption, the decline in yield, and the decline in effective capacity, all resulting from the activation of the quartz under high temperatures.

Of course, a refiner forced to switch his source of bauxite has an alternative to increased operating costs. He can modify his refinery to process the substitute bauxite efficiently, but modifications are expensive and require the plant to lie idle for some months. For example, it was estimated that modification of the Gove (high-temperature) refinery to refine Weipa (mixed hydrate) or Darling Range (trihydrate) bauxites efficiently would cost approximately $115–170 million and a similar amount to modify Alcoa's or Comalco's refineries to take Gove bauxite.[18] At these costs, modification is only an extreme option; it is not

Table 2.3 Hypothetical comparison of costs of producing one ton of alumina from a mixed-hydrate bauxite in a high-temperature refinery and a low-temperature refinery.

Assumptions

The bauxite contains 50% total active alumina (30% trihydrate, 20% monohydrate), and 3% reactive silica. (These specifications are of a mixed bauxite, such as Weipa bauxite.)

Bauxite cost = $20 per ton

Caustic soda cost = $150 per ton

High-temperature refinery

2.2 tons of bauxite at $20 per ton	$44.00
0.07 ton of caustic soda at $150 per ton	10.50
	$54.50

materials handling capacity	1 million tons of alumina
dry mud residue	0.75 ton per ton of alumina produced

Low-temperature refinery

3.9 tons of bauxite at $20 per ton	$78.00
0.12 ton of caustic soda at $150 per ton	18.60
	$96.60

materials handling capacity	564,000 tons of alumina
dry-mud residue	2.2 tons per ton of alumina produced

---

surprising that very few actual cases of significant refinery modifications of this type have occurred. Once a refinery has been set up to take bauxite from a particular deposit, or from deposits of ore having very similar characteristics, chances are that the refinery's managers would have to perceive a major long-run change in the supply balance of bauxites of different types to change the specifications of the plant. Another option for the refiner, open only at the outset, is to design a refinery that can take bauxites of different types. Martin Marietta Corporation's plant in the Virgin Islands and Showa Denko KK's Yokohama plant are such refineries, but they are less cost-efficient than are specialist plants. Because the costs of alumina represent about 40 percent of the average total costs of (nearly full capacity) primary aluminum production, fairly small variations in refining efficiency can be important. In any case, most of the refineries designed to take a mixture of bauxites are producers of specialty aluminas, products that account for only about 8 percent of alumina production and that flow into other industries.

Table 2.4 Hypothetical comparison of costs of producing one ton of alumina from a trihydrate bauxite in a low-temperature refinery and a high-temperature refinery.

Assumptions

The bauxite contains 50% total active alumina, all of which is trihydrate, 3% reactive silica, and 8% quartz. (These specifications are typical of Caribbean bauxites.)

Bauxite cost = $20 per ton

Caustic soda cost = $150 per ton

Energy = $15 per ton of alumina capacity in the low-temperature plant. Capital costs based on $600 per ton of alumina capacity financed 50:50 by debt and equity, and including interest on debt, depreciation on equity, and maintenance = $54 per ton of alumina capacity in the low-temperature plant.

Low-temperature refinery	
2.2 tons of bauxite at $20 per ton	$44.00
0.07 ton of caustic soda at $150 per ton	10.00
energy costs	15.00
capital costs	54.00
	$123.00

High-temperature refinery	
2.36 tons of bauxite at $20 per ton	$47.20
0.13 ton of caustic soda at $150 per ton	19.50
energy costs (consumption up 15%)	18.50
capital costs	62.10
	$147.30

The bauxite-refinery specificity problem can also be relieved, but only slightly, by blending and beneficiating bauxite from one or several sources. No amount of blending will change the basic chemical properties of a bauxite, but sometimes marginally adjusting the content proportions is possible. For example, Alcoa of Australia blends its bauxite to control silica content, while Weipa bauxite is wet-screened to remove the fine particles that are largely silica-bearing kaolin. In its Hurricane Creek, Arkansas, alumina plant, Reynolds finds blending advantageous because "although this alumina plant can operate exclusively on Arkansas bauxite, the Arkansas bauxite must be used in mixture with imported bauxite of high grade in order to achieve production at maximum design capacity." [19] Such advantages are not always easily available, however, because blending is limited by the texture of some bauxites; for example, soillike bauxites, such as Jamaican bauxite, are physically difficult to blend in significant volumes.

While the technical links between bauxites and refineries have the effect of tying mines and refineries together, there is another set of factors that is increasingly tightening mine-refinery relationships. The set of factors includes the widespread distribution of the world's major bauxite deposits, the vast distances between the deposits and the primary aluminum smelters, the low value of bauxite at the mine's front door relative to freight rates, and the more than 100-percent reduction in material volume during refining.

Table 2.5 provides information on the regional distribution of bauxite, alumina, and primary capacity for both 1960 and 1977. Notice that the increasing majority of the world's bauxite production capacity is in the relatively underdeveloped and isolated

Table 2.5 Regional distribution of bauxite, alumina, and primary capacity, 1960 and 1977 (percentages based on equivalent tons of primary).

Region	Bauxite		Alumina		Primary	
	1960	1977	1960	1977	1960	1977
Major source regions						
Caribbean[a]	67.6	35.3	9.0	15.0	0.0	0.5
Australia	0.0	30.1	0.3	20.9	0.3	2.5
West Africa[b]	5.0	19.6	0.0	2.4	0.0	1.6
Total	72.6	85.0	9.3	38.3	0.3	4.6
Major use regions						
North America	7.0	2.1	70.2	29.6	73.1	46.7
Europe	12.9	7.3	14.7	17.9	18.6	26.7
Japan	0.0	0.0	4.3	9.4	3.4	12.9
Total	19.9	9.4	89.2	56.9	95.1	86.3
Other regions	7.5	5.6	1.5	4.8	4.6	9.1
Total	100.0	100.0	100.0	100.0	100.0	100.0

Source: Data described in Appendix A.

a. Includes Jamaica, Guyana, Surinam, Dominican Republic, and Haiti.
b. Includes Guinea, Ghana, and Sierra Leone.

regions of the Caribbean, Australia, and West Africa. This trend will almost certainly continue, but the role of the Caribbean region will gradually decline and will be taken over by Brazil: reserves in the non-Communist world are located 35 percent in West Africa, 28 percent in Australia, 15 percent in Brazil, 11 percent in the Caribbean, 5 percent in Europe, and 4 percent in Asia. So the world's major bauxite mines are distant from one another, but they are also distant from the major metal-consumption points. Table 2.5 indicates that North America, Europe, and Japan contain the great majority of the world's smelting capacity (86 percent in 1977), and while this will decline in the future because of increasing power costs and pollution-control problems in these areas, they will continue to dominate fabrication and consumption of aluminum products.

Given this spatial pattern, bauxite, alumina, or primary, or all three, must be transported large distances at high costs. For example, in 1977 Weipa bauxite had an Australian free on board (f.o.b) price of about $16 per ton, but a delivered cost in, say, the U.S. Gulf Coast of about $25 per ton, implying transport costs of 36 percent of delivered price. In contrast, Jamaican bauxite sold at just under $25 per ton, but its transport costs were only about 8 percent of that. This price structure meant that bauxite costs were about 50 percent of the operating costs of Gulf Coast refineries, and in the case of Weipa bauxite, bauxite transport costs alone were about 17 percent of refinery operating costs.

Clearly, bauxite is a low-value bulk commodity, and because refining cuts the volume per primary-equivalent ton by at least 50 percent, there emerges an obvious incentive to locate refineries near bauxite mines. The incentive is quite strong, for, as Table 2.6 shows, the great majority of bauxite is either refined locally or is shipped to the nearest major consuming region. With the addition of the approximately 12 million tons of bauxite produced in regions other than the four regions listed in the table, almost 60 percent of bauxite output in 1975 was refined locally, and 33 percent was refined in the nearest major consuming region (Australia-Japan, 5 percent; Indonesia-Malaysia-Japan, 2 percent; Caribbean–North America, 16 percent; and West Africa–North America–Europe, 10 percent). It should be noted, however, that the high proportion of bauxite refined

Table 2.6 Refining locations for bauxite from major producing regions 1977[a] (thousands of tons; percentages in parentheses).

Producing region	Refining location				Total production
	Japan and Taiwan	North America	Western Europe	Local	
Australia	3,478 (13)	19 (1)	3,739 (14)	18,834 (72)	26,070 (100)
Indonesia and Malaysia	1,918 (100)	0 (0)	0 (0)	0 (0)	1,918 (100)
Caribbean	74 (1)	12,433 (59)	298 (1)	8,242 (39)	21,047 (100)
West Africa	0 (0)	3,736 (30)	3,881 (31)	4,705 (38)	12,322 (100)
Totals	5,470 (9)	16,371 (27)	7,918 (13)	31,781 (52)	61,357 (100)

Source: Metallgesellschaft A. G., *Metal Statistics 1967–1977*, (Frankfurt: Metallgesellschaft, 1978).
a. As inferred from import and export statistics.

locally has occurred only recently. Table 2.5 shows that between 1960 and 1977, the source countries' share of alumina capacity rose from 9 to 38 percent, while the user countries' share fell from 89 to 57 percent, a change largely caused by shifting mine locations and transport costs. One final important point is that, of the 60 percent of bauxite refined locally, most of it is refined in plants that are more or less next door to the mines and is transported relatively short distances by train, truck, or conveyor.

The evidence therefore indicates that there are strong economic incentives to locate refineries next door to mines, incentives that became important in the 1960s and that are becoming more important as time progresses. But because the major bauxite mines are located in isolated and otherwise undeveloped areas distant from each other, mines and refineries are locked in pairs, at least to the extent dictated by costs of transporting ore from the nearest other mine or refinery.

The special, technical relationship between bauxite type and refinery design, combined with the transport-cost advantages of back-to-back mine and refinery operations, produces a situation where the majority of the world's bauxite flows from mines to refineries via transactions that, without vertical integration, would be bilateral monopoly or small-numbers bilateral oligopoly exchanges. The trend, particularly because of the transport-cost factor, is toward strengthening bilateral relationships between mines and refineries.

Segmentation of the Alumina Market

Alumina, like bauxite, is heterogeneous. The degree of heterogeneity is less, but it still has the effect of breaking the market down into several segments between which substitution is far from perfect. The major division splits the market into two, the sandy alumina segment and the floury alumina segment, and substitutability between them is very low. In 1977 the sandy segment constituted about 73 percent of the total alumina market, the remaining 27 percent being floury aluminas.[20] Within each segment the aluminas are quite similar, but minor differences do inhibit substitution.

Sandy and Floury Segmentation. Refineries and primary smelters are usually specific to one type of alumina. The great majority of alumina transactions are therefore intrasegmentary. But alumina type is apparently independent of both the original bauxite type and the eventual primary-metal type. That is, it is technically possible to refine any bauxite into either sandy or floury alumina, and both types of alumina can produce the same metal. However, the design and operating characteristics of the refineries and smelters of sandy aluminas differ markedly from those of floury aluminas, and, of course, these characteristics affect cost structures; here lies the explanation of choice of technology and, hence, of alumina type. The initial choice of technology tends to be in smelting, where, at the planning stage of building a smelter, there is considerable flexibility in the ratio of capital to power, the optimal ratio depending upon the relative prices of capital and electrical power. Sandy aluminas require a heavy power input but a low capital input, relative to floury aluminas. Given that power costs have historically been higher in Japan and Europe than in North America, it is not surprising that sandy and floury refineries are located in different regions of the world. The North American refineries and the Caribbean refineries (owned almost exclusively by the North American majors) are overwhelmingly producers of sandy alumina. The only exception is the relatively small refinery in the Virgin Islands owned by a second-tier producer, the Martin Marietta Corporation. In Japan, floury alumina predominates, as it does to a lesser degree in Europe. Africa and the Middle East (Guinea and Turkey) produce mainly floury aluminas; the other significant alumina-producing area, Australia, produces the sandy types.

But this regional pattern is changing. During the 1970s two major changes occurred that disturbed the traditional distribution by type of refinery and smelter. First, the cost of electrical power from new sources increased rapidly (initiated by the rise in world oil prices), particularly in the United States. Second, Alcoa invented equipment to modify existing sandy-alumina smelters so that air pollution from the smelters would be cut significantly, the result of research presumably stimulated by antipollution legislation of 1972. Importantly, the modification (known as hooded pots and dry scrubbing) works only with sandy alumina. The rise in power costs discouraged sandy alumina production while the antipollution legislation worked in the opposite direction. The evidence suggests that the force promoting sandy alumina is the strongest: all newly planned refineries will produce sandy alumina, and several refineries that produce the floury types have been or will be converted to produce the sandy type. On the basis of announced plans for new refineries, extensions to existing refineries, conversions of existing refineries, and closings of refineries, the proportion of total alumina capacity in sandy aluminas will have increased from 73 percent in 1977 to 82 percent by 1980 and to 84 percent by 1985.[21] These predictions include the conversion of four floury refineries to sandy refineries: Pechiney Ugine Kuhlmann's (PUK) Salindres plant in France, the Friguia consortium plant in Guinea, Nippon Light Metal's Tomakamai plant in Japan, and the Gove joint-venture plant in Australia.

Let us return to the crucial issue of plant flexibility and alumina substitutability. An alumina refiner has little choice, apart from making major modifications in the plant, in which type of alumina — sandy or floury — to produce. In the refining process, following digestion and filtration, the process liquor consists largely of sodium aluminate. From this the alumina is precipitated and then calcinated; it is during these later stages that the sandiness or flouriness of the alumina is determined. The two types of alumina are chemically very similar, but they have different physical properties that particularly affect handling and moisture absorption. The plant design for the precipitation and calcination of sandy alumina is quite different from that required for floury alumina, and large numbers of tanks, pipes, and other equipment are involved. Modification is therefore expensive. For example, the modification of the Gove refinery to produce sandy rather than floury alumina is estimated to cost $35 million, which is approximately 10 percent of the book value of the entire Gove complex or 3 percent of its current replacement value.[22] There is no doubt that the Gove joint venturers regard the switch to sandy alumina as a long-run, probably permanent, decision. Note, however, that this sort of conversion is not nearly as expensive as conversion of the plant to process a different type of bauxite.

Technically it is possible to design refineries that produce both sandy and floury alumina, but these incur higher capital and operating costs. To achieve economies of scale and to operate at capacity at all times is difficult in such plants, but some refinery operators, such as Japan's Showa Denko, prefer flexibility, despite its greater cost, to being locked in to only one segment of the alumina market (or to a particular bauxite type), and despite greater efficiency achieved. "The excelling qualities of Yokohama's [refinery] technology are well demonstrated by its ability to handle both trihydrate and mixed-hydrate bauxite with its fully-established bauxite dissolving process, and also to produce floury as well as sandy type alumina."[23] Showa Denko's desire for flexibility is not surprising, since it relies on arm's-length markets for all of its bauxite and for some of its alumina.

At the smelting stage, however, there is some substitutability between sandy and floury aluminas. There are basically two versions of the Hall-Heroult smelting process: the prebaked anode-cell technique for sandy aluminas and the Soderberg anode-cell technique for floury types. It is possible to switch alumina types, but process efficiency suffers. The productivity of a continuously operating smelting pot falls typically by only about 2 or 3 percent, but pot failures become much more common. This has the effects of cutting effective capacity and increasing maintenance costs. Of course, smelters using the new hooded pots – dry scrubbing technology for pollution control are forced to use sandy alumina if the decline in pollution is to be at all significant. The costs of fines and loss of the pollution-control authorities' good will from excess pollution are already sizable and will probably increase in the future.

Operators of primary aluminum smelters also have the option of converting their smelting technology to process a different alumina efficiently. For example, during the 1970s the Aluminium Corporation of South Africa (Alusaf) converted its smelter from floury alumina to sandy alumina. Two independent and reliable sources informed me that Alusaf made the conversion to escape the "unfair" prices for floury alumina charged it by Alusuisse, which owned 22 percent of the corporation. The Alusuisse-Alusaf dispute was eventually litigated, hence my sources requested to remain anonymous.

Substitutability. Aluminas differ in more than just sandiness or flouriness, and within each of these two types are aluminas having minor differences in chemical properties that affect smelting efficiency. Some idea of these differences is given by noting the typical range (in percentages) of the chemicals composing, say, a sandy alumina:

Al_2O	98.5000%
SiO_2	0.005 – 0.040
Fe_2O_3	0.005 – 0.040
TiO_2	0.004 – 0.005
P_2O_5	<0.002
V_2O_5	<0.001
ZnO	<0.010
Na_2O	0.040 – 0.800
Loss on ignition	0.050 – 1.000[24]

The width of the ranges indicates the differences that are acceptable for efficient operation, and although they may amount to only fractions of a percentage point, they can affect the smelting process and the purity of the final metal. Traditionally, each of the major firms has its own, slightly different alumina that "fits" best with its smelters, but the extent of the differences requiring real technical changes is not great, if indeed such differences exist at all. Practically, the important point is that smelter operators learn over time the special smelting requirements of their regular supplies of alumina. The productivity of greenfield smelters rises significantly over the first few months or even years of their operation, reflecting both the "art part of smelting" (as one manager put it) and the familiar learning-curve phenomenon. Even small variations in the chemical composition of a smelter's regular alumina supply can upset smelter productivity (and smelter managers, so I am told!). There is considerable evidence of technical problems in smelters in companies' annual reports, industrial journals, and so forth, and the problems quite often involve matching a particular alumina with a particular smelter.

Effects of Transport Costs. Alumina, like bauxite, is reduced in its volume by the next stage of aluminum production; hence there is an incentive to minimize transport costs and to locate refineries and smelters back-to-back. Because new refineries are often now located adjacent to bauxite mines in bauxite-producing countries, one might also expect smelters to be located near refineries, tightening refinery-smelter relationships and lowering transport costs. But, the magnitude of these effects is small and is not likely to become particularly greater in the future, because alumina is a much more valuable commodity than bauxite, and even lengthy ocean routes add only about 10 percent to f.o.b. prices. Furthermore, alumina costs are a smaller proportion of smelting costs, and other costs (particularly power) have at least an equal impact on smelter location. During smelting, a volume of alumina is usually reduced by less than 50 percent, whereas in refining, a volume of bauxite is reduced an average of 75 percent. The location of pairs or small groups of technically complementary refineries and smelters therefore has only a minor effect on buyer-seller relationships in the alumina market.

Alumina's heterogeneity does not have the effect of breaking the market down into bilateral monopolies, as bauxite's does, but, as I will show, the alumina market is a small-numbers market anyway, particularly on the seller's side. The sandy-floury division of it is therefore important, because it cuts down the number of potential traders in an actual alumina transaction. This makes the arm's-length market for alumina even thinner than the currently estimated 10 percent of total exchanged alumina, because any potential trader is really operating in only one of the market's segments.

Bilateral Monopoly, Transactions Costs, and Market Failure

So far I have argued that the bauxite market, and to some extent the alumina market, would, in the absence of vertical integration, consist of a number of bilateral monopolies and oligopolies. This is so because of three major factors. First, substantial minimum efficient scales of operation relative to total market size, particularly in the past, and in regard to alumina refining, have limited the number of efficiently sized plants. Second, complementary technical relationships between pairs or small groups of vertically related plants have the effect of encouraging long-term exchange relationships because of the higher operating or capital costs associated with substitution. Third, the large reductions in volume of raw material to final product in refining and smelting, the spatial distribution of bauxite deposits and markets for finished aluminum products, and the high costs of transport, relative to explant prices, often foster the back-to-back location of mines and refineries in isolated places and discourage substitution. The next step is to show why reliance upon arm's-length spot transactions in bilateral monopolies and bilateral oligopolies is unsatisfactory, and why vertical integration should be preferred.

The analysis of this proposition will be applied principally to the bauxite market, which illustrates it very effectively. In the case of pure bilateral monopoly — that is, a single bauxite seller and a single bauxite buyer — well-known theory predicts that only in very special circumstances will a unique and stable equilibrium exist between the two parties. Assuming for the moment that a bauxite transaction is fully described by price and quantity, there are only two outcomes that are both determinate and sensible for a bilateral monopoly. The first is defined by the price and quantity that would result if the buyer was a monopsonist facing many competing bauxite suppliers, and it would occur in the unlikely event that the alumina refiner was overwhelmingly more powerful than the bauxite miner. The second is defined by the price and quantity that would result if the seller was a bauxite monopolist facing many competing buyers, and it would occur in the similarly unlikely event that the bauxite miner's power overwhelmed the refiner's. These extreme outcomes form part of the boundary of feasible outcomes, but to illustrate their unreality consider an upstream aluminum world consisting only of Alcoa of Australia's balanced bauxite-alumina complex, but where the mines were owned entirely independently of the refineries. Is it reasonable to assume that either of the two parties would completely dominate the other? The general answer is obviously no.

Having rejected the polar cases, bilateral monopoly becomes "indeterminate with a vengeance." [25] But assume that the two parties make the rational decision at the outset to maximize joint profits—a very reasonable assumption, given the sorts of circumstances that could prevail in bauxite-alumina bilateral monopolies. Under this assumption, the quantity of bauxite exchanged is determinate, but the price is still indeterminate within the range consistent with nonnegative profits for both parties. "Within the range lying between these 'zero-profit limits', the *price* is determined by relative strength . . . For all prices *other than that measured by the ordinate of the intersection of the marginal-cost curve with the marginal value product curve* [that is, the price that happens to equate supply and demand] the profit-maximizing contract must include an all-or-none ("take it or leave it") clause." [26] There is nothing "natural" or "expected" about the price that happens to equate supply and demand. The exchange price can be determined only after bargaining, a process that in the eyes of the bargainers can produce "winners" and "losers," and hence the motivation to haggle. If the range of feasible prices is wide, the potential "win" or "loss" is large and long, hard negotiations can often be expected. In fact, the negotiations will probably continue until one of the parties sees its marginal net benefits from haggling turn negative. While the parties are bargaining over how a cake of a constant size is to be sliced in two (that is, in a constant-sum game), the size of both slices is effectively being reduced by the costs both parties are incurring in bargaining. Here the bargainers have their one common interest: to reduce bargaining costs.

Although the quantity of bauxite exchanged is determinate under joint profit-maximization, it depends upon conditions in the final output-market (in this case, the alumina market) and upon conditions in the original input-market (in this case, the market for mining leases). If both of these markets are competitive, then mining-refining joint profit maximization leads to the same quantity of throughput that would occur if the entire industry were perfectly competitive. But neither of these conditions holds in the aluminum industry, there being, in the extreme, a chain of successive monopolists, monopsonists, or both, at least up to the primary-metal market. Under these circumstances even joint profit maximization among *all* of the stages with market power does not lead to the competitive throughput, but at least it leads to the throughput that would occur if there was only *one* monopolized stage. This outcome is preferable to that which would occur under nonjoint (but individual firm) profit-maximizing in a successive monopoly-monopsony situation. because it leads to a higher output rate and to higher industry-wide profits, a privately and socially superior state of affairs.[27] The general result is that whenever there are at least two adjacent monopolistic or monopsonistic stages of production in a vertical chain, joint profit-maximization can only increase and therefore improve the industry's output rate, relative to nonjoint (but individual firm) profit-maximizing behavior.

In a single-period bilateral-monopoly model, that is nearly the end of the story. But consider the much more interesting and realistic situation of a long-term, multitransaction relationship between the bilateral monopolists, occurring in a dynamic world where costs, demand, technology, and so on are often changing. Under these circumstances the parties are continually haggling; whenever one of the important parameters exogenous to the bargain changes, one of the parties may believe the balance of power has swung its way and instigate a new round of negotiations before the next spot transaction. The costs of these continual negotiations include the obvious ones such as legal fees and management time and effort, but also the costs of idle capacity during protracted negotiations, the risk of a permanent impasse, and the risk of an opportunistic coup by the opposition. The parties have a joint incentive to avoid these transactions costs, but, at the same time, they must preserve their conflicting private interests in the bargains over price. Merger, or vertical integration, is one solution to this "Catch-22" situation. Common ownership also has the advantage of ensuring that the throughput rate is the jointly optimal rate, and that the joint profit "cake" is maximized. (These ideas, and the substantiation of them that follows, were inspired by the recent work of Oliver Williamson.[28])

Before extending the analysis of the long-term dynamic bilateral-monopoly situation, I return to the simple static model and show that its predictions regarding bargaining problems and costs are qualitatively robust when its specifications are modified to capture more closely several aspects of the actual bauxite market. Consider first the bauxite-market reality that for an individual grade of bauxite, there are other, substitute bauxites, some of which are probably quite good substitutes. This has the effect of narrowing the bargaining range but not the qualitative result. The same conclusion is probably justified when the model is extended from bilateral monopoly to bilateral oligopoly, at least if one assumes that mutual dependence is well recognized throughout the system. But bilateral oligopoly could put joint profit-maximization under more strain and, hence, widen the set of possible outcomes. Finally, recognition should also be given to the reality that price and quantity are not the only parameters important in a bauxite transaction: quality, delivery schedules, the point when the property rights are transferred, and so on, are also relevant and open to negotiation. In principle, these parameters tend only to alter the effective price, but in a bargaining situation they probably complicate and lengthen the haggling process by increasing the number of variables upon which agreement must be reached.

While substitute bauxites, and bilateral oligopoly rather than bilateral monopoly, may have the effects of narrowing the bargaining range and cutting down on transactions costs, a combination of several of the industry's basic structural features has the opposite effect by severely aggravating potential bargaining problems. The first feature is the high proportion of average costs that are fixed, both in bauxite mining and alumina refining, but particularly in refining. At normal and subnormal operating rates, marginal costs are an unusually low proportion of average costs, and to stay in business in the short run, only marginal costs need be covered. The bauxite miner's business is viable in the short run if the price received for bauxite covers variable costs (royalties and resource taxes, and the variable portions of wages and transport costs, to mention the major ones). Such a price could be quite low, relative to average costs, at least in the large, modern mines or during periods of depressed demand. On the other hand, the alumina producer could be forced into a very high price for bauxite because (1) bauxite costs are a low proportion of average costs (about 30 percent on average), (2) other variable costs are only of about the same magnitude in total, and (3) the fixed factor-proportions of the alumina production process mean that input substitution is impossible. On these rough figures, the price of alumina could be doubled relative to normal, and variable costs would still be covered.

These production cost structures mean that the feasible price range is wide, which immediately increases the incentive to bargain and, therefore, presumably the costs. But the production cost-structure also means that the price range and either party's notion of a "fair" price are highly sensitive to variations in largely exogenous variables, such as ocean freight rates, bauxite royalties, power costs, caustic soda costs, exchange rates, and so on, variables that have fluctuated historically quite often, sometimes sharply. Given a change in such a variable, it would be surprising if the disadvantaged bilateral-monopoly party did not attempt to adjust the price before the next spot transaction. The justification for the adjustment could be economically rational, but the occasion could also be used for opportunistic bargaining.

Apart from variations in other costs and, hence, the occasion for renewed price negotiations, variations in the final demand prompt renegotiation of both quantity and price. Variations in final demand are also common and large, and they can have major implications for bauxite and alumina producers, because of the irregular behavior of average and, particularly, marginal cost curves at about capacity in both mines and refineries. At below capacity, marginal costs are much smaller than average costs, but at about capacity, marginal costs accelerate quickly. The curves theoretically important in bilateral monopoly, namely, the bauxite miner's marginal and average cost curves and the alumina refiner's marginal- and average-value product curves, change slope and intersect at about capacity. Consequently, a change in final demand, and hence a shift in the alumina producer's demand curve, can cause a change in the optimal quantity of bauxite to be transacted and probably a much bigger change in the limits of the feasible price range. The point is that a bauxite miner and an alumina refiner, locked into a situation of spot transactions within a bilateral monopoly, continually buffeted by exogenous variations in relevant variables, will frequently be forced into the costly exercise of renegotiating prices and quantities.

The cost structures of bauxite and alumina production pose financial risks as well as bargaining costs. The width of the feasible-price range means that if a distinct power imbalance arose, the powerful party could, in the short run, force a bauxite price that would allow the weaker party only to cover variable costs. The powerful party could, in other words, expropriate the weaker party's return on capital (interest, principal, and dividends). But the strength of this argument depends crucially upon the knotty question "how long is the short run?" If bauxite price squeezes are likely to occur only for very brief periods, then they pose no great threat to the unintegrated operator. It is easy to think of a number of factors that could, in this situation, affect the length of the short run (as it is understood by economists). But there is one structural feature of the industry that could systematically have the effect of making "the short run," as far as bauxite mining or alumina refining are concerned, a devastatingly long period of time. That feature is the high barriers to exit, in all cases a problem to refiners and also a problem to owners of the large, infrastructure-intensive mines. The expensive and long-lived physical assets (plant, port facilities, rail lines, townships, and so forth) are in most cases of very little value to anyone outside the aluminum industry, because they are either industry specific, and in some cases even bauxite specific (such as an alumina plant), or spatially immobile (such as Gove's Nhulunbuy township in undeveloped northern Australia. So, even if a disadvantageous bauxite price means that the cash flow covers only variable costs, creditors have little choice but to wait and hope; bankruptcy would just leave them with a collection of highly illiquid and low-valued assets. With sunk capital and minimal salvage value, debtors and equity holders alike would prefer to see the business continue as long as more capital is not required — and even then, more capital might be made available if prospects for future profitability existed.

Under these sorts of circumstances, a distinct imbalance of power within a bilateral monopoly could make "the short run" long enough to be a major threat to many refiners and to some miners. The argument applies not only to the extraction of profit by one party from the other, but also to the distribution of losses during periods of recession. The financial risks of independent bauxite mining or alumina refining are therefore substantial, and it is not surprising that the availability of debt finance for unintegrated upstream projects is typically conditional upon specific marketing arrangements, usually long-term contracts.

In summary, if the bauxite market operated on the basis of arm's-length spot transactions in the context of a collection of bilateral monopolies and oligopolies, the independent miners and refiners would be faced with frequent and expensive bargaining sessions and be continually running the financial risk of exploitation by bilateral partners. These two problems are logically separate, but they both arise because of the same set of basic, structural features: bauxite heterogeneity, specialized refinery design, capital intensity, and asset longevity and specificity. The frequent industry comments about "security of supply" or "reliable markets," both at "prices competitive with the integrated majors," often can be reduced to these issues.

To avoid the problems associated with reliance upon spot markets, firms are forced to use other mechanisms for vertical coordination. One of these other mechanisms is, of course, internal organization, or vertical integration, and the evidence indicates that it is indeed the favored mechanism. But the choice of mechanism for vertical coordination is not just binary; there are other alternatives, such as long-term contracts, or integration via joint ventures. The abilities of these other mechanisms to overcome the problems of bilateral monopolies and oligopolies in trading are examined in later chapters, but several other possible reasons for spot-market failure in bauxite and alumina need to be treated first.

Integration and Information

The heterogeneity of bauxite, the segmentation of the bauxite market, and the technical and spatial specificity of refineries motivate bauxite-alumina integration for a reason other than the desire to lessen the costs of transactions and the financial risks in trading situations that end up being bilateral monopolies or oligopolies. While such a desire applies to the operational phase of the mine-refinery relationship, that is, to the phase *after* what Williamson calls the initial-contract award stage, the reason for integrating argued in this section applies *during* that stage. When the going refiner (or a potential entrant) is planning a new refinery, he must make a decision about which segment of the bauxite market he is going to trade within, because once he has designed and constructed his plant he will have constrained severely his ability to trade in the other segment. The refiner wants to design and locate his refinery to suit the characteristics and location of a bauxite that has good long-run supply and cost prospects, a decision that requires accurate information about the bauxites of different types and in different regions. Such information may be more reliable and accurate if acquired first-hand, and thus the refiner will have an incentive to be active in mining, or at least in exploration and in the market for mining leases. Such activity represents in itself a type of upstream integration and, combined with the earlier operational reasons, encourages complete vertical integration. I call this additional reason for integration the information-acquisition reason.

The strength of the information-acquisition reason depends upon the small-numbers structure of the bauxite-supply industry, but the general idea that integration can improve investment planning if processing capital must be committed before operation has recently been proven for a competitive industry by

Kenneth Arrow.[29] Arrow's model differs somewhat from the case of bauxite, but his results are illustrative. His model is of a fully competitive industry with an upstream raw-material producing stage and a downstream raw-material processing stage. The supply of each upstream firm is a random variable positively correlated with the output of all other upstream firms; it cannot be altered by any decisions, but the firm knows its supply one period in advance. Demand for the processed product is nonrandom, and the demand function is known by all firms, but downstream firms must choose their quantity of capital one period in advance. The downstream-stage technology is homogeneous and has a positive elasticity of substitution between the two inputs, raw material and capital. The raw material is homogeneous, and its market clears through price during each period. Arrow shows that if there is no vertical integration to begin with, a downstream firm will have an incentive to buy one or more upstream firms, because this improves his forecast of the spot price of upstream product and therefore his ability to choose the level of capital. As Arrow stresses, the advantage of integration is *not* to ensure in advance a quantity of raw materials, nor does it afford protection against scarcity as reflected in high prices, but rather it allows the firm to predict the market quantity of raw material, and thus the price of the final output, before investing. It can thus make a more informed investment decision.

In Arrow's model, three crucial features produce the incentive to integrate. First, upstream firms have useful information otherwise unavailable to downstream firms. Second, downstream capital is durable and takes time to put in place. Third, information about the upstream industry cannot be sold independently of the product itself. Each of these can be seen to apply to the miner-refiner relationship, though for somewhat different reasons and in somewhat different ways.

There is little doubt that the firm owning a bauxite deposit knows more about the size and composition of the deposit than anyone else does, and except under special circumstances, this is closely guarded information. It might also have a better idea of the availability of other deposits within its geographical region. For example, Alcoa of Australia surely knows more about southwestern Australia's bauxite potential than, say, its Northern

Hemisphere customers do. The bauxite miner is also aware of the variations in the bauxite within a given deposit and can adjust the composition of the output. When Comalco extended its Weipa mine in 1972, "an important consideration . . . was the maintenance of a balanced programme designed to extend and conserve the ore body by the appropriate selection and blending of various grades of bauxite."[30] The mine operator also has access to another piece of valuable information, namely, any likely future changes in mining costs, resulting from, say, variations in overburden characteristics.

The application of Arrow's result also requires that refining plants are long lived, that it takes time to build them, and that they are bauxite-specific. The information presented in Chapter 1 on alumina plants strongly supports the first two requirements. The bauxite-specificity requirement is too extreme, because plants can usually be modified, but this does not affect the qualitative predictions of the model; modifications are expensive and for the long run. The fact that the alumina-refining capital stock is slow to adjust means that the markets for the various types of bauxite can experience extended periods of disequilibrium relative to the conditions that would hold if the capital stock could be economically turned over more rapidly. And this is why a refiner can pick a "winner" or a "loser" when choosing the kind of bauxite and technology he will use.

The same logic applies to decisions about refinery location and technology. Of course, the argument relies upon the fact that alumina refineries are specific to the aluminum industry and therefore next to useless for any other purpose. The implied low salvage value of a refinery outside the industry means the refiner is locked into the industry, as well as the bauxite type and location he has chosen. The high proportion of refining costs that are fixed capital costs means that other costs (such as the cost of the bauxite) can increase greatly before the refiner will walk away from his refinery. The miner's information advantage and the vulnerability of refiners after they have committed their capital give mine developers an incentive to supply false information during the initial–contract award stage so that their bargaining position will be strong in the post–contract award stage.

For upstream integration to be useful it must somehow improve the downstream firm's supply of information, and for this to occur there must be something wrong with the market for information. In Arrow's model the market for information does not exist, because of the rather peculiar specification that information about the upstream product cannot be sold independently of the product itself. It is impossible, for example, for market research firms to collect, analyze, and sell reliable information on future industry prospects. When the upstream industry is competitive, this specification seems somewhat artificial, but in the case of bauxite it is easy to see why a market for information about bauxite deposits might be inclined to fail. The reason is what Williamson calls "information impactedness," a condition that exists when the true underlying circumstances relevant to a transaction are known to one or more parties but cannot easily be discerned by others. In such situations, arm's-length exchanges can be hazardous because of strategic misrepresentation, or put more simply, because of calculated lying by the one or more parties possessing the information. In this case, it is the owners of bauxite deposits who are in the potentially more manipulative position.

Williamson argues that the problem is most extreme when opportunism and bounded rationality are combined with small numbers and information asymmetry. Opportunism and bounded rationality are presumed always to exist, so bauxite traders are not unusual on these counts. Furthermore, information asymmetry is not a necessary condition, although it does, as in the bauxite business, exacerbate the problem. The vital ingredient is therefore small numbers, and this feature is certainly true of the market for bauxite deposits. At any point in time there is a limited number of untapped bauxite deposits which are feasible economically and available for exploitation. If each is owned by an independent party, the bauxite-deposits supply industry would be oligopolistic. Here the relevant industry boundary is the *entire* bauxite-deposit supply industry, not one of its segments, because during the contract-award stage refiners have still not committed themselves to the segment they will rely upon for commodity trade. So while *commodity* trade occurs in segments that approach monopolies on the supply side (and the demand side), bauxite-*information* trade occurs industry-wide.

This is important because the oligopolistic rather than monopolistic structure of the industry-wide market inhibits collusion and joint profit-maximizing behavior. If the bauxite-information market during the contract-award stage was a bilateral monopoly, or something close to it, the bauxite owner would supply accurate information to his processing partner, because otherwise the joint profit available to both would be reduced. Calculated lying would not be consistent with joint profit-maximization during the operational stage of the relationship. On the other hand, such lying would also not occur if the bauxite-deposit industry were a large-numbers industry, because, as Williamson pointed out,

> one of the remarkable attributes of large-numbers competition is that it serves to safeguard buyers against opportunistic representations of suppliers who enjoy an information advantage. Thus, even though suppliers may be much more fully appraised of certain attributes of the transaction, this is of little consequence if buyers can continuously elicit competitive bids in the marketplace. The competitive process in these circumstances makes it unprofitable for any party to engage in strategic behavior.[31]

To summarize the argument, and to put it in more practical terms, the owner of a bauxite deposit has an incentive to produce falsely optimistic information about his deposit to attract as many refiners as possible to commit themselves to him as a supplier. For example, he can select appropriate samples for assaying and pilot-plant testing, he can overestimate reserves, he can underestimate overburden depth, and so on, and he is in a position to do so. As a result, his arm's-length customers may build capacities in excess of his capacity, and thus he immediately has a superior bargaining position when the commodity trading begins. To avoid outcomes like this, refiners have an incentive to integrate across the information market, and they do this by undertaking their own exploration programs and by owning their own inventory of mining leases.

As to why internal organization is preferred by refiners as a means of acquiring information, the most important point is that internal organization serves to attenuate incentives to exploit information impactedness. The firm's internal authority and performance-auditing schemes largely prevent the mining division from passing false information to the refining division. The firm's internal communication codes and auditing powers also act to overcome the basic information asymmetry itself.

Industry Structure, Behavior, and Integration

The motives for upstream integration that arise from the special structural traits of the overall industry and the behavioral patterns that correspond to these structural traits should now be considered. For the most part, the complications of bauxite's and alumina's heterogeneity and the market failure they cause are assumed not to exist in the industry. This absence draws attention to the distinction between vertical integration motivated by failure of a heterogenous commodity's market, and vertical integration motivated by structural failure of a market. Although these two causes of vertical integration work together in practice and probably interact with each other positively, I want to establish that either one can independently still cause vertical integration. By industry structure and behavior I mean the standard, familiar theory of industrial organization, revolving around concentration, barriers to entry, pricing behavior, and so on.

Integration as an Element of Behavior

Previous studies of the aluminum industry, such as those by Wallace and Peck, have concluded that vertical integration as a *structural* feature of the industry is an important barrier to entry into the industry and is at least a partial explanation of why the industry is so highly concentrated. This line of reasoning takes vertical integration as given and then quite correctly uses theory and evidence to derive what patterns of behavior it produces. This will be pursued below, but first, it is established that the industry has other basic structural features that promote vertical integration as a form of *behavior*. Briefly, the argument is that bauxite mining, alumina refining, and primary smelting each has structural features that even without vertical integration would still produce moderate to high firm concentration at that stage.

Each vertical pairing of the three necessarily linked stages could confront problems of either of two types, according to how symmetrically the power in each of the two bilateral markets is distributed. Symmetrical market power in bilateral situations amounts to bilateral oligopoly and the problems discussed earlier, a likely event in the bauxite market. On the other hand, asymmetrical market power leads to the exploitation of the weaker stage by the stronger stage, a likely event in the alumina market and a problem for primary aluminum producers. Both of these problems can motivate firms to integrate vertically.

To develop this argument, assume a model of the industry where bauxite and alumina are homogeneous and no transport costs exist, thus eliminating the basic reasons, previously discussed, for vertical integration. Assume further that since the industry's birth, vertical integration has been prohibited, but that by some miracle the market has still grown and developed just as it has in reality. We therefore have three industries rather than one: bauxite, alumina, and primary aluminum. It is probable that in our hypothetical world, the bauxite industry would be moderately, tending toward highly, concentrated. This would result from two sources of barriers to entry. First, there is the absolute cost barrier resulting from the limited number of bauxite deposits having comparable factors such as quality, location, overburden, royalties, and local political stability. Going firms tend to control the most favorable deposits and, in the process, gain a cost advantage over potential entrants. Detailed information has already been presented (see Chapter 1 and Table 2.5) describing the international location of commercially feasible bauxite deposits. Although there always has been and still is plenty of bauxite, the comparable costs of mining a potential ton of ingot at a particular point in time are what matters. Given this important consideration, the absolute cost barrier has always existed.

During the last twenty years or so, however, bauxite mining has had to confront another entry barrier. The push into undeveloped areas, into a poorer quality of deposits, or both, have had the effect of creating substantial scale economies in bauxite mining. An efficient mine for the early 1980s might cost $500 million, add 8 to 10 percent to the world's capacity and suffer a significant average (largely fixed) cost disadvantage at less than minimum efficient scale. The new entrant has the choice of attempting to find and secure the rights on a suitable deposit, to find the capital, and to face the marketing problems of adding 10 percent to the world's supply, or of operating at a cost disadvantage, at least over the medium run. Taken together, the barriers to entry into bauxite mining are significant. In the terms introduced by Joe Bain in his seminal book on barriers to entry, they can be classifed as "substantial to very high." [32]

In alumina refining, substantial economies of scale present the classic barrier to entry and have always done so. The long-run average cost curve falls up to a capacity that today would add 3 to 4 percent to the world's capacity and that would cost between $250 million and $500 million, and the curve rises quite steeply below minimum efficient scale. The new entrant also faces absolute cost disadvantages, owing to his lack of experience in the technically sophisticated task of designing and operating a refinery, and possibly also owing to penalty interest rates caused by his lack of credibility as a successful refiner. Rating these barriers to entry on Bain's classification scheme again yields a classification for alumina refining of substantial to very high entry barriers.

Barriers to entry into primary smelting are probably moderate to substantial. They are qualitatively very similar to the barriers in alumina, but at most half the height. Two previous studies have put them into Bain's "substantial" category, but with respect to just the U.S. economy.[33] The bulk of the primary aluminum market in the 1980s is at least intraregional (North America, Europe, and so on), if not worldwide. This widespread distribution has the effect of lowering entry barriers caused by scale economies, as evidenced by the relatively large number of new entrants over the last fifteen years. But transport costs and trade restrictions are still sufficient to keep barriers in the moderate to substantial range.

In our model of the aluminum industry, where vertical integration is barred, it has thus been shown that one of the stages of production has moderate to substantial barriers to entry and two have substantial to very high barriers. On the basis of the theory of industrial organization and previous empirical studies, it can confidently be predicted that barriers to entry of these magnitudes would lead to moderate to high levels of firm concentration. There is some uncertainty in the literature regarding the extent to which concentration is a causal function of more basic structural features, such as barriers to entry, but in my opinion the dependence of concentration upon barriers to entry is strong and becomes stronger as the period of time under consideration increases from, say, several years to ten or twenty years. Given moderate to high concentration, the theory and evidence for oligopolistic markets imply that mutual dependence would be recognized, meaning that the firms in each stage, or industry, would attempt to "gang up on" and extract rents from their mutual suppliers, customers, or both.

But if concentration, mutual-dependence recognition, and collusion are moderate to high in each of the bauxite, alumina, and primary industries, then the model predicts two vertically back-to-back bilateral oligopolies. The prices and quantities occurring in the two markets are theoretically indeterminate and depend principally upon the degree of collusion within each stage and the relative degrees of collective market-power at each stage. Countless scenarios are possible, but in all scenarios, apart from those having market outcomes approximating perfect competition, incentives for vertical integration will come from: (1) the costs of bargaining, contracting, and so on, and (2) intermediate-product prices differing from the sellers' marginal costs or the buyers' marginal-value products.

Integrating because of the costs of bargaining or contracting does not require elaboration. This incentive is likely to become stronger as the overall degree of collusion increases and as the bilateral power-balance becomes more even; it would therefore be more important for bauxite-alumina integration than for alumina-primary integration, given the relatively high, and similar, concentration of firms in the bauxite and alumina industries.

Integrating because of unsatisfactory intermediate-product prices can be motivated by either the desire of relatively weak buyers to avoid paying above marginal cost for inputs or the desire of relatively strong sellers to exploit any downstream elasticities of input substitution. These two motivations are quite different and deserve separate treatment. The first will occur in a market where the upstream sellers successfully collude and have enough power to force the downstream buyers to pay a price above minimum average cost for the intermediate product. This market power asymmetry is quite likely in the model of the alumina market, where a primary aluminum producer has an incentive to integrate back into alumina either to appropriate the oligopoly rents for himself or to be a party to destroying them if other primary producers integrate back as well. The market-power asymmetry is necessary, because when it is significant but symmetrical, the market is a bilateral oligopoly and the mutual incentive to integrate comes from wanting to avoid bargaining costs. Such a situation would be more likely in the bauxite market. But in the alumina market, even if the primary aluminum producer has an incentive to integrate and is allowed to do so in the model, he has to be able to scale the entry barriers that were the source of the oligopoly rents in alumina to begin with. Or put another way, if he can scale the barriers, why can't everyone else? I will take up this issue later on; it is sufficient now to have shown that primary producers have this incentive to integrate back to alumina.

When integration is motivated by the desire of relatively strong sellers to exploit downstream elasticities of input substitution, it is theoretically possible for the upstream firms to benefit from integrating forward. For example, an alumina producer earning oligopoly profits by selling alumina at a price exceeding minimum average cost can further benefit by integrating into primary if the production function for primary is characterized by positive elasticities of substitution between alumina and any other input factor or factors.[34] Existing downstream firms select an inefficient input combination by underutilizing alumina because of its high price, although doing so is privately optimal. The integrated alumina-primary producer, on the other hand, may be able to select a more efficient point on the smelting production function by performing his optimization calculation with the price of alumina equal to marginal cost. Two potential sources of additional gain exist: first, a decrease in the unit costs of primary production that *exceeds* the difference between alumina's marginal cost and market price, and second, gains in margin or volume resulting from a new primary pricing policy. These gains are difficult to see intuitively and lengthy to model and derive, but all gains necessarily depend upon substitutability between inputs in the downstream production process, a condition unmet in either primary smelting or alumina refining. The bauxite-alumina conversion ratio and the alumina-primary conversion ratio are fixed (for any given pairing of grades), virtually independently of the quantities applied of capital, labor, and so on. There is a slight tradeoff between plant sophistication (capital) and conversion ratios (material input), but it is insensitive to the sorts of relative price changes that could actually occur in the aluminum industry. Summing up, it is unlikely that forward integration by an alumina firm would produce benefits from a reorganization of input ratios.

I have argued that the basic structural features of the upstream aluminum industry are such that the barriers to entry into each individual stage are sufficient to produce a substantial to high concentration of firms in bauxite and alumina, and a moderate to substantial concentration in primary. If the resulting collusion produced a power symmetry on the two sides of a market, a likely event in the bauxite market, parties on both sides would be motivated to integrate to avoid the costs and risks of trading on markets that are bilateral oligopolies. On the other hand, if a power asymmetry occurred, probable in the alumina market, then the weaker parties would have an incentive to integrate upstream to get the raw material at cost of production. Vertical integration under either of these circumstances is, in the final analysis, a result of industry structure.

Integration as an Element of Structure

Using a simple model of the aluminum industry in which vertical integration is prohibited, I have shown that vertical integration caused only by industry structure would occur if the prohibition against it were lifted. Let me now take a large step closer to reality by allowing such vertical integration to exist as a structural factor. In this circumstance, integration fosters patterns of behavior that are generally advantageous for integrated firms and that require a high degree of vertical integration throughout the industry. In a dynamic setting, vertical integration as a structural factor can perpetuate itself because of the benefits it indirectly accrues for the firms. The industry life-cycle model explained the original reasons for the high degree of vertical integration; this section helps explain why it has remained higher than the life-cycle model would predict.

Integration and Concentration: Levels and Trends. Now that vertical integration has been readmitted to the list of structural elements, the list is now a good approximation of reality in the industry. Consequently, actual data from the industry can be used to quantify the structural elements that play important roles in my argument. I focus on three structural elements: the balance of an individual firm's vertical integration, the concentration of sellers in the industry, and the concentration of buyers.

Table 2.7 gives integration-balance ratios for the six major firms of the two upstream markets, presented at four equidistant points in time over the twenty-five-year period of 1955 through 1979. The ratios use alumina capacity as the denominator, bauxite or primary capacity as the numerator, and are presented in

Table 2.7 Ratios of bauxite-alumina and primary-alumina capacities for the six majors, 1955, 1963, 1971, and 1979 (in percentages at start of year).[a]

Ratio	1955	1963	1971	1979
Bauxite / Alumina				
Alcoa	119.9	117.5	96.9	104.6
Alcan	98.9	90.5	86.5	71.8
Reynolds	102.2	94.6	112.2	89.1
Kaiser	93.8	156.3	118.5	105.3
PUK	96.8	83.0	56.1	62.4
Alusuisse	57.0	45.0	83.1	90.2
Total group	102.5	102.9	93.7	90.6
Primary / Alumina				
Alcoa	69.2	89.1	65.3	47.5
Alcan	80.9	68.4	92.0	102.3
Reynolds	74.9	81.4	93.6	83.2
Kaiser	99.5	92.9	60.8	71.6
PUK	95.5	88.8	79.5	81.0
Alusuisse	78.1	61.9	173.9	106.5
Total group	79.8	80.1	81.0	73.2

Source: Data described in Appendix A.
a. Based on plant capacity data in primary equivalents.

percentages. There are two main facts to notice. First, each firm has throughout the period operated in all three stages, and with only several notable exceptions, the ratios indicate operation within the neighborhood of balance. (Note when assessing this latter point that, *industry-wide*, the bauxite/alumina ratio and the alumina/primary ratio typically range between 105 and 130 percent, discounting in large part the "excesses" of bauxite and "deficiencies" of primary implied in the table.) Second, both ratios have declined for the majors as a group, and for most of the individual firms (Alusuisse being the notable exception).

Table 2.8 shows the same firms' shares of capacities and six firm concentration ratios, for all three stages of production. The data for bauxite represent a firm's share of the selling side of the bauxite market, while the data for primary represent a firm's share of the buying side of the alumina market. The data for alumina represent a firm's share of the market for buying bauxite *and* for selling alumina. The first obvious point is that both seller and buyer concentration have been high for both intermediate-product markets, a fact strongly reinforced when it is recalled that these are for the world industry. In most individual nations, typically only one to three of the majors account for 80 or 90 percent of capacity. Second, it is very clear that the concentration of firms in each stage of production has steadily declined, particularly that of bauxite sellers.

The important point here is that throughout the observation period a small group of firms had a large share of each production stage and hence could operate virtually independently of the rest of the upstream industry. The shares of the two intermediate-product markets not represented by *potential* intracorporate transfers were small, leaving a potentially thin market for outsiders. Data on *actual* transfers are not available, but my strong impression, gleaned from personal contact with the industry, is that the bulk of actual bauxite and alumina exchanges were intracorporate, and most of the rest were intermajor.[35]

Effects of structure on conduct. Given this industry structure, consider the plight of a firm wishing to enter the industry. The high concentration and the limited free market in the upstream aluminum industry mean that the potential entrant must choose from several difficult options, options that were even less attrac-

Table 2.8 Shares of the six majors in world bauxite, alumina, and primary capacities: 1955, 1963, 1971, and 1979 (in percentages at start of year).[a]

Stage of Production	1955	1963	1971	1979
Bauxite				
Alcoa	28.2	20.0	19.1	23.5
Alcan	25.6	22.4	14.1	8.1
Reynolds·	16.4	13.7	10.6	6.7
Kaiser	11.0	17.3	12.3	8.1
PUK	4.7	6.7	5.3	4.5
Alusuisse	2.3	1.9	2.1	3.5
Total[b]	88.2	82.0	63.5	54.4
Alumina				
Alcoa	24.8	18.0	23.0	27.6
Alcan	27.3	26.3	19.0	13.9
Reynolds	16.9	15.4	11.1	9.2
Kaiser	12.3	11.7	12.2	9.4
PUK	5.1	8.6	11.0	8.9
Alusuisse	4.2	4.6	2.9	4.8
Total[b]	90.6	84.6	79.2	73.8
Primary				
Alcoa	20.4	16.9	17.1	15.1
Alcan	26.2	19.2	19.9	16.3
Reynolds	15.0	13.4	11.8	8.8
Kaiser	14.6	11.6	8.4	7.8
PUK	5.8	8.1	10.0	8.3
Alusuisse	3.9	3.0	5.8	5.9
Total[b]	85.9	72.2	73.0	62.2

Source: Data described in Appendix A.
a. Based on plant capacity data in primary equivalents.
b. Equals the six-firm concentration ratio.

tive prior to the mid-1960s than they are now. The first option is to enter the industry fully integrated into all stages of production, namely bauxite mining, alumina refining, primary smelting, and fabrication of final products. The major alternative option is to enter only one or two stages, the popular combination being smelting and fabrication. (Entry into primary smelting is traditionally regarded as "entry into the aluminum industry," unlike entry into fabrication.) By examining the problems associated with the options it becomes clear that the going aluminum firms (principally the majors) have substantial advantages over new entrants or potential entrants, a condition maintained largely through vertical integration.

The main problem with the option of fully integrated entry is the volume and nature of the resources that must be committed. The obvious one is capital, assuming for the moment entry at minimum efficient scale. At the extreme, an entrant wanting a fully balanced and efficient scale operation would have to have at least $2 billion, over half of this for the several smelters and semifabrication plants needed to balance a refinery of minimum efficient scale. This sort of capital requirement would strain the enthusiasm of any potential entrant's management and board of directors, and more important, the entrant's access to the capital market. The latter is Bain's familiar "absolute capital requirements" barrier to entry, which is based on the belief that individual firms face increasing capital costs, or capital rationing, as the size of finance requirements increases (ceteris paribus). It is highly likely that most potential entrants could not raise $2 billion to enter the aluminum industry, while those that could would often experience a higher average cost of capital than going firms. The underlying assumption here is that the capital markets do not value the rate of return or the solvency advantages of being fully integrated versus being single-stage as much as they discount for the risk associated with a large capital sum being tied up with a single firm. But this is just the sort of imperfection in the capital market usually assumed to cause absolute capital requirements barriers to entry.

The new entrant would also have to find several other crucial resources, particularly, a suitable bauxite deposit, power for the smelters, technical expertise to design the plants, and management experienced in the industry. But because each of these resources would also have to be found by new single-stage firms entering the stage for which the resource is specific, and because each resource tends to be used only in a single stage, the vertically integrating entrant faces the same costs for it as do nonintegrating entrants. An exception might exist in the case of senior technicians and managers experienced in aluminum, because such personnel resources are limited in supply and would largely be in the employ of going firms. The new entrant seeking perhaps 10 to 20 such people to design and run the integrated operation may have to offer higher average compensation packages than the single-stage entrant requiring only three or four such people. This amounts to an absolute cost disadvantage, but in perspective it is probably of little importance.

The fully integrated, efficient-scale entrant would also have to confront the traditional economies-of-scale barrier, namely the problem of quickly securing a downstream market share commensurate with half a million tons of primary (approximately 4 percent of the 1980 world market). Note, however, that entry as a vertically integrated firm, rather than as a single-stage firm, only adds to this problem to the extent that the integrated entrant ends up with a larger market share than the single-stage entrant. This will arise when the single-stage entrant enters a stage of production with a relatively small minimum efficient scale. This quite general proposition is an important practical consideration in the aluminum industry, because smelting and fabrication, the historically popular stages for entry, have much smaller minimum efficient scales than does refining.

The entrant who believes that balanced integration is essential has two alternatives apart from efficient-scale entry. The first is entry at less-than-efficient scale. It has the advantage of cutting down on capital costs and the required market share, but the disadvantage of increased unit costs. Data presented earlier indicate that cost penalties would be considerable, particularly in alumina production. The second alternative is to locate other potential entrants with similar aspirations, or going firms with plans for expansion, and to form joint-venture plants. This alternative would be particularly attractive in bauxite and alumina, and it has the strong advantage of simultaneously satisfying all of the constraints. There are problems with joint ventures as well, but there is no doubt whatsoever that their blossoming in the upstream aluminum industry has been in part a response by entrants to entry barriers.

So far it has been assumed that successful entry requires complete integration; it is now time to examine this assumption. What, for example, would be the problems associated with entry as a specialist in primary-aluminum production who would rely upon arm's-length supplies of alumina (ignoring here the down-stream integration strategy)? And what about the bauxite miner who would rely upon arm's-length sales, or the specialized refiner who would rely upon arm's-length markets for both input and output? Briefly, the problem with single-stage entry is that the specialist must be a buyer *or* seller in a market where a small group of integrated firms constitutes almost all of the other *potential* buyers *and* sellers. If the integrated firms successfully collude, they can, as a group, dictate terms to the specialized firm to the extent of controlling its rate of return or even driving it out of business. It is here that the high levels of concentration evidenced earlier play a necessary role.

Before examining the methods that the integrated firms could use to control specialized producers, it is necessary to show that conditions favor sufficient oligopolistic coordination among the majors to allow the unity of group behavior needed to keep specialist producers "under control." A thorough treatment of this issue would be a lengthy undertaking, involving a rigorous analysis of the multitude of factors affecting oligopolistic coordination that have arisen in theoretical and empirical studies of oligopoly.

But because the aluminum majors and the markets they operate in have characteristics that are mostly quite conducive to coordination, the following brief point-by-point treatment is adequate. (It is somewhat of a digression from the argument here, however.)

1. Only six firms collectively control major shares of the three upstream markets (recall Table 2.8). It is unanimously believed that fewness promotes coordination.

2. Furthermore, the size distribution of the majors can be seen to be conducive to coordination. The market-share data in Table 2.8 show clearly that Alcoa dominates the other five, a pattern supported by history and admitted frankly by the other majors. The only possible challenger to Alcoa is Alcan, originally an Alcoa subsidiary. The remaining four have quite similar market shares, which should encourage their tacit collusion, since they would be well aware of the others' situation.

3. The majors have very similar vertical and horizontal structures. They are similarly integrated vertically, they each have

production and selling operations in all major regions of the world, and they have each invaded each other's home market. Strategic symmetry on these planes encourages cooperation.

4. The firms use the same basic technologies, have very similarly sized plants, and have similar cost structures.

5. The firms' products are commodities (in the sense used in marketing studies); although the products are not all homogeneous, quality differences are easily measured. The products also are unbranded and undifferentiated. The major variables requiring coordination are price and quantity, the two variables usually considered the easiest to coordinate in an oligopoly.[36]

6. Only one of the majors, PUK, has widely diversified into other industries. Kaiser and Schweizerische Aluminum AG (Alusuisse) diversified during the 1970s, however. It is not obvious how these differences affect cooperation, although I am inclined to believe that cooperation declines as the number of diversified firms and their degrees of diversification increase.[37] That five of the six majors are totally (Alcoa, Alcan, and Reynolds) or heavily (Alusuisse and Kaiser) dependent upon aluminum improves their understanding of each other's position and makes them less inclined to upset an equilibrium upon which their entire business depends.

7. The average financial performances and financial structures of the majors are very similar, which is both an assistance to, and possibly an indication of, successful cooperation.

8. Most of the majors have ample opportunity for, and give evidence of, effective interfirm communication. Here I have in mind the sort of communication modeled by Stigler and Michael Spence, rather than the explicit, direct communication one immediately thinks of ever since the U.S.'s electrical equipment conspiracy of the 1950s.[38] In particular, aluminum firms regularly make public quite specific plans for new upstream projects or plant expansions, a practice known as capacity signaling. The information is usually published well in advance and contains data on size, cost, location, and so on. Such information is extremely important in an industry where capacity additions are lumpy and take time to implement. My observations are that aluminum firms constantly monitor the financial press for market signals, which they mention frequently and use immediately

to modify company plans. There are countless examples of capacity signaling, but a very explicit one came from Alusuisse during a period of industry-wide excess capacity. In its 1971 report to shareholders, the directors lectured, "In our opinion the problem of excess capacity in the aluminum industry can only be solved if the producers postpone their expansion plans until demand catches up with existing capacities, and the large inventories of primary aluminum have been reduced. We have drawn the consequences from this situation and have correspondingly cut back production." [39] It has been suggested that joint ventures between the majors provide yet another opportunity for the exchange of information and the development of cooperative patterns of behavior. This is examined in Chapter 4.

Taken together, these factors facilitating coordination seem quite powerful. There is one strong factor working in the opposite direction, however, and that is the cost structure of the upstream industry. The high proportion of average costs that are fixed makes price cutting in times of excess capacity more attractive than production cutbacks—for the individual firm that is, not for the group. Very little is known about pricing behavior in bauxite and alumina (besides, most prices are just transfer prices), but there is a lot of evidence that the industry has problems with recalcitrant firms in the primary aluminum market. [40] Overall though, both theory and evidence strongly suggest that the aluminum majors can, and often have, successfully coordinated their upstream operations. The most important variable for coordination is quantity (that is, capacity).

Given the ability of the majors to coordinate their behavior, and given that they are the "buyers" *and* the "sellers" that execute the great majority of transactions on the bauxite and alumina "markets," they have the potential as a group to give any unintegrated entrant a very rough introduction to the industry. They have two principal methods of doing so. First, they can use a price squeeze either to allow the single-stage firm barely to stay in business, or to drive it out of business. The mechanics of a price squeeze are easy to see: for example, in the case of a specialized primary-aluminum producer, the integrated firms would sell alumina to him at a price that would prevent him from undercutting them in the primary-aluminum market or in downstream product markets, or even at a price that would make him run at a loss. The specialist has no choice, because the majors have monopoly power over the alumina market — in fact, this is the stage they have always dominated most completely (refer back Table 2.8). Similarly, an independent bauxite supplier can sell only to the majors, and here they have monopsony power. A specialist alumina producer would be the proverbial "meat in the sandwich," a predicament rendering the producer apparently so vulnerable that it has prevented such a specialist from *ever* emerging.

Second, the majors can use the possibly even more destructive method of quantity rationing. They can refuse to trade with specialists, or they can use them to absorb the cyclicality of final demand, and given the considerable cyclicality in aluminum demand and the heavy fixed costs, that would be most attractive. The proposition that rationing in an intermediate-product market between two vertically linked stages of production can motivate a firm to integrate vertically has been demonstrated by Jerry Green.[41] He shows that an intermediate-product market afflicted with price inflexibility and stochastic final demand, and the temporary shortage and gluts that they imply, will incite all firms to adopt perfectly balanced integration strategies. Unintegrated firms get caught because they must make production plans (and hence input plans) before the realization of exogenous demand becomes known, a crucial feature, which coincidentally is identical to the specification that "runs" Arrow's model of vertical integration and information. Green's rationing rule is of the all-or-nothing variety, and his model's product is unstorable; such specifications are generally unrealistic, definitely for aluminum, but as he points out, less-severe specifications would not alter the qualitative results. Bauxite and alumina can both be stored indefinitely, so inventory is one possible insurance against rationing, but, as I detailed previously, storage cost can be very high relative to the value of the product.

The ability of the majors to squeeze prices, ration unintegrated firms, or to do both is probably not as complete as I have implied, but the risk does not have to be very high to deter entry. The cost, specificity, and durability of upstream assets mean that a specialized entrant is playing an expensive game, and a game from which exit is extremely unattractive. If the majors wish to deter single-stage entry, a sensible wish if they earn above-normal profits, they have to be capable of only moderate price squeezing or rationing.

In summary, the majors have an incentive to retain full and balanced integration as a means of restricting entry. Entrants or unintegrated firms have an incentive to become vertically integrated to avoid price squeezing or rationing by the majors. The integration behavior of the firms that have entered the industry in the last several decades is quite consistent with these propositions. Table 2.1 showed that the typical strategy of the fourteen private, post-1955 entrants has been, first, entry into primary and fabrication to secure a foothold in the market, and then to integrate upstream later. Barriers to entry prevent immediate complete integration, but the intention and often the practice is to integrate, possibly because of price squeezing or rationing; as Comalco's Mark Rayner puts it, smaller producers need to integrate "to obtain raw materials at cost levels closer to those achieved by the major fully integrated producers." [42]

Interfirm Differences in Upstream Integration

The theory developed in this chapter indicates that there are strong motivations for firms in the upstream aluminum industry to be integrated across mining, refining, and smelting. We would therefore expect to observe that individual firms have integrated structures. The theory also implies that balanced capacities across the three stages are preferable, because intermediate-product markets can then be circumvented completely. Another prediction, therefore, is that integrated firms will have approximately the same capacity (in primary equivalents) in mining, refining, and smelting. The industry-wide data indicate that, on average, these expectations are fulfilled, but observation also reveals that there are some one- and two-stage producers, and a few producers with quite imbalanced capacities across the stages in which they operate. Validation of the theory requires an explanation of the unexpected behavior of these firms.

The method I have selected to explain this behavior involves the estimation of three cross-sectional ordinary least-squares regression models aimed at identifying those characteristics of an individual firm that are associated with incomplete and imbalanced integration. The estimated versions of the models are presented in detail in Appendix B, so only a summary is required here. The first model has as its dependent variable the number of stages of production out of three (bauxite, alumina, and primary) in which the forty-seven basic aluminum firms included in the sample were active in 1979. The second model has as its dependent variable the bauxite-alumina capacity balance of each of the thirty-five out of forty-seven firms that were active in mining, refining, or both in 1979. The third model has as its dependent variable the alumina-primary capacity balance of each of the forty out of forty-seven firms active in refining, smelting, or both in 1979.

A variety of possible explanatory variables was tried, chosen both deductively (from the theory) and inductively (from examining any special characteristics of unintegrated firms). As the details in Appendix B reveal, a number of modestly significant explanatory variables were discovered, together explaining 18 percent of the variation in the first dependent variable and about 30 percent in the other two dependent variables. What follows is a description of the logic behind each of the useful explanatory variables and a discussion of its implications for the validity of the theory.

The most significant variable in the estimated models is the number of years since a firm entered the upstream aluminum industry. The longer a firm has been involved in the industry, the more likely it is to have complete, balanced integration. This result comes as no surprise, given the empirical evidence (Table 2.5) regarding the strategies for vertical integration of firms entering the industry since 1955. Furthermore it is not at odds with the theoretical prediction that firms prefer complete and balanced integration; it merely shows that the barriers to entry into upstream aluminum prevent instant arrival at an ideal vertical structure.

However, the link between years since entry and vertical structure is not significant as far as bauxite-alumina balance is concerned. Firms with bauxite-alumina capacity imbalances do not show a significant tendency to alleviate their imbalances over time. These firms have used arrangements across the bauxite market apart from vertical integration, and to understand this we have to look at their other distinguishing characteristics. The model using firms' bauxite-alumina balances as the dependent variable shows that there are two types of firms that have imbalances: Japanese firms and firms indigenous to bauxite source countries. As I will show in detail in the next chapter, these firms trade bauxite at arm's length among each other, arrangements that have arisen for a variety of largely noneconomic reasons. Until recently, the Japanese national strategy was one of noninvolvement in direct investment in resource projects in other countries, and because Japan has had no bauxite deposits of its own, its aluminum producers have been forced to buy bauxite at arm's length. Their demand engendered several arm's-length bauxite suppliers in Australia and Southeast Asia. So the imbalances of the Japanese firms and their suppliers were caused and sustained by a national policy, and hence they were prevented from behaving in a manner consistent with the theory. Recently, Japan has begun to encourage overseas investment by its firms that use raw materials; a policy change caused by experiencing precisely the sorts of problems with arm's-length markets predicted by the theory.

The only other variable consistently linked with firms' vertical structures is a dummy variable that equals 1 for state-owned firms. These firms tend to be involved in fewer stages of production and have more imbalanced capacities than other firms. These relationships were suggested by the data, and they probably result from state-owned firms' being less sensitive to the risks associated with arm's-length trading than privately owned firms. State-owned firms may justify the risks on political grounds, such as the need for a domestic smelter for security reasons or for reasons of national status. Governments may also care less about the financial implications of opportunistic exploitation by trading partners because losses can be absorbed more easily, or can even be disguised, in national budgets.

One other variable that was weak statistically but that always had the expected sign was a measure of firms' product specialization. As a firm's estimated percentage of sales from aluminum industry products increases, so too does its vertical balance. This relationship was hypothesized on the grounds that aluminum specialists prefer to avoid the risks associated with arm's-length trading, while in contrast, firms diversified into other industries can more easily absorb the risks. The statistical weakness of this variable may have been owing to measurement errors, because it was estimated very roughly for a number of firms.

So although the estimated models explain only a limited amount of the variation in the three dependent variables, those explanatory variables that do have some statistical significance are not in conflict with the overall theory. Most firms do have complete and more or less balanced integration, and those that do not are either working toward that end or for some reason are better capable than most firms of absorbing the risks associated with reliance upon arm's-length markets.

Summary

By dichotomizing vertical organization into vertical integration and arm's-length interfirm markets, it has been shown that the aluminum industry is 80 to 90 percent reliant upon vertical integration for its upstream coordination. Stigler's life-cycle theory of vertical integration explains why vertical integration became so common, but it fails to explain why it has continued at such high levels.

The technical fact that bauxites and aluminas are heterogenous commodities, and that, consequently, pairs of vertically adjacent plants are technically complementary, means that without vertical integration, firms would operate in bilateral monopolistic or oligopolistic markets. The bargaining costs and financial risks associated with these market structures cause market failure, and firms resort to the relative efficiency of internal organization. This type of integration is motivated by market failure and not by anticompetitive behavior, and hence it improves the industry's allocative and technical efficiency. Enforced disintegration would not be in the industry's or the public's interest. But integration can also be advantageous for going firms because it can maintain high barriers to entry and therefore restrict entry, or encourage integrated entry at less-than-efficient scale. Integration under these circumstances is anticompetitive and not in the public's interest.

Integration into bauxite mining may also result from the desire of refiners to acquire information to aid in the efficient planning of refining facilities. Without integration into bauxite mining, refiners are vulnerable to the opportunistic behavior of miners. Integration for this reason promotes efficiency and is in the public's interest.

The incentives for upstream integration must be strong, because most firms are integrated across mining, refining, and smelting and have approximately balanced capacities across the three stages. Furthermore, many of the firms that do not have complete and balanced integration are pursuing strategies to take them in that direction. The only significant group of firms for which this generalization does not apply is a group of state-owned firms.

3 Upstream Long-term Sales Contracts

Empirical data show that the bauxite and alumina markets are those of a bilateral monopoly or a small-numbers bilateral oligopoly; I have argued that under such structures, spot markets fail in the sense that they involve transactions costs that can be reduced by substituting internal organization for market exchange. But, as Williamson points out, in a dynamic bilateral oligopoly, vertical integration is not the only alternative to spot markets; on what I have called the vertical organization continuum between spot markets and internal organization Williamson identifies two discrete alternatives: a complete, "once-for-all" contract, and a series of incomplete, sequential contracts. Indeed, the series of contracts is the alternative to internal organization that the aluminum firms actually consider as a practical alternative for upstream vertical organization — spot transactions tend to be used only when short-term or unexpected surpluses and shortages arise. The purpose of this chapter is to examine, theoretically and empirically, bauxite and alumina sales contracts, including their strengths and weaknesses, and when and why they do and do not occur.

By *sales contracts* I mean formal arrangements for strictly arm's-length transactions. This "strictly arm's-length" qualification is important: it eliminates from my discussion here all transactions between plants or organizations that have any common ownership, either direct or indirect. Furthermore, it has the effect of eliminating from my analysis the contracts used to organize the supply of bauxite or alumina into several major joint-venture operations. For example, 70 percent of the bauxite feed for the massive Queensland Alumina, Limited (QAL) consortium's refinery is supplied via long-term contracts between Comalco (the bauxite seller), and Alcan, Kaiser, and PUK (the bauxite buyers who together hold 70 percent of the equity of QAL). But Comalco owns the other 30 percent of QAL (and directly supplies this same proportion of the bauxite), and most important, it is part of the QAL joint-venture contract that Alcan, Kaiser, and PUK will purchase their bauxite exclusively from Comalco (with one caveat in the case of Alcan). The point is that the bauxite contracts are part of the joint-venture contract, and a crucial part at that; for this reason contracts of this type will be analyzed in the chapter on joint ventures. These contracts differ from strictly arm's-length contracts in ways that bear directly on the whole concept of vertical organization. The distinction has been made explicit at this stage because within the industry, and in everyday usage, *contracts* is usually taken to include the contracts associated with joint ventures.

I am not concerned with the differences in legal status between the contracts discussed in this chapter and what have been called spot transactions; most likely, to the extent that spot transactions occur, they involve agreements that are contractual in the legal sense. Here, I am more concerned with the temporal element. The contracts discussed in this chapter are what are normally called long-term contracts, typically of ten- or twenty-years' duration, that involve formal, legal documentation.

Long-term Arm's-length Contracts: Theory and Application

Consider first the possibility of once-for-all contracts for organizing exchanges between buyers and sellers. A once-for-all contract is a contract that fully specifies the terms and conditions of sale (price, quantity, quality, delivery, and so on) between the two parties, from some specified date until the unspecified, distant future, according to a set of rules and formulas that embrace all possible future contingencies. That is, at any point in time after the contract has become operational, whatever the past, prevailing, and expected economic climate, the contract will generate the complete terms of the next transaction.

Once such a contract was formulated, it would overcome all of the important limitations associated with spot transactions or incomplete, sequential contracts. Costs of future transactions would be minimal and risks would be eliminated, while at the same time the increased capital outlay for more expensive, specific, and durable assets involved in vertical integration would be avoided. But, there is no point in expanding on these virtues of once-for-all contracts, because for other reasons they are infeasible, if not impossible.

> The dilemma posed by once-for-all contracts is this: lest independent parties interpret contractual ambiguities to their own advantage, which differences can be resolved only by haggling or, ultimately, litigation, contingent supply relations ought exhaustively to be stipulated. But exhaustive stipulation, assuming that it is feasible, is itself costly. Thus although, if production functions were known, appropriate responses to final demand or factor price changes might be deduced, the very costliness of specifying the functions and securing agreement discourages the effort. The problem is made even more severe where changing technology poses production redesign issues. Here it is doubtful that, despite great effort and expense, contractual efforts reasonably to comprehend the range of possible outcomes will be successful.[1]

In other words the crucial feature of a once-for-all contract, its completeness, is probably impossible in most practical situations. This problem, of course, is familiar to students of the work on general equilibrium by Kenneth Arrow, Gerard Debreu, and their collaborators: "When environmental uncertainties are so numerous that they cannot all be considered . . . or, what comes perhaps to much the same thing, when any particular environmental risks are so hard to define and to distinguish from each other that it is impossible to base a firm betting or insurance contract upon the occurrence or non-occurrence of any of them, then for this reason alone it is impossible to have a system of contingency . . . markets."[2] These problems of excessive numbers, undefinable risks, and indistinguishable events are not problems of logic but of human limitations. That human beings are incapable of listing all possible future states of the world and specifying optimization rules, all at nonprohibitive costs, is a result of what Herbert Simon calls "bounded rationality"—"*the capacity of the human mind for formulating and solving complex problems is very small compared with the size of the problems whose solution is required for objectively rational behavior in the real world.*"[3] Even if complete once-for-all contracts were possible in a situation of bounded rationality and uncertainty, Williamson argues that opportunism (self-interest pursued with guile) and information impactedness (information asymmetry between parties to a transaction) would cause problems in contract enforcement, such as unambiguously determining the states of the world that have actually occurred in the world. For any or all of these reasons, then, it is reasonable to declare that once-for-all contracts are not a feasible means of organizing vertical exchanges.

Incomplete, sequential contracts are, however, a realistic alternative to spot transactions and vertical integration. Such contracts do not specify completely all terms, timing, and contingencies; they operate over some prespecified time period; and they arrange, at the time they are drawn up, for opportunities to allow adaptations to be made in response to changes in the state of the world. Such contracts must definitely be renegotiated at the termination of the specified time period, including the presumably simplest options of duplicating the previous terms or of breaking the buyer-seller relationship altogether. Nevertheless, because of their incompleteness in a dynamic world, their execution also usually involves frequent specifications of the terms of individual transactions (precise delivery dates, prices, grades, and so forth), and significant periodic adjustments of the overall contract, all *within* the specified time period.

The principal advantage of sequential contracts over spot transactions is that they offer some security on specific, durable assets, and allow investments to be amortized with more confidence. Although this advantage encourages lengthening the duration of such contracts, their incompleteness does subject the parties to trading or business risks, in the sense that changes in the state of the world not covered fully by the contract can render the original, mutually acceptable terms either "unfair" to one of the parties or jointly suboptimal. If one of the parties is disadvantaged while the other gains at his expense, the disadvantaged party may face a choice between honoring the now unattractive contract or accepting the costs and risks of litigation. If both parties desire to renegotiate the contract, as they might if the viability of the disadvantaged party is at risk under enforcement of the original terms, then the costs of haggling and the risks of opportunistic bargaining, the same problems that occur during spot transactions, must be faced.

In view of these problems, an optimal specific-term contract can be imagined. It is characterized by a duration, a degree of term specificity, and a level of completeness representing the best tradeoff between the need for security against fixed assets, the avoidance of trading risks associated with being locked into an incomplete contract, the costs and risks associated with contract renegotiation, and the costs and risks associated with leaving unsettled the fine details of actual future transactions under the contract. A number of factors impinge on the outcome of this optimization process in any particular exchange situation, but the most important include the level and nature of the uncertainty surrounding possible states of the world in the future; the links between the uncertainties and (ultimately) cash flow and profitability; capital intensity and the durability and degree of specificity of capital; and finally, the number of potential parties available for contracting.[4]

Applications to Bauxite and Alumina Markets

Rather than push this analysis further in general terms, a task already undertaken successfully by Williamson, it is more expeditious to trace the relationships for the bauxite and alumina markets alone. I have already demonstrated quite extensively the causes and effects of having a small number of potential parties available for contracting, which is particularly a problem after an initial contract has been let. Furthermore, I have shown that capital in the upstream stages appears in large, durable, and specific chunks. Together, these factors would encourage longer terms (to assure a reasonable return on capital) and relatively exhaustive contingency clauses (to minimize the renegotiation problems caused by small numbers). But another set of factors is working against both these tendencies, namely, the extent and nature of uncertainty. Briefly, there are several factors that recent experience has shown are highly variable and unpredictable, and upon which the economic performance of upstream operators who rely on long-term contracts is highly sensitive. These factors limit the extent of contingency clauses and keep contracts in effect for shorter terms.

One of the most important uncertainties during recent years has come from the advent of flexible exchange rates, rapid inflation, and international differences in inflation rates. These variables have had quite drastic effects on the real home-currency prices paid and received on international bauxite and alumina contracts, the great majority of contracts in these commodities being international. Such changes in effective prices can produce considerable tension between trading partners and can undermine the whole concept of a long-term international contract. As I will show, problems of these types have caused considerable trading losses, renegotiations, and some friction over the terms of bauxite and alumina contracts in the 1970s. Without significant exception, as far as I am aware, all contracts written in the late 1960s denote prices in the U.S. dollar—and it was during those years that long-term contracts for bauxite, and to a lesser extent for alumina, first took on quantitative significance; most of the contracts were of ten- or twenty-years' duration.

Another series of events during the early 1970s had a severe, disruptive effect on existing contracts, which for the most part lacked appropriate contingency clauses. The increase in the price of oil in 1973 set the ball rolling; repercussions for the aluminum industry included disproportionate cost of production implications for bauxite, alumina, and primary, and sharp increases in the relative cost of transport. The power-intensive smelting stage was worst hit by production-cost increases, particularly those smelters using oil-generated power: by 1975, Japanese smelter operating costs were over 30 percent higher than average international costs and almost 75 percent higher than costs in the U.S. Pacific Northwest, the discrepancies arising almost entirely from changes in the relative costs of oil, coal, and hydroelectricity.[5] Production cost increases owing to higher oil prices were much more modest in alumina refining and even smaller in bauxite mining, but the impacts of the consequent sharp increases in freight rates hit bauxite the hardest, then alumina, and, to a lesser degree, primary.

The behavior of the Organization of Petroleum Exporting Countries (OPEC) also demonstrated to the bauxite source countries how effective such a cartel could be, and although the International Bauxite Association they formed has failed to achieve a monopolistic price for bauxite, taxes and royalties in those countries have increased massively, though differentially. For example, Jamaican taxes and royalties rose during the 1970s about tenfold: by the end of 1975 they were $15 per ton, almost 80 percent of the total f.o.b. price, compared with about $1.70, 45 percent of the total f.o.b. price, in 1970. In Surinam, however, taxes and royalties were about $2, 40 percent of the f.o.b. price, in 1970, but increased "only" to $12.50, 60 percent of the f.o.b. price, by the end of 1975.[6] All of these changes in the state of the world, but particularly the bauxite royalties and taxes changes, have influenced drastically the effective terms of many contracts in bauxite and alumina and have forced long and hard renegotiations. While integrated firms also faced the same cost pressures, interstage prices and quantities presumably were adjusted quite simply. And here lies a general point: the problem with incomplete long-term contracts is not that they fail to protect the parties from changes in the state of the world, for such changes are largely independent of vertical organization, but rather that adaptation to the changes is costly, risky, and open to opportunistic bargaining. Adaptation when transactions are organized internally is, in contrast, a process of cooperative adjustment.

A final example of a series of events, not embraced in long-term contracts, that has disturbed some alumina contracts is the arrival of the era of environmental awareness, antipollution legislation, Alcoa's invention of a low-pollution, smelter technology, and its use specifically with sandy alumina. Consequently, floury-alumina contracts have not fared well, and there has been at least one case of litigation against a firm that withdrew as a buyer from a floury-alumina contract.

A Case Study of Contract Failure

A good illustration of some of the problems associated with long-term contracts became public when in 1975 the Anaconda Company filed a lawsuit in a U.S. federal district court seeking to have the Reynolds Metals Company uphold its commitments on a 1972 alumina contract between the two aluminum firms.[7] That contract included an agreement that Reynolds would supply Anaconda with 327,000 tons of alumina from 1977 to 1978 at a price between $77 and $84 per ton, the actual price to depend upon market conditions at the time. As is typical of sales contracts within the industry, Anaconda was allowed flexibility in the distribution of the 327,000 tons over the two years, and accordingly it notified Reynolds late in 1974 that it intended to purchase 109,000 tons in 1977 and 218,000 tons in 1978. But in April, 1975, Reynolds informed Anaconda that the alumina would not be delivered at the prices specified in the contract, and that price renegotiations would be necessary, because of the rising costs of alumina production.

Prior to Anaconda's filing the suit and "going public" with the dispute, the problems with the contract were not at all surprising, given the major changes in other prices occurring at the time, and they were certainly not atypical of contractual relations throughout the industry. Indeed, it is probable that the great majority of bauxite and alumina contracts written before 1973–1974 underwent price renegotiations at about the same time. Even by the time of the suit's filing, alumina production costs were running about $110 to $130 per ton, while U.S. spot-market alumina prices were $150 to $165 per ton, both substantially higher than the contract's $77 to $84 per ton, and expectations for 1977–1978 prices and costs would certainly have been higher still. The Reynolds-Anaconda 1972 contract was clearly incomplete, particularly with respect to cost contingencies, and the two parties had left themselves open to the business risks, renegotiation cost risks, opportunistic bargaining risks, and even litigation cost risks. The contract, as a mechanism for coordinating a commodity flow over time between two independently owned and heavy fixed-cost stages of production, had failed, or at least was on the road to failure. Notice that more than six months passed between Anaconda's notification to Reynolds of its 1977–1978 quantity requirements and its filing of the lawsuit, sufficient time for the two parties to have undertaken considerable private negotiations and for each party to have considered carefully its predicament and optimal strategy.

The surprising and atypical aspect of the Reynolds-Anaconda dispute is that it went as far as the filing of a lawsuit. This is even more surprising when one recalls that since 1969 Reynolds and Anaconda had been (and still are) joint venturers, along with Kaiser, in a large and seemingly successful bauxite-alumina project in Jamaica (Alumina Partners of Jamaica, known as Alpart). Anaconda's decision to file the suit, a move that the company had probably previously threatened and that Reynolds therefore "encouraged" by default, could have had only a negative impact on the cooperation required for the successful running of Alpart. Anaconda's motives for taking the contract dispute to law must have been very strong.

There are several factors that may explain Anaconda's behavior. First, there was a historical precedent for it: when Anaconda first entered the aluminum-smelting industry in 1955, it secured its alumina supply through a 1956–1960 contract with Reynolds, but Anaconda cancelled the contract in 1958 in favor of a contract on better terms with Kaiser. The memory of this event, an event that could feasibly have been precipitated by Reynolds's setting an "unreasonable" price on the alumina transfers, could have had the effect of making the parties more antagonistic in the 1975 renegotiations than they otherwise would have been. Second, and doubtlessly more important, was the industry-wide excess of alumina capacity over primary capacity that existed at the time of the 1975 dispute. A number of other alumina producers probably would have been willing to supply Anaconda if Reynolds successfully defended the suit. In this context Anaconda could have exploited the opportunistic bargaining allowed by the incompleteness of the contract. Third, and because Reynolds apparently would not submit to Anaconda's short-term bargaining power advantage, Anaconda filed the lawsuit and made public the dispute as a means of making credible the seriousness of its threat. As Thomas Schelling argues in his theory of the strategy of conflict: "It is typical of strategic threats that the punitive action—if the threat fails and has to be carried out—is painful or costly to both sides. The purpose is deterrence *ex ante,* not revenge *ex post.* Making a credible threat involves proving that one would have to carry out the threat, or creating incentives for oneself or incurring penalties that would make one evidently want to."[8] A court battle over the contract would certainly have been poor public relations for each firm, both within the industry (regarding the firm's reputations as "good guys" to do business with) and outside the industry (regarding the public airing of how upstream aluminum industry prices were *actually* determined). These eventualities could of course be avoided if Reynolds gave way and offered a deal sufficiently attractive to Anaconda that it would accept a "winner's" out-of-court settlement, but this option was available to Reynolds only because Anaconda had (deliberately) forced itself into a corner in which it would have to stay to preserve (or create?) its reputation as a tough bargainer, one not easily susceptible to stand-over tactics employed by the aluminum majors. It could be said that Anaconda had put the ball in Reynolds's court, and the only court available for a return shot was a U.S. district court.

Some ten months after Anaconda filed the suit, the two parties held a pretrial conference, and six months later still, in November 1976, it was announced that the parties had agreed to an out-of-court settlement. The settlement involved cancellation of the 1972 contract and Reynold's paying $4 million to Anaconda. "The $4-million payment works out to $11.11 a [short] ton, considerably less than the difference between the 1972 contract prices and the prices Anaconda will have to pay if it elects to buy the alumina elsewhere."[9] At the same time, it was announced that for the next five years Anaconda would swap its Alpart alumina for alumina from Reynolds's Corpus Christi, Texas, refinery; in other words, Anaconda would not be involved operationally in Alpart, a change that coincided with Reynolds's taking over the management responsibility of Alpart (a takeover prescribed in the original Alpart contract). It is not known whether the alumina swap was part of the settlement on the contract dispute, or if either party was a net gainer in the swap arrangement, but one possible inference is that either or both of the firms wanted to avoid the frequent intercompany contact that would have been involved via Alpart when Reynolds took over its management. After the contract dispute, the chances of amicable cooperation in Alpart may have seemed slim.

Apart from a net gain that Anaconda may have won via the alumina-swapping deal, the facts seem to indicate that Anaconda was the loser in the two-year dispute: the supply contract was cancelled, and the $4 million cash transfer was insubstantial. But by the time the out-of-court settlement was agreed to, late in 1976, the Anaconda Company was destined to undergo a major change in ownership structure, the timing of which coincided remarkably with that of the out-of-court settlement; it was a change that had important implications for Anaconda's aluminum-business strategy. In July 1976, the Anaconda board and shareholders had agreed to merge the company with the oil producer Atlantic Richfield, a company with a cash position and cash generation capacity that could easily arrange an alumina contract on the arm's-length market or scale the entry barriers into new refining capacity. Although this occurred in July, it was not until November 2 that a Federal Trade Commission request for a preliminary injunction toward cancellation of the merger on antitrust grounds was denied by a U.S. district court. It was only several weeks after the court's decision, a decision subsequently affirmed by a U.S. circuit court of appeals in January 1977, that Anaconda made the seemingly unattractive out-of-court settlement with Reynolds.

Since the Atlantic Richfield – Anaconda merger and the Reynolds-Anaconda out-of-court settlement, Anaconda's alumina supply strategy has taken a new tack. By the end of 1976, Anaconda's alumina requirements in excess of the swap deal with Reynolds were "provided by a contract under which Anaconda has agreed to purchase 360,000 [short] tons of alumina per year through 1990 at competitive prices from a source outside Jamaica." [10] The cancellation of the contract with Reynolds clearly caused no great problem — it is possible that this new contract was arranged *prior* to the out-of-court settlement with Reynolds — but even with the new contract all signed and sealed, Anaconda subsequently announced a $140 million commitment to take a 25 percent share in a new 800,000-ton refinery in Ireland that Alcan had been attempting to float on a joint-venture basis for several years. Anaconda will receive 200,000 tons of alumina annually from the Irish refinery, which, when combined with the company's entitlement from Alpart and the Reynolds swap, would make Anaconda self-sufficient in alumina even without the new contract (given its 1977 primary capacity). The Irish joint-venture prospect may have existed before Anaconda allowed its contractual relationship with Reynolds to be severed, but in any case, its merger with Atlantic Richfield would have promised such prospects. (As an interesting aside, the third joint venturer in the Irish refinery is the Dutch firm Billiton. Since 1970 Billiton has been a wholly owned subsidiary of the oil major Royal Dutch Shell. It does not require much speculation to imagine how Billiton [Shell] and Anaconda [Atlantic Richfield] became involved in such a "well oiled" joint venture.)

Some Positive Aspects of Contracts

So comparison of the characteristics of term contracts and the features of the bauxite and alumina markets indicates that contracts cause severe problems, even if they are of optimal length. Their provisions are undoubtedly superior to those of spot transactions because of their additional security, but contractual organization suffers relative to internal organization through its poor ability to adapt smoothly, cheaply, and optimally to changes in the state of the world. Clearly, these inferences about the capability of a firm's internal organization to adapt require some justification. Extensive studies of internal organization, including most notably the work of Williamson and Arrow, argue that because the outcome of any adjustment or decision is internal to the firm, and because the firm has internal incentives and controls that tend to promote cooperation rather than competitive confrontation, the firm has adaptability properties superior to those of arm's-length contract markets, at least under the sorts of circumstances prevailing in the bauxite and alumina markets. More specifically, the internalization of transactions has the advantage of encouraging investment in organizational infrastructure in ways that permit efficient information processing, encouraging cooperation via hierarchies of authority and by fiat, and having greater credibility, intelligibility, and rapidity in its communications.[11]

Because the strengths of internal organization have been well studied and because there is nothing particularly special about aluminum firms' organizational capabilities, there is no need to expand on these points. But there are two points I want to make that will be quite useful later in the chapter. First, internal organization itself is neither costless nor frictionless, principally for bureaucratic reasons, and suffers from "organizational failure" analogous to the market's suffering from "market failure." Second, because the organization can fail, internal organization is not a unitary concept; the firm has a choice of designs for its internal organization and selects one to accord with the firm's situation and business. Transactions costs explain both the decision to shift a transaction from the market into the firm and, within the firm, what organizational form will be chosen. Note, though, that it is "market failure" rather than "organizational success" that pushes aluminum firms toward the internalization of transactions.

My case against long-term contracts this far is probably too harsh. For one thing, as I show below, contracts in bauxite and alumina have increased in recent years to the point where they are a significant means of vertical coordination. Furthermore, there is some evidence that interfirm contract negotiation is not altogether an antagonistic affair. For example, Galbraith, in his theory of the corporation-dominated "economic planning system," grants a major role to the system of interlocking contracts. He argues that if firms were the opportunistic profit maximizers assumed in my argument so far, then contract negotiation would be so time consuming that it would choke the free-market system.[12]

Galbraith's explanation is that, because firms are growth maximizers subject only to a modest profit constraint, there is one set of contractual terms that is more or less jointly and singularly optimal for each buyer-seller pair. While it is clear that a given quantity of product to be exchanged will be jointly optimal, as is the case with profit-maximizing bilateral monopolists, it is not obvious that the growth-maximization assumption makes agreement on price any easier than it is in profit maximizing. Nevertheless, I am inclined to believe that, to the extent that contract negotiation and execution is a peaceful process, it is because of the ability and inclination of firms and their managers to develop informal interfirm social and institutional relationships.

In an empirical study into noncontractual relations in business, Stewart Macaulay, an academic lawyer, found that businessmen often find it unnecessary or undesirable to plan exchange relationships completely and seldom use legal sanctions to adjust these relationships or to settle disputes. Macaulay's evidence indicates that detailed formal contracting and enforcement is considered expensive in one way or another, and that incomplete contracting and informal enforcement serve an economizing purpose — precisely one of the major advantages, I have argued, motivating vertical integration. Just as internal organization fosters cooperation, an atmosphere of cooperative flexibility can also exist among firms.

"Businessmen often prefer to rely on 'a man's word' in a brief letter, a handshake, or 'common honesty and decency'— even when the transaction involves exposure to serious risks." [13] Macaulay found that such informal relationships are acceptable because, with care at the outset that both parties understand the primary obligation on each side, there is little room for what he calls "honest misunderstandings or good faith differences of opinion" about the nature and quality of each party's performance. This is assured by a number of effective nonlegal sanctions, such as the time-honored maxims of conduct that, "Our firm does not welsh on a deal," or, "We produce a good product and stand behind it." Furthermore, personal relationships across the boundaries of the two organizations exert pressure for conformity to expectations; for example, the salesman for the selling firm may, for reasons of friendship and moral suasion built up through repeated personal contact, feel an obligation to the purchasing agent of the buying firm at least equal to his obligation to the production manager of his own firm. More generally, firms feel compelled to perform to expectation to protect their long-run business success. For one thing, there are cost advantages and psychological reasons for wanting to perpetuate a harmonious relationship with a particular supplier or customer;

interfirm flows of information and behavioral patterns take time to develop but make life much more stable.

Furthermore, the way in which a firm behaves in a particular exchange relationship will color its general business reputation and affect its relationships with other firms. In general, a firm trading on an arm's-length market has at least partial control over other firms' perceptions of its commercial policies and practices relating to trading on that market. The firm that controls its reputation thereby also influences other firms' expectations about its behavior, and hence can indirectly influence the strategic behavior of other firms. As Schelling often stresses, in mixed-motive small-numbers bargaining situations, the ability to get the other party to *believe* your threats, promises, and so forth is crucially important. For example, in the context of long-term sales contracts, a reputation for dealing in a "straight and fair" manner enhances the firm's credibility as a trading partner. This is advantageous because it saves on haggling and policing costs, but on the debit side, such a reputation can only be established and maintained if the firm passes up chances to profit from opportunistic behavior. Here the firm faces a tradeoff between foregone opportunistic profits on the one hand and transaction-cost savings on the other. So it can be seen that trading via long-term contracts on an arm's-length market is itself not a simple procedure.

Industry-wide Bauxite and Alumina Contracts

By considering the factors that affect the efficiency of contracts as a means of vertical coordination, and by examining their character in and impact on the upstream aluminum industry, the prediction has been made that contracts are unlikely to be a major medium for bauxite and alumina exchanges. This section tests the prediction against the available data on upstream contracts.

Figure 3.1 graphs data that roughly measure the significance of contracts as a means of planning and executing exchanges among the aluminum industry's three upstream stages of production. The bauxite percentage is an estimate of the average proportion over the indicated three-year period of world alu-

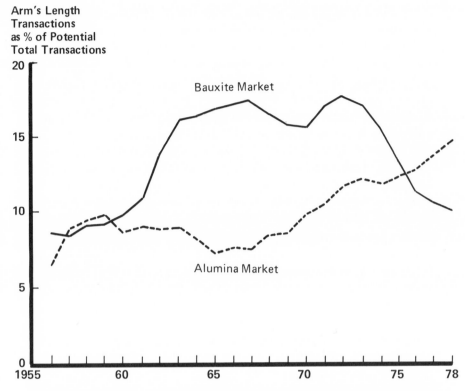

Arm's Length
Transactions
as % of Potential
Total Transactions

Figure 3.1 Strictly arm's-length transactions as a percentage of potential transactions in the bauxite and alumina markets: three-year centered moving averages of annual percentages, 1956–1978. *Source:* Data described in Appendix A. See Stuckey, "Vertical Integration and Joint Ventures in the International Aluminum Industry," p. 174, for details.

mina capacity that was potentially reliant upon *strictly* arm's-length bauxite transfers. This is the alumina capacity that would have required arm's-length bauxite if all potential bauxite transfers between mines and refineries with any common ownership had been exploited. The alumina market's percentages reflect the proportions of primary capacity reliant upon arm's-length alumina.

Before analyzing these data, several points about them should be made. First, they are only rough estimates; they were derived as residuals from the data on plant capacities and ownership and not from explicit data on actual contracts. This means they are overstated to the extent that firms rely upon spot transactions to secure supplies, but the information I have on this from miscellaneous sources indicates that very few firms *plan* to use spot transactions. Second, the reader may have noted an apparent inconsistency between these data in Figure 3.1 and the data presented in the testing of the life-cycle theory (AVIB and PVIA). The latter measured the degree of vertical integration and showed downward trends over the period 1956 to 1978, implying residuals (arm's-length transactions) with upward trends and higher absolute levels during the 1970s than are found in Figure 3.1. The inconsistency is the greatest for the bauxite market, because obviously the graph for bauxite in Figure 3.1 does not have a significant trend one way or the other. The explanation is that the contracts used to organize the supply of bauxite and alumina into several major joint-venture operations have been removed from Figure 3.1, as explained at the beginning of this chapter. It is these quasi-integration arrangements that have been on the increase, relative to both vertical integration and strictly arm's-length transactions, particularly in bauxite, and they fall more appropriately into the category of joint-venture transactions.

Keeping these qualifications in mind, Figure 3.1 indicates that contract-transactions are a relatively minor medium for upstream vertical coordination. Between 1955 and 1979, an average of only 13.5 percent of alumina capacity was obliged to rely upon strictly arm's-length supplies of bauxite. Smelters were even more fully covered by integrated alumina sources—an average of only 10 percent of alumina remained untied. Even though the equivalent data for other industries are not available to demonstrate that these levels are "low," the levels are quite consistent with the a priori predictions. The evidence suggests that the costs and risks associated with contracts are greater than the costs and risks associated with other forms of vertical organization, most notably, vertical integration.

Figure 3.1 also indicates that there have been differences and changes in the degree of contracting in the bauxite market, relative to the alumina market. The historical record shows that, for the most part, contracting has been proportionally greater in bauxite than in alumina, particularly during the 1960s. However, during the 1970s, contracting in bauxite declined quite rapidly to the point where in 1979 only 11 percent of potential bauxite supplies to refineries were by necessity arm's length. In contrast, contracting in alumina has been on the increase, reaching 16 percent in 1979. The earlier theory should be capable of explaining these trends: as Williamson points out, "Both firms and markets change over time in ways that may render inappropriate an initial assignment of transactions to firm or market." [14]

It will be recalled from Chapter 2 that the main cause of market and contract failure in the aluminum industry is small-numbers bargaining problems, and there have been changes in this element of structure. The changes from 1955 to 1979 were an increase in the number of basic aluminum firms — in particular, firms not integrated across bauxite, alumina, and primary or firms with unbalanced integration across the three stages — and concomitant declines in the concentration of bauxite, alumina, and primary production. In the bauxite market, the number of basic producers jumped from fifteen to twenty-four and the number of basic consumers, from fourteen to twenty-six during our observation period; the nonmajors' shares of capacity increased from 12 percent to 43 percent in bauxite and from 11 percent to 26 percent in alumina. There are more potential traders, and they now control significant shares of the markets. Similarly, in the alumina market, the number of basic producers almost doubled (from fourteen to twenty-six), and the number of basic consumers more than doubled (seventeen to thirty-five); the nonmajors' share of primary capacity rose from 15 percent to 31 percent. Here again, the market potentially thickened. Furthermore, in each case the entry of new producers lifted the number of potential traders in any given exchange situation from, say, three or four to, say, seven or eight, and it is over this sort of range that we might expect a significant decline in mutual dependence recognition, collusion, and so on.

The theory predicts that these changes should have led to an attenuation of the small-numbers bargaining problems that make contracts hazardous, and therefore to an increase in the use of contracts. This is upheld certainly with respect to the alumina market, but the bauxite market displays the opposite trend. The explanation is that although in the alumina market small-numbers conditions result largely from industry-wide fewness, in the bauxite market they result much more from commodity heterogeneity, plant specificity, and transport costs. Here conditions have been worsening as the industry has expanded into more-distant and lower-grade deposits, causing pairs of mines and refineries to be more securely locked together and making contracts potentially more troublesome. The result has been the decline in bauxite contracting depicted in Figure 3.1.

This decline is probably also due to a worsening in another of the factors that affect the efficiency of contracts. In Williamson's terms, the other factors, apart from small numbers, are uncertainty, opportunism and bounded rationality, the only possible candidate for deterioration being uncertainty. The bauxite graph in Figure 3.1 indicates an upward trend in contracting during the 1960s and early 1970s and a decline since 1972. This pattern is consistent with the degree of *revealed* uncertainty with respect to at least flexible exchange rates, rapid inflation, the oil crisis, and the arrival of the International Bauxite Association, events which severely disturbed many of the large contracts written in the late 1960s. Possibly, the demise during the early 1970s of the post–World War II era of growth and stability combined with these specific sources of contract problems to cause upstream firms to reappraise their assessments of contracts as a transactional mechanism because of increased uncertainty about the future.

As I have shown, the major cause of integration is market failure, which in turn is due to small-numbers trading situations combined with, principally, uncertainty and barriers to exit. In the bauxite case, small-numbers trading situations were seen to derive largely from mine-refinery technical complementarity and transport costs; these conditions are unlikely to subside in the future, and indeed, they could well intensify. On the other hand, small-numbers trading situations in the alumina market were seen to arise at least as much from the industry's structural factors (concentration of firms in alumina and primary) as from special refinery-smelter relationships. Small-numbers conditions will be attenuated slowly because, first, market growth and entry of new firms will increase the number of traders, particularly the number of alumina buyers, and second, special refinery-smelter relationships will ease as sandy alumina increasingly predominates floury alumina.

The implication is that contracting in alumina will increase, at least relative to contracting in bauxite, a trend in contrast to the industry's experience during the 1960s but consistent with its post-1972 experience. Furthermore, increased contracting is consistent with announced plans for new smelters, refineries, and mines to come onstream in the 1980s. Close study of the plans published in the *Engineering and Mining Journal*'s annual surveys of mine and plant expansion and of statements in companies' annual reports indicate that the major refineries under construction will be fed with bauxite under arrangements that cannot be described as strictly arm's length. The principal refineries are Alcoa of Australia's Wagerup plant (in-house bauxite), the Reynolds–Billiton–Broken Hill Proprietory Company, Limited, (BHP) Worsley project in Western Australia (in-house bauxite), and the Alcan-Billiton-Anaconda plant in Ireland (to be supplied with Trombetas, Brazil, bauxite, a consortium project including Alcan and Billiton). The Trombetas bauxite project is by far the largest bauxite development for some time, and all of its output will go into refineries somehow connected to at least one of the eight members of the consortium. There do not seem to be any new bauxite developments that will rely upon strictly arm's-length outlets. The implication is that the industry-wide proportion of alumina capacity requiring arm's-length bauxite will continue to decline.

On the other hand, it appears that smelters relying upon arm's-length purchases of alumina will continue to increase. A study of the smelting capacity coming onstream between 1979 and 1985 indicates that maybe 50 percent of new capacity will be owned entirely independently of refineries, an enormous increase from the 16 percent of smelting capacity so owned in 1979. Alcoa of Australia is likely to supply a significant proportion of this unintegrated capacity via long-term alumina contracts. The evidence is consistent with the theoretical prediction that alumina-primary integration will decline proportionately in the future.

Evidence from Firms

More direct and explicit evidence on the use of sales contracts as a vertical coordination mechanism is available by observing the strategies and performance of individual firms that rely upon arm's-length markets for an important slice of their businesses. With the industry-wide picture already drawn, it is revealing to observe how several of the arm's-length traders operate and fit into an industry where arm's-length markets are thin.

The Bauxite Market

Table 3.1 lists all of the bauxite producers that have in recent years been important arm's-length sellers of bauxite and gives some idea of the magnitude of their operations and their contracted customers. Note that there are only eleven sellers in the list, a small number, given that in 1977 there were twenty-nine basic bauxite producing firms. If the five producers that rely upon Eastern Block outlets are assumed not to operate on the "free" market, then we are left with only six producers, two of which account for about 70 percent of the "free" market. Comalco is the only seller with a strong connection in the aluminum industry, its 45-percent owner Kaiser, but this connection is of little significance in its arm's-length dealings. Since 1970 Billiton has been a subsidiary of Royal Dutch Shell and is the vehicle for Shell's diversification into minerals. While this connection gives Billiton "long purse" potential, it is probably otherwise unimportant. Aside from these qualifications, the sellers are small, single-business organizations.

Table 3.2 presents similar information about the principal bauxite buyers. There are approximately ten alumina producers, from a worldwide total of twenty-six, that must purchase bauxite at arm's length to operate their alumina refineries at full capacity. By far the most important are the three Japanese producers, Sumitomo, Showa Denko, and Nippon Light Metal, constituting a little over 50 percent of the market, and PUK with about 22 percent.

Definitely the most voluminous arm's-length bauxite exchange relationships have been those between the Australian

Table 3.1 Arm's-length sales required for full-capacity bauxite mining (in equivalent tons of primary aluminum) and principal known customers, 1977.

| Seller | Sales | | Customers |
	Tons	Percentage of firm's capacity	
Comalco (Australia)	920,000	40%	Nippon Light Metal, Showa Denko, Sumitomo, Pechiney Ugine Kuhlmann (PUK), Vereinigte Aluminium-Werke (VAW)
Gove Alumina (Australia)	105,000	17	Nippon Light Metal, Showa Denko, Sumitomo
Aneka Tambang Mining[a] (Indonesia)	210,000	100	Japan
Billiton Maatschappij (Surinam)	290,000	53	Largely North America; possibly Reynolds
Guyana Bauxite and Berbice Mines[a] (Guyana)	520,000	74	Largely Canada and the United States
Four Greek producers	620,000	100	Largely the U.S.S.R. and Eastern Europe
Office des Bauxites de Kindia[a] (Guinea)	520,000	100	Largely the U.S.S.R.

Source: Data described in Appendix A, companies' annual reports for 1977, and import-export statistics in *Metal Statistics,* 1977.

a. A majority or all of the firm is state owned.

and Southeast Asian producers, and the Japanese aluminum firms. These relationships grew rapidly from the 1950s along with the Japanese aluminum industry, the primary capacity of which grew at a compounded annual rate of 15 percent between 1955 and 1976. The bauxite-trade pattern associated with these relationships is explained easily by the traditional real theory of international trade: Japan had no bauxite endowment, while Southeast Asia and particularly Australia had large endowments; capital, labor, and technology were relatively abundant in Japan; Japan had a large and rapidly growing domestic market; and

THE ALUMINUM INDUSTRY

Table 3.2 Arm's-length purchases required for full-capacity bauxite refining (in equivalent tons of primary aluminum) and principal known suppliers, 1977.

Buyer	Purchases		Suppliers
	Tons	Percentage of firm's capacity	
Nippon Light Metal (Japan)	300,000	100%	Comalco, Gove Alumina
Showa Denko (Japan)	320,000	100	Comalco, Gove Alumina, Aneka Tambang, Ramunia Bauxite
Sumitomo (Japan)	450,000	100	Comalco, Gove Alumina, Aneka Tambang, Ramunia Bauxite
Taiwan Aluminium Company[a] (Taiwan)	40,000	100	Comalco
Pechiney Ugine Kuhlmann (PUK) (France)	450,000	35	Comalco
Vereinigte Aluminium-Werke (VAW) (West Germany)	125,000	26	Comalco
Guilina (West Germany)	70,000	100	Open market; suppliers vary
Reynolds (United States)	150,000	11	Possibly Billiton
Revere (United States)	95,000	48	Unknown
Phelps Dodge (United States)	75,000	100	Unknown

Source: See Table 3.1.
a. A majority or all of the firm is state owned.

finally, the two regions were close geographically, given the global distribution of bauxite deposits and final markets. But these factors do not explain why the trade is largely via intercorporate arm's-length transactions rather than the industry's norm of intracorporate transfers. The explanation seemingly lies in

Japan's national strategy, before the 1970s, of noninvolvement as either host or source country in foreign direct investment, and in the skills and efficiency of the globally pervasive and almost unique Japanese trading enterprises. It is no coincidence that of Japan's five aluminum firms, three are subsidiaries of trading firms (Mitsubishi, Mitsui, and Sumitomo) among the top ten, two of which (Mitsubishi and Mitsui) are clearly the largest trading enterprises in Japan. Apparently the supplying firms in Southeast Asia and Australia were initiated and grew to accommodate the Japanese strategy.

Support for these generalizations and pertinent evidence on a number of issues I have raised about contracts come from an examination of the history of bauxite contracts between Comalco, the world's largest bauxite producer after Alcoa and by far the largest arm's-length supplier, and Comalco's Japanese customers. Comalco was formed in 1956 following the discovery (in 1955) of a potentially commercial bauxite deposit at Weipa, Queensland, and by the turn of the decade the company had determined that the deposit was commercially viable, subject only to the availability of markets.

> By 1961 trial shipments of 10,000 tonnes each were made to Japan and Bell Bay, Tasmania. The ore had to be loaded by means of small lighters which ferried it out to a ship. In 1962, *after long negotiations,* the first contracts for supplying bauxite to Japan were signed. Starting in 1963, a minimum of 600,000 tonnes of ore was to be shipped to Japan over three years. These contracts were particularly significant in that several Japanese firms had agreed to *modify their alumina plants to allow for the slightly different nature of Weipa bauxite.* From this small start, Weipa today [1975] is the source of over 50 percent of Japan's bauxite imports [emphasis mine].[15]

From the beginning, then, the necessarily long-term and bilateral nature of bauxite seller-buyer relationships was recognized: negotiations were long and therefore expensive, Japanese refineries had to be modified, and Comalco's growth was entirely dependent upon gaining sales contracts prior to sinking capital in specific and durable assets.

The fixed costs and risks for both parties in an arm's-length bauxite relationship demand long-term, formal contracts, including specifications for prices and quantities. Comalco's contracts are certainly long in duration: by 1970 the company had contracts running to 1997, and contracts to 2008 were under negotiation. Options on some contracts were dated to 2041! While the details of these next-century contracts probably were not taken too seriously by the contracting parties, they may have been included to make explicit and to formalize the expected long-term nature of the exchange relationships. It is interesting that, as far as I am aware, the only time Comalco has made public relatively comprehensive data on the duration of its contracts was in the prospectus it published in association with its first sale of shares to the public; potential shareholders would have seen such information as relevant to their calculations of Comalco's net present value at the time. The prospectus also indicated that contracted quantities plus options were in excess of existing capacity plus plans for expansion, presumably a comforting imbalance for potential equity holders.

The common practice in specifications for quantities in contracts between Comalco and its Japanese customers is to specify an aggregate quantity over ten or twenty years, rather than to fix annual quantities. Some stability from year to year is normally achieved by stipulating a minimum quantity per annum, but sufficient flexibility in the actual quantity exchanged is left to allow the buyer to adjust to the cyclical ups and downs in the industry and to pass the "market message" through to the supplier. That contracts allow for quantity variation at the outset is a reflection of the mutual recognition that joint profit-maximization in a bilateral monopoly facing uncertain demand often requires quantity adjustment. It is interesting, and also consistent with the theoretical prediction, that quantity adjustments between Comalco and its customers do not seem to have been a source of major conflict between the parties, and this conclusion holds for a period when the volume performance of the Japanese aluminum industry fluctuated quite violently, as Table 3.3 shows. Indeed, quantity coordination seems to have been handled quite precisely, the one-year phase inconsistency between Comalco-Japan shipments and the other two indicators of growth probably being due to differences in when the measurements were made.

Table 3.3 Volume fluctuations in Comalco-Japan bauxite transactions (annual percentage charges in tonnages), 1971–1977.

Year	Alumina production	Comalco-Japan bauxite shipments	Japanese bauxite imports
1971	24.7%	38.5%	27.5%
1972	2.6	0.0	7.0
1973	20.9	− 7.0	12.4
1974	− 9.4	− 5.9	− 5.4
1975	−13.1	−18.8	−13.3
1976	− 9.8	15.4	− 7.0
1977	26.4	16.5	24.4

Source: Metal Statistics, 1975–1979, and Comalco Ltd., *Annual Report,* 1971–1977.

The claim that such coordination is the result of relatively peaceful negotiation has been supported by my discussions with Comalco personnel, but it is also consistent with the calm and understanding tone used in annual reports to describe the quantity fluctuations on contract sales during the 1970s. For example: "Bauxite sales to Japan declined slightly during 1976. Factors which influenced demand were the considerable stocks of bauxite and alumina built up in Japan during 1975 and a reduction in output from Japanese smelters to adjust inventories. The company does not expect a large increase in sales to Japan in 1977 since the local industry has yet to recover fully from the 1975 downturn and is still completing organizational changes." [16] This sympathetic attitude is all the more significant given the poor quantity performance of Comalco's Japanese contracts, relative to the company's European contracts, and especially its tied-outlet contracts during the same period, a fact given statistical support below.

The relatively amicable renegotiations of quantities specified in Comalco's Japanese contracts also stands in contrast to the nature of price renegotiations in the same contracts. Most of Comalco's bauxite contracts written by the early 1970s contained fixed prices in U.S. dollars, and the only formal price-adjustment formulas included in the contracts related to variations in the alumina and silica content of any particular shipment. From Comalco's point of view, the real $A price on such contracts plummeted between 1970 and 1976 because of two sets of factors: first, inflation in Australia and the devaluation of the U.S. dollar; and second, depressed demand, excess capacity, and hence downward price pressure in the world's aluminum industry. Without the first set of factors, the bilateral-monopoly model predicts a downward shift in the feasible price range along with the decline in the joint-profit maximizing quantity. The shifts are shown in Figure 3.2, using Comalco and the Sumitomo Aluminum Smelting company as seller and buyer, and 1970 and 1976 as the two years. Assuming that all the variables determining the actual original price in U.S. dollars ($U.S.) within the feasible range remained constant between 1970 and 1976, or varied in a manner leaving the parties' relative bargaining strengths unchanged, the model predicts a decline in price in 1976 (from, arbitrarily, P_{70} to P_{76} in Figure 3.2). Of course, this simple model assumes that Comalco would have been willing under these circumstances to enter into renegotiations on price.

But forces external to the aluminum industry, operating at the same time, caused a decline in the real $A price (arbitrarily, P_{70} − P_{76}^*) that was undoubtedly much greater than the decline predicted by the model. To give some idea of the magnitudes, from 1970 to 1976 the average annual U.S. list price for primary aluminum rose by 54.4 percent, while the U.S. wholesale price index rose by 65.8 percent from June 1970 to June 1976, implying a decline in the "real" aluminum price of 11.4 percent. Very roughly, this is the sort of decline we might expect in the model from P_{70} to P_{76}. However, accounting for Australian inflation and the change in the $US/$A rate, the decline from P_{70} to P_{76}^* was something like 53 percent! And furthermore, the decline from P_{70} to P_{76}^*, if measured in 1970 yen, was about 70 percent.

So for reasons outside the control or influence of Comalco or its Japanese customers, the effective price in their bauxite contracts swung away widely from the original equilibrium, and in a direction and by a magnitude that seem "unfair" to Comalco, relative to the 1976 price that would have been struck if the parties relied upon spot transactions. To the extent that this is true, we have a classic example of the disadvantages of incomplete long-term contracts. There is no doubt that Comalco saw

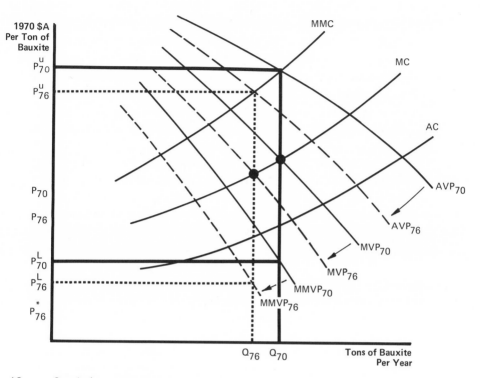

AC   = Comalco's average cost curve
MC   = Comalco's supply curve or marginal cost curve
MMC   = The curve marginal to Comalco's supply curve
AVP   = Sumitomo's demand curve or average value product curve
MVP   = Sumitomo's marginal value product curve
MMVP   = The curve marginal to Sumitomo's marginal value product curve
Q   = Joint profit maximizing quantity
P^u = The upper price limit
P^L = The lower price limit
P   = Assumed equilibrium price
P^* = Actual price
70, 76 = Year

Figure 3.2 Comalco-Sumitomo hypothetical bilateral-monopoly showing the effects of a decline in Sumitomo's final demand between the two years 1970 and 1976.

the situation as grossly unfair: in every annual report from 1972 to at least 1977 the company made quite explicit reference to the damaging effects of the fixed-priced contracts on profitability, and the attempts to renegotiate prices with overseas customers.[17] Price renegotiations were first mentioned in the 1972 annual report, but even so, by 1975 it was admitted that "the company's continued efforts to obtain improved prices for bauxite and more adequate compensation for increased costs have been met with only partial success." [18] By 1977 it seems that some further gains had been made, particularly in compensation for currency realignments, but renegotiations were still underway.

Throughout the difficult years of the early to mid-1970s, Comalco and each of its Japanese customers had strong incentives to maintain viable long-run bilateral relationships. The thinness of the arm's-length bauxite market outside of their own exchange relationships, their relative geographical proximity, and their bauxite-refinery complementarity dictated that they "stick together" even under adverse circumstances. Furthermore, Comalco and two of its major Japanese customers, Sumitomo and Showa Denko, had become partners in the Bluff smelter in New Zealand in 1972, and the firms had plans for other joint ventures in Australia as the economics of aluminum production in Japan continued to worsen relative to that in most other countries. Comalco's willingness to continue to supply bauxite at a price low enough to allow Japanese refineries and smelters to maintain operation and achieve some return on relatively new plant can be interpreted as a long-term investment by Comalco to ensure access for its bauxite to Japan's aluminum end-product market, regardless of where the intermediate stages of production would take place. Such a strategy was consistent with the obvious long-run infeasibility of alumina and primary production within Japan and has been rewarded recently with the announcement that Comalco will be a 30-percent partner with four Japanese firms (50 percent) and Kaiser (20 percent) to build and operate a 180,000-ton-per-year smelter at Gladstone, Queensland. The smelter will use exclusively alumina refined from Comalco bauxite, and, not coincidentally, Sumitomo is a 21.5 percent partner in the venture. Such outcomes, being mutually advantageous to Comalco and the Japanese firms, are not to be taken for granted, as evidenced by the fact that Japanese firms have also become participants in planned refineries and smelters in Indonesia, Brazil, and Venezuela, with a combined primary equivalent capacity of 850,000 tons.

Although Comalco's entry and rapid growth in the upstream

aluminum industry crucially depended upon long-term contracts with Japanese producers, and more recently with VAW
and PUK in Europe, the company's strategy is to decrease dependence upon strictly arm's-length transactions. As Comalco's
share of the world bauxite market has grown to about 13 percent, its dependence upon arm's-length sales has fallen from 80
percent in 1965 to only about 30 percent today. One of the
reasons for its preference toward tied outlets, apart from the
problems associated with long-term contracts, on which I have
already elaborated, is that Comalco has initiated successfully two
consortium refineries that take Comalco bauxite exclusively and
that have proven to be very stable users of the ore. The consortium contracts contain clauses that strongly encourage full-capacity utilization of the refineries, even when the industry is in a
slump, which in turn ensures a regular volume outlet for Comalco's bauxite. The consortia's favorable role for Comalco as
volume outlets has been important. For example, in the bad
slump of 1975 when worldwide alumina-capacity utilization ran
at only 78 percent, Comalco's arm's-length shipments fell by 24
percent, while tied outlet shipments actually rose by 15 percent.
The strong performance of the tied outlets allowed Comalco to
run at 91 percent of capacity.[19]

The available evidence on Comalco's Japanese bauxite contracts therefore strongly supports the theoretical predictions.
The extensive contractual relationships arose only because the
Japanese aluminum firms were prevented from integrating upstream, but with the unexpected events of the 1970s, the incompleteness of the contracts rendered them unreliable and inefficient. Renegotiations have been long, expensive, and probably
unpleasant, particularly with respect to price. The bilateral monopoly character of the relationships meant that Comalco was
forced to accept the unfavorable turn of events. One outcome
has been a determined attitude by Comalco to develop new tied
outlets.

The Alumina Market

The structure and the composition of the firms involved in the
arm's-length alumina market in 1977 are described in Table 3.4,

Table 3.4 Arm's-length sales and purchases required for full-capacity refining and smelting of alumina (in equivalent tons of primary aluminum), 1977.

Seller	Sales		Buyer	Sales	
	Tons	Percentage of firm's capacity		Tons	Percentage of firm's capacity
Alcoa	1,816,000	44.9%	Mitsubishi	358,000	100.0%
			Alumax	200,000	100.0
			National Steel	163,000	100.0
			Aluminios Argentinos	43,000	100.0
			Aluminium Bahrain[a]	120,000	100.0
			Iranian Aluminium[a]	45,000	100.0
			Egypt Aluminium[a]	100,000	100.0
			Aluminium South Africa	82,000	100.0
Kaiser	519,000	35.4	Anaconda	110,000	40.4
Reynolds	240,000	17.3	Phelps Dodge	52,000	41.3
Martin Marietta	42,000	20.0	British Aluminium	38,000	27.0
Pechiney Ugine Kuhlmann (PUK)	171,000	13.2	Riotinto Zinc	33,000	100.0
Vereinigte Aluminium-Werke (VAW)[a]	102,000	21.3	Vereinigte Metallwerke Ran-shofen-Berndorf Austria[a]	81,000	100.0
Metallgesellschaft	54,000	100.0	Det Norske Nitridaktiesels-kap Norway[a]	48,000	100.0
Guyana Bauxite[a]	180,000	100.0	Norsk Hydro	120,000	100.0

Source: Data described in Appendix A.

a. A majority or all of the firm is state owned.

Note: Although Alcoa's known customers are listed, buyer-seller relationships for the remaining firms in the table could not be ascertained with sufficient confidence for their inclusion.

Summation of the two tonnage columns indicates that potential arm's-length alumina supply is almost 50 percent greater than potential arm's-length alumina demand. Perhaps 20 percent of this gap can be explained by the use of alumina in other industries, while the rest reflects the fact that in 1977 alumina capacity was greater than bauxite capacity. It is quite possible that some of the sellers listed did not sell any alumina in 1977, and probable that they all sold less than their potential.

revealing several dissimilarities between the buyers and sellers. The selling side of the market is clearly dominated by one firm, Alcoa, with almost 60 percent of the potential supply; it also includes three of the other majors, which together can sell another 30 percent. There are only eight suppliers, but they own 63 percent of worldwide alumina capacity; only 34 percent of this, however, relies upon arm's-length outlets. In other words, the important members of this group have substantial smelting facilities of their own. In contrast, the buying side of the market consists entirely of second-tier or small, state-owned enterprises; the only truly large member of the group is Mitsubishi. But buyers are quite numerous: fifteen of the total of thirty-five basic primary producers worldwide are arm's-length buyers. The buyers are mostly young firms, nine having begun in the 1970s and two in the late 1960s, and in total they own only 15.8 percent of worldwide primary capacity. Finally, and very much in contrast to the alumina sellers, twelve of the fifteen buyers rely upon arm's-length purchases for *all* of their alumina requirements, including the eight known to buy (probably exclusively) from Alcoa.

Given these structural differences between the two sides of the alumina market, theory predicts that the market power of the sellers as a group is greater than the market power of the buyers. Concentration on the selling side is high, and most of the sellers are not totally reliant upon arm's-length sales; on the other hand, the buyers are small, unconcentrated, geographically dispersed, and in most cases, totally reliant upon arm's-length purchases. As sandy alumina increasingly dominates floury alumina, and as substitutability of aluminas increases, the power imbalance between the group of sellers and the group of buyers will become more important, because bilateral relationships between each buyer-seller pair will weaken. Under these circumstances, it can be expected that the sellers could, on average, charge an alumina price above the marginal cost of production. This is so because during periods of high capacity utilization the small, strictly arm's-length buyers of alumina would have no alternative but to buy from the small group of powerful sellers. And at least in the case of the primary aluminum producers like Aluminios Argentinos, Aluminium Bahrain, Iranian Aluminium, Egypt Aluminium, and Aluminium South Africa, all domestic monopolists, the above marginal cost of alumina could probably be passed on in the prices for primary through protectionist policies on ingot importations, policies that the local government would probably be willing to provide if the "national champion" aluminum firm's viability was under threat.

The rapid growth in the size of the potential arm's-length alumina market has been due largely to Alcoa's strategy of becoming an arm's-length supplier of alumina. The development, execution, and success of this strategy is worthy of analysis, partly because it bears on the narrow subject of contracts, but also because it demonstrates how one firm, the industry's oldest and largest, has modified its entire vertical strategy to best suit the changing conditions in a dynamic industry. For many years prior to the introduction of this strategy, Alcoa was fully integrated, from bauxite mining to downstream fabrication, with balanced capacity in each consecutive pair of production stages (with the exception of a consistent excess of primary capacity for its downstream capacity). This original strategy of balanced and full integration is consistent with the life-cycle theory of industry-wide vertical integration, in the sense that Alcoa's own life cycle and the industry's life cycle were much the same thing until about 1950, by which time Kaiser and Reynolds had been created, and Alcan had become an independent firm effectively as well as officially. But by the early 1960s, Alcoa's overwhelming dominance of the industry was under attack from several directions, and there were signs that the industry's status quo was unlikely to last for long. A reassessment of Alcoa's strategic position was called for.

To begin with, the demand for aluminum was growing rapidly along with, and indeed ahead of, the world's gross national product, and the growth was likely to continue. The other majors were matching Alcoa's growth in all stages of the industry, and possibly even more important, there was an unprecedented entry of new firms. In the United States, two copper majors, Anaconda and Revere, had entered the aluminum industry, and two diversified corporations, the Olin Mathieson Chemical Corporation and Harvey Aluminum had also entered. Outside the United States, several new producers had sprung up, while the West German state firm, VAW, and the three Japanese producers were expanding. In the aggregate, the new entrants were involved more heavily in smelting and fabrication than in mining and refining, as would be expected, given the much greater barriers to entry to the upstream stages. Of course, the free markets in bauxite and alumina were still extremely thin in the early 1960s, and hence new entrants were attempting to become integrated upstream. The potential for arm's-length markets must have occurred to Alcoa, given the entry of small primary producers.

Alcoa's room to maneuver in primary and downstream production was being limited by the aggressive strategies of the other majors. In the U.S. downstream market, for many years Alcoa's "birthright," Alcan and Reynolds in particular were quite explicit in their desire to achieve an increased market share, to the extent that Alcoa's previously unquestioned role as price setter was tested.[20] At the same time, Alcoa was under the close surveillance of U.S. antitrust authorities, particularly in the downstream U.S. market, a fact the company was reminded of forcefully in the early 1960s, when the U.S. Justice Department challenged Alcoa's 1959 acquisition of Rome Cable Corporation, a producer of copper and aluminum cable, and its 1960 acquisition of Cupples Products Corporation, a fabricator of aluminum for architectural uses. In the Rome Cable case, the Supreme Court upheld the Justice Department's suit under the Clayton Act. That decision was based on questionable economic logic, and it reversed an earlier, district court decision permitting the merger. Finally, as if Alcoa's domestic problems were not enough, the company suffered a humiliating "defeat" when Reynolds won control of British Aluminium in 1959. Alcoa and Reynolds had both been seeking independent control of the then attractive monopolist of the British industry for several years, and Reynolds won control in a classic stock-market coup, headlined in London's *Daily Mail* as the "35-Million Pound Battle for Britain."[21] Apart from losing face, Alcoa also lost instant control of the Commonwealth's markets.

As a result of Alcoa's ordeal with the other majors, new entrants, and the antitrust authorities, the company's performance slumped: between 1956 and 1964 its sales grew by only 20 percent overall, while Kaiser, Reynolds, and Alcan each experienced growth of over 50 percent. At the same time, Alcoa's stock price fell by nearly two-thirds.[22] Under these circumstances it is not surprising that the company developed a new competitive strategy. As one journalist put it in 1962, "Alcoa is no longer behaving like the poor little rich boy of the aluminum business, too proud to fight. It is facing up to the requirements of today's fierce competition and is hustling for a profit in the marketplace, just like companies that came up the hard way."[23] Alcoa's major long-term strategic change has been its concentration of investment in the upstream industry rather than across-the-board investment to maintain balanced integration. By adopting this strategy, Alcoa has distinguished itself from the other majors, and the evidence is beginning to indicate that its financial performance and strength are also distinguishing it from the others, and in a direction favorable to Alcoa.

From a position of near balance across the four stages of production in 1960, Alcoa in 1979 had over twice as much upstream capacity as downstream capacity. This gave the company approximately 25 percent of the worldwide bauxite and alumina capacity (measured in primary equivalents), with about half of the potential alumina output available for third-party sales. The transition from balanced to imbalanced integration is well described in Figure 3.3 by the ratio of alumina capacity (in primary equivalents) to primary capacity. The ratio for Alcoa shows a steady increase, a trend consistent with my argument that Alcoa's bias in favor of bauxite and alumina is the result of a deliberate long-run strategy probably originating in the early 1960s. The table also highlights how Alcoa's strategy has diverged from the strategies of the other majors; the only other firm with a comparable strategy is Kaiser.

Alcoa of Australia has been Alcoa's major vehicle for the implementation of the new strategy. The Australian subsidiary now has over 40 percent of the company's bauxite and alumina capacity, and if the company's announced plans for expansion in the next several years come to fruition, the subsidiary's share will rise to 50 percent. In a lengthy 1962 *Fortune* magazine article reviewing Alcoa's unhappy position in the late 1950s and early 1960s, and describing "the once complacent giant's" strategies

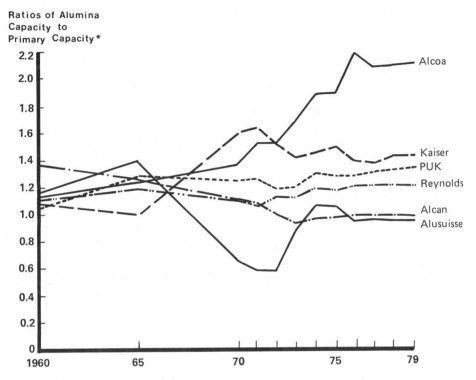

Ratios of Alumina
Capacity to
Primary Capacity*

* Based on primary equivalents at start of year

Figure 3.3 Ratios of alumina capacity to primary capacity of the majors, 1960–1979. *Source:* Data described in Appendix A. See Stuckey, "Vertical Integration and Joint Ventures in the International Aluminum Industry," p. 205, for details.

for "striking back," the long-run implications of the 1961 formation of Alcoa of Australia were forecast with notable accuracy.

Alcoa's biggest new investment outside the Western Hemisphere is an extensive venture in Australia, in association with several Australian companies, which will cost about $100 million. It involves bauxite mines, ore refineries, and facilities to smelt about 44,000 tons, which is close to Australia's present consumption . . . But Alcoa is counting on a rapid increase in Australian consumption, and also *expects to use the Australian plants as a base for serving the whole Pacific-area market.*

Moreover, Alcoa President Litchfield, who has made a specialty of international operations, explains that *the company went into Australia because of the long-run potential of low-cost supplies of bauxite and coal close by a good smelter site.* Says Litchfield: "There's a strong possibility of over-capacity in Australia for a while, but these trolley cars come along only once and you've got to get on them" [emphasis mine].[24]

It is quite clear that Alcoa's plans for its Australian subsidiary were more than just to set up a small, integrated operation to serve the small Australian market. The quotation and other sections of the article also indicate that the journalist was rather fixed in his impression that aluminum firms always desire balanced integration, but President Litchfield seemed quite open to the possibility that trolley cars do not necessarily stop at domestic consumption levels.

The main reason for Alcoa's decision to concentrate on bauxite and alumina was probably the realization in the early 1960s that the inevitable growth in aluminum demand, combined with the low barriers to entry into downstream activities and the relatively low barriers into smelting, meant that the two downstream stages were destined to become less concentrated and more competitive. The exmonopolist had already found the beginnings of that market structure unpalatable. But the upstream barriers to entry were still high, and with limited new deposits and continually increasing minimum efficient scales of operation in mining and refining, the barriers were likely to stay high in the foreseeable future. Alcoa's response to this forecast was to become a bulk, low-cost producer of alumina, both to be the supplier for the new entrants into smelting and at the same time, to remove the need for the entrants to integrate upstream.

At first glance this might seem a second-best strategy, because if the barriers to upstream entry were likely to stay high, collusion among the majors could undermine the profitability of the new entrants by charging above-marginal costs for alumina (or even rationing it). But there would have been a weakness in such a policy: upstream barriers *could* be scaled by the small producers if they formed mining and refining joint ventures, a strategy that new entrants were beginning to exploit by the early 1960s. For example, two of the four new entrants to the U.S. industry had secured bauxite and alumina supplies by forming the industry's first upstream joint ventures ever. In 1956, Olin and Revere formed the Ormet Corporation (Olin Revere Metals Corporation), a joint venture (each owned 50 percent) across refining, shipping, power generation, and smelting, which added a significant 8 percent to both U.S. refining and smelting capacities. At the same time, Olin organized a large bauxite-alumina joint venture in previously untapped but richly endowed Guinea, using the bauxite-starved but experienced European producers to hurdle the technical and capital barriers to entry. (The other partners were PUK, British Aluminium, Alusuisse, and VAW.) Olin and Revere demonstrated that, first, it was possible for small, inexperienced firms to break into the aluminum industry, and second, that integrated entry, as well as independence from the majors as feedstock suppliers, was also possible. While Olin's and Revere's boldness was never rewarded, both firms suffering frequent losses, leading to Olin's exit from the industry in 1973–1975 and Revere's attempted partial exit in 1976–1978, their entry was sufficient to cause the industry to begin to rewrite the rules of the aluminum game.

Alcoa was quick to begin its role as a supplier of upstream products by supplying Ormet's Burnside, Louisiana, refinery with bauxite from the company's wholly owned subsidiary in Surinam. Since then, the company has managed to secure the bulk of the long-term, strictly arm's-length alumina contracts that have been written around the world, most of them through Alcoa of Australia. At least as far as the Australian subsidiary is concerned, upstream capacity and plans for expansion, at any point in the subsidiary's eighteen-year history, have been backed fully by medium- to long-term alumina contracts. Alcoa's bauxite-alumina expansions have been coordinated neatly with the entry into smelting and expansion of the following firms: Mitsubishi Light Metal Industries (1963), Alumax (1965), National Steel (1969), Aluminium Bahrain (1971), Iranian Aluminium (1972), Aluminos Argentinos (1974), Egypt Aluminium (1975), and Dubai Aluminium (1981). The neat coordination has, of course, been no coincidence; both parties typically announce the contracts along with the plans for entry or expansion. Information on the performance of the contracts is limited, but it appears that they have been mutually satisfactory, with Alcoa probably maintaining the position of exclusive supplier in each case. According to Alcoa of Australia's annual reports, most customers have honored their contractual obligations, even during the 1975 slump, and production has been close to capacity. To the extent that the evidence is available, then, contracts have performed well as a mechanism for the vertical coordination of refineries with smelters.

This brief history of Alcoa's strategy to become an arm's-length seller of alumina is somewhat tangential to the subject of this chapter, but it does support my earlier claim that long-term contracts are becoming an efficient form of vertical organization between the refining and smelting stages of production. From the fact that the industry's leading firm is now a heavy arm's-length seller of alumina we can infer that contracts are efficient, at least from the seller's point of view.

Market and Contract Failure and the Structure of Internal Organization

Earlier in this chapter I introduced the point that the internal organization of exchange is not a costless or frictionless process, and that it can suffer from organizational failure just as markets can suffer market failure and contractual coordination can suffer contract failure. It is not a foregone conclusion, then, that when the costs of using the market or contracts are in some sense "high," as I have argued they are in aluminum, that internal organization will always be preferred. It is quite possible that in any particular situation the costs of internal organization will be even higher. Recognition of the existence of internal organization costs, combined with the observation that internal organization can take on a variety of forms, leads to the proposition that in any given exchange situation, one form of organization may be better than another, or ultimately, that there exists an optimal organizational form. It is this optimal form (or structure, to use the popular word) that should be compared with the best other alternative mechanism for exchange coordination.

What, then, are the costs of internal organization, or alternatively, what are the forces that can lead to organizational failure?

The answer has been well researched and is well known by any senior manager, but a brief summary here serves as a basis for the arguments that follow.[25] Internalizing an additional stage of production or function insulates the enlarged organization from the outside market for the good or service involved, with the result that, in the short run at least, there may be no credible alternative sales outlet or source of supply. Such a situation allows for managerial discretion, in the sense that the managers directly involved in the internal transactions can use their special knowledge of the "real facts" and their access to a source of internal information used for audit, personnel performance measurement, and so on, to promote their own or their sub-group's interests at the expense of the total organization. Internal organization may also have the effect of cutting off sources of potential information on suppliers' and customers' research and know-how. To the extent that the addition of another stage of production or activity significantly increases the size of the firm, a number of problems may arise. Bounded rationality may mean that the additional internal communication required may be performed less efficiently, a phenomenon Williamson calls "control loss." Bureaucratic insularity may also arise, because as organizations get larger, senior managers can better insulate themselves from the critical eyes of lower-level personnel and shareholders, allowing the seniors both to engross themselves in their work and to entrench. Finally, many studies of organizational behavior have shown that as organizations get larger, the individual's sense of "belonging" and being "a part of the team" may decline, performance along with it.

But as has been clearly demonstrated by several writers, notably Alfred Chandler and Oliver Williamson, the tendency for a firm to suffer organizational failure as it adds stages and functions can be arrested up to a point by changing its internal structure.[26] Structure in this context is considered "the design of the organization through which the enterprise is administered. The design has three aspects: first, the authority and responsibility of each executive; second, the kinds of information that flow along the lines of communication among executives; and third, the procedures established for channeling and processing the information."[27] The reasons why internal efficiency can improve with a change in structure are numerous and sometimes quite complex. In empirical studies, the analysis of structure is usually limited to the level of those senior managers who report to the chief executive directly. Such studies have shown that most firms above a very modest size have a structure at the senior management level based on functional lines (production, marketing, finance, and so forth), geographical areas, or product lines. The single-product firm operating in geographically undiversified markets and production sites tends to be pyramidally structured along functional lines (the U-form, in Williamson's terminology), but as the firm expands across product lines, geographical areas, or both, its management efficiency comes under strain from what Williamson calls "control loss" and "subgoal pursuit." Consequently, the firm will adopt a divisionalized structure, one based on geographical areas or product lines (the M-form) with a pyramidal functional structure within each division, a change that often improves the management's efficiency and makes the firm superior to an otherwise equivalent firm having the original structure.

Authority, responsibility, and information flow up and down a firm's organizational lines much more efficiently than across them. Therefore, one of the major criteria for selecting the optimal structure is to ensure that the people and the information flows required for day-to-day management are kept within the one line. Correspondingly, divisionalization will be successful only if interdivisional coordination is needed relatively infrequently and mainly for longer-term management, such as capital budgeting and strategic decision making. These principles have been found by John Stopford and Louis Wells also to apply to multinational firms, with the added complication that when a firm becomes multinational, it first adds an international division that has a status similar to that of its domestic divisions, but if the international division grows to approach the size of the largest domestic division, then it is dissolved, and all the domestic divisions become worldwide divisions.[28]

The importance of organizational structure for firm performance recently has been demonstrated statistically by Henry Armour and David Teece. From studying the history of twenty-eight U.S.-based petroleum firms over the period 1955 to 1973, they found that return on stockholders' equity was about two percentage points higher for M-form firms than U-form firms. Their findings are particularly important for this study, because the oil industry and the aluminum industry are very similar in a number of the factors that impinge upon organizational form, including, of course, high degrees of mine-to-market integration in firms. Armour and Teece concluded "that the efficacy of internal exchange is a function of organizational form (and hence that the appropriate division of economic activity between firms and markets is a function of organizational structure)," a statement that applies to the aluminum industry as well.[29]

Given these general findings on corporate organizational structure and my hypothesis that aluminum firms desire upstream integration to avoid market and contract failure, what organizational structures would be predicted for aluminum firms? Concentrating on the undiversified firms such as Alcan and Alcoa, the observation that they are large, single-product, highly multinational, and integrated across all functional areas suggests that their structures would be based on functions or areas, either on a worldwide scale or on a domestic scale with an international division. But whichever of these structures actually exists, if the need for close coordination of the upstream stages is as important as I have maintained, an integrated aluminum firm would be expected to have a senior executive and a major division, or something akin to them, to manage those upstream operations.

The reason for this expectation is that the characteristics of the upstream aluminum industry make the efficient planning and management of a worldwide integrated upstream operation a highly demanding task. Close coordination from the short run through the long run is required to determine the quantity, quality, and timing of bauxite and alumina flows to achieve an optimal balance between capacity utilization rates, transport costs, the meeting of long-term contractual commitments, the fulfillment of joint-venture contractual obligations, and coordination with joint-venture partners. Quite small variations in most of these factors have disproportionately large effects on efficiency. The implication is that a worldwide upstream operation requires the close coordination available only within a single management line, a line amounting to a worldwide functional division (production). Such a line would fit neatly into a firm having an overall worldwide functional structure, but it would be in some conflict with a worldwide area structure or a domestic divisions–international division structure.

Alcoa, Alcan, and Reynolds

Compactly, the hypothesis states that if the characteristics of the upstream aluminum industry are such that spot markets and long-term contracts fail to achieve efficient vertical coordination, and if firms elect to internalize transactions to improve coordination, one would expect them to choose an organizational structure well suited to achieving upstream coordination. Acceptance of the hypothesis is a necessary condition, strictly speaking, for my arguments regarding market and contract failure to remain forceful. The empirical test is to determine whether or not aluminum firms have such structures.

The hypothesis cannot be tested with very great precision — first, because "well suited" is a rather vague criterion; second, because the firms' structures are inferred from the limited information available in public sources (particularly, lists of senior managers and the descriptive titles of their positions given in annual reports); and third, because the sample of firms is small, because of the exclusion of the diversified aluminum producers, firms in which the major divisionalization is by product and in which the structure *within* the aluminum division is not apparent from published sources. The sample consists of Alcoa, Alcan, and Reynolds; although it is small, it includes the three largest producers (though whether Reynolds is the third largest depends on the criterion used). The descriptions of these firms' structures are brief here, but they are supported by detailed descriptions in traditional box-diagram form in Appendix C.

Alcoa is the largest and oldest firm in the industry. At the top of its management hierarchy it has an executive committee consisting of the chairman, the president, and four executive vice presidents. One group of vice presidents, in charge of various functions, report directly to the chairman, and another group report to the president; most of them have worldwide responsibility. The chairman is assisted by the lowest-ranking executive vice president, while the three senior executive vice presidents are responsible for operations, each managing one stage, or several vertically consecutive stages, of production: one is in charge of primary products; another, mill products; and the third, allied products (that is, final-user products). The operating divisions are thus structured on the basis of the vertical stages of production. The Primary Products Division is a classic example of a worldwide functional division, for it is almost totally concerned with managing worldwide production. The Mill Products Division and the Allied Products Division are best classified as regional functional divisions, the former having a role in production (semifabrication) and in marketing, and the latter mainly in marketing, in North America. Their overseas activities occur mostly within partially-owned subsidiaries and are the responsibility of the International Division, headed by a nonexecutive vice president who reports directly to the president.

Although Alcoa does not have one of the pure structures discussed above, it is fairly close to having a worldwide functional structure. This is highly unusual, even for a single-product firm concerned with the international rationalization of production; according to Stopford and Wells, such firms almost always have regional divisions. "Greater control and a more far-reaching rationalization of production might be achieved if, instead of regional divisions, the organization had a Stage 2 [U-form] structure in which each functional department had worldwide responsibilities. But this structure is seldom adopted, even by firms with only a single product line. The marginal gains of increased rationalization of production and lower costs are normally judged to be more than offset by losses in marketing effectiveness." [30] Apparently, worldwide upstream production coordination is more important to Alcoa than to most multinational firms, too important to risk control loss, squabbles, and so on, between regional divisions. This point is further emphasized by the recent history of Alcoa's organizational structure: until the 1970s Alcoa had three "textbook" worldwide functional divisions (production, sales, and finance-legal), but it finally yielded to the marketing pressures to decentralize and produced the present organization. Importantly, though, the upstream production activities retained their worldwide functional character and in fact were made separate divisions, probably because of the company's rapid upstream internationalization during the 1960s.[31]

Finally, the organization within Alcoa's primary products division lends further support to the argument that upstream integration requires the most exacting coordination internal organization can offer. The executive vice president of primary products has a vice president of operations directly under him, who, in turn, has three supporting vice presidents for operating primary metals, operating alumina and chemicals, and operating raw materials. The division obviously is oriented toward production; it observes the stages of production I have distinguished, and, most interesting, it has two general managers at the top, rather than the one in the other divisions, to coordinate its activities. It seems reasonable to infer that intradivisional coordination is a large and important task for the managers.

Further evidence regarding the size of the task comes from an examination of the number and global distribution of Alcoa's upstream facilities. As Table 3.5 shows, Alcoa in 1979 had thirty-two separate upstream plants (nine mines, eight refineries, and fifteen smelters). Only thirteen of these plants were located in the United States, the remaining nineteen being scattered widely throughout the world. Alcoa's primary products division was responsible for organizing a complex set of interplant commodity flows, including third-party transactions, tolling, and swaps, in a way that optimally balanced objectives (mainly cost) against a number of constraints, probably frequently binding, (such as shipping routes and costs, technical complementarity between plants, plant capacities, and so on).[32]

In Canada's Alcan, organizational structure is based on three multinational *regional divisions* headed by regional executive vice presidents, who report to a group of three senior executives (the chairman, vice chairman, and president). The President is also supported by five nonoperating vice presidents, a secretary, and a treasurer. This M-form area structure is not surprising, given Alcan's unusual history, originating as it did from Alcoa's international division. When Alcoa was forced in the late 1920s to divest its international operations, the resulting independent

Alcan consisted of an internationally diverse collection of plants, markets, and subsidiaries. Amazingly, the firm was organized in a correspondingly haphazard fashion until the late 1960s, at which time an incredible thirty-three chief executives of subsidiary companies all reported directly to the president in Montreal! A 1972 article in *International Management,* somewhat tongue in cheek, commented that "the structure was uncomplicated by such distractions as divisions or regional profit centres," but went on to say that "finally, Alcan hired U.S. management consultants McKinsey & Co.," who prompted the creation of three worldwide line divisions (raw materials, smelting, and fabricating and sales) headed by executive vice presidents.[33]

The new structure corresponded to what might be expected, given the work of Chandler, and Stopford and Wells, and given its similarity to Alcoa's structure, but it survived only a few years. Unlike Alcoa's line divisions, Alcan's separated its processing of raw materials from smelting to form two separate divisions; coordination between the two had to rely upon informal horizontal connections within the divisions, or horizontal connections right at the top, via the Group Executive Committee (composed of the president and executive vice presidents). With the close coordination I have argued is necessary between bauxite, alumina, and primary, it is not surprising that one of the "major weaknesses of the existing structure" was "the heavy responsibilities of the Executive Committee which still preoccupied itself with both planning and strategy, *as well as daily operating problems*" [emphasis mine].[34] So the first modification of the McKinsey-inspired structure was predictable: "On January 25, 1973, the smelting and raw materials line divisions were amalgamated. It was argued that economic interdependence and use of common process technology meant that the amalgamation made economic, managerial and technical sense."[35]

Although this change may have solved upstream coordination problems, Alcan's great geographical diversity apparently resulted in too many reporting relationships and information flows within the divisions, particularly in the fabricating and sales division. The data in Table 3.5 show Alcan's regional diversity: thirty-one of its thirty-seven plants in 1979 were located outside its base country, they were distributed throughout a wider range

Table 3.5 Regional distribution of upstream capacity of Alcoa, Alcan, and Reynolds, 1979 (percentages of each firm's worldwide capacity in primary equivalents).

Firm and region	Bauxite		Alumina		Primary	
	Percentage of capacity	Number of plants	Percentage of capacity	Number of plants	Percentage of capacity	Number of plants
Alcoa						
North America	4.2	1	31.6	3	77.7	9
Caribbean and Central America	39.5	3	23.6	2	5.7	2
South America	1.6	1	1.8	1	3.1	1
Europe	0.0	0	0.0	0	8.9	2
Africa and the Middle East	12.5	1	0.0	0	0.0	0
Asia	0.0	0	0.0	0	0.0	0
Australia	42.3	3	43.1	2	4.6	1
Worldwide	100.0	9	100.0	8	100.0	15

Alcan

North America	0.0	0	30.4	1	42.1	5
Caribbean and Central America	38.5	2	27.4	2	0.0	0
South America	5.3	1	2.9	1	2.8	1
Europe	6.0	1	0.0	0	29.7	7
Africa and the Middle East	34.4	1	0.0	0	0.0	0
Asia	15.9	3	26.6	4	23.2	6
Australia	0.0	0	12.7	1	2.1	1
Worldwide	100.0	8	100.0	9	100.0	20

Reynolds

North America	14.7	2	74.4	2	86.9	7
Caribbean and Central America	85.3	3	16.0	1	0.0	0
South America	0.0	0	0.0	0	4.5	1
Europe	0.0	0	9.6	1	2.8	1
Africa and the Middle East	0.0	0	0.0	0	5.8	2
Asia	0.0	0	0.0	0	0.0	0
Australia	0.0	0	0.0	0	0.0	0
Worldwide	100.0	5	100.0	4	100.0	11

Source: Data described in Appendix A.

of regions than were any other aluminum firm's plants, and the regions outside North America were proportionally much more important for Alcan than for any other aluminum firm. So, in 1975 the worldwide functional divisions were replaced by the current regional divisions. The structure within each of the new divisions is also based on geography: ten general managers for different areas or countries report to the regional executive vice presidents.

Although one hopes that the new area structure has solved Alcan's geographical diversity problems, it does not seem at first glance to be consistent with either my hypothesis regarding the need for close upstream coordination, or the January, 1973, amalgamation of raw materials and smelting. If ten area general managers, each presumably motivated to achieve intra-area goals, can successfully coordinate bauxite flows between eight mines (in six countries) and nine refineries (also in six countries), and alumina flows between the nine refineries and twenty smelters (spread across ten countries), then upstream coordination must not be a very difficult task. But fortunately for my hypothesis (and fortunately for Alcan), the company's new structure includes one more manager, whose existence strongly supports my hypothesis. Under the executive vice president of the largest regional division (the Western Hemisphere) is an area general manager of basic raw materials. Although he is only on the third tier of management, he has corporate-wide responsibilities. "The supply and movement of raw materials (bauxite, alumina, petroleum coke, etc.) to Alcan group companies, the sale of raw materials to third parties and the planning function for Alcan's needs and investments in this sector of the business are handled *throughout the Alcan group* by a management organization in Montreal known as the Basic Raw Materials Area." [emphasis mine].[36] So here is a company that has found from experience that it must be structured by region because of the diversity and importance of its overseas operations, but at the same time, it is forced to have a formally recognized group that cuts right across the regional divisions to assure upstream coordination.

The third large, single-product, integrated aluminum firm is the Reynolds Metals Company. Reynold's organizational structure does not fit neatly either the textbook models or my hy-

pothesis. The company is headed by three senior executives—
the chairman and chief executive officer, the vice chairman, and
the president and chief operating officer. Twenty-two officers
report directly to the chief operating officer; eleven of them
appear to have corporate-wide staff or related functions, six are
downstream-product general managers, two are subnational regional general managers, one heads the international division,
and the remaining two are responsible for primary metals and
aluminum supply. The relative status of these officers cannot be
determined from published information, but it seems that Reynolds believes in having all bases covered: the second level of
management includes functional managers, product managers,
regional managers, and staff officers.

Apparently four officers are responsible for upstream production management: the executive vice president international
(who, in 1979, was one of the three members of the Reynolds
family active in the firm's management); a vice president for
primary metals; a vice president for aluminum supply; and a vice
president for purchasing and transport. If this is an accurate
summary of the real upstream management structure, then efficient coordination of this area of the business would be problematic, if Reynolds were to develop the upstream complexity Alcoa
and Alcan have. But Table 3.5 indicates that Reynold's upstream
facilities are relatively few in number and are concentrated
geographically. In 1979 the firm had only twenty plants; eleven
of them were in the United States, and an additional five were in
nearby Jamaica, Haiti, and Venezuela. Of these sixteen plants,
eleven were on or very near the Gulf of Mexico, and one was
across the Caribbean Sea in Venezuela. The other four plants of
the total of twenty were nonmajority-owned overseas joint ventures: in two of them Reynolds held only small shareholdings and
had negligible management input, and the other two were only
several years old. The situation for bauxite and alumina was even
simpler than for the overall firm upstream. Reynold's Jamaican
bauxite fed the Corpus Christi, Texas, refinery; its Haitian mine
and its two mines in Arkansas fed the Hurricane Creek, Arkansas, refinery; and the Alpart joint venture in Jamaica ran its
balanced back-to-back mine and refinery operation independently.

Obviously, Reynolds's upstream operations are considerably

less complex than either Alcoa's or Alcan's (or any of the other major producers' for that matter), and, consequently, planning and tactical management requirements are fewer. It can therefore be concluded that Reynolds's loosely structured upstream organization is not in contradiction with my hypothesis; on the other hand, though, neither is it good support for the hypothesis. Looking to the future, Reynolds has announced plans that will take it into a more internationally diverse and greater number of upstream plants (particularly, the Worsley bauxite-alumina project in Western Australia and the Trombetas bauxite project in Brazil). I predict that Reynolds will be forced to restructure its internal organization as these and other developments become operational, though this may take many years, judging by the speed of adjustment Reynolds has displayed in the past. It is interesting to note that in Chandler's study of more than seventy large U.S. corporations, Chandler found that "the few firms among those studied here that remained family held have tended to be slower in changing both structure and strategy than the others."[37] Reynolds has always been partially owned, and predominantly managed, by the Reynolds family, a characteristic that distinguishes it from the other majors.

In summary, at least two major, integrated aluminum firms, Alcoa and Alcan, have internal organizational structures that include a functional line headed by a general manager, with corporate-wide and worldwide responsibility for the coordination of upstream operations. This indicates that upstream management demands the organizational structure that is best able to achieve maximum internal coordination. It is also consistent with Chandler's finding that one characteristic common in functionally organized enterprises is that the coordination problems of a chain of vertically integrated production processes are so intricate and important that they demand the attention of top management. Chandler puts copper, nickel, steel, aluminum, paper, and glass firms into this category.

Chandler also finds that firms of this type tend to be product specialists, showing little sign of diversifying into other industries. The apparent reason for this is that when a single organization consists of a vertical chain of sub-businesses, it can handle no more than one business efficiently. The problem probably arises at the executive level, where the bounded rationality of executives and their preoccupation with vertical coordination problems leave them little managerial capacity for product diversification. The structures of Alcoa, Alcan, and Reynolds are consistent with this, although the other three majors have diversified into other industries.

Finally, and most important, the evidence presented here supports the finding that arm's-length contracts are not usually the most efficient means of upstream coordination in aluminum. The evidence is indirect, but it shows that when upstream coordination is internalized, it demands the most sophisticated and intricate internal organizational design available for functional management. It is therefore not surprising that arm's-length contracts in bauxite and alumina, when they have arisen, have not been very successful.

Summary

In this chapter, I have explored theoretically and empirically the use of long-term sales contracts as a form of vertical organization connecting bauxite mining, alumina refining, and primary smelting. The theory of contracts in uncertain, small-numbers trading situations, combined with the characteristics of the upstream industry, predicted that sequential long-term contracts would generally not be a successful mechanism for achieving vertical coordination. It was shown that during the 1970s the main reasons for contract failures were contractual incompleteness, flexible exchange rates, inflation, and the cost of production and relative price disparities brought about by the rise in oil prices. These problems were illustrated in the failure of the 1972 Reynolds-Anaconda alumina contract.

The theoretical predictions were supported in large part by industry-wide data on the use of contracts, which indicated that contracts are relied upon for only about 10 percent of potential upstream transactions. But, there was some evidence that the number of alumina contracts could well increase in the future, although probably not the number of bauxite contracts. A study of Comalco and Alcoa, by far the world's largest arms-length sellers of bauxite and alumina, respectively, upheld that conclusion. I explained that the rapid growth in bauxite contracts between Australia and Japan during the late 1960s was a result of the unusual strategy adopted by the Japanese aluminum industry and Japan's Ministry for International Trade and Industry (MITI), rather than of a change in the fundamental forces discouraging reliance upon arm's-length trading in bauxite.

I also introduced the idea of internal organization failure, and I argued that in some circumstances contracts are quite workable. But when bauxite and alumina exchanges are internalized, efficient coordination between the upstream stages of production requires an organizational structure including an upstream line division, which supports the notion that upstream vertical coordination is a difficult task.

4 Upstream Joint Ventures

The existence of joint-venture firms is a fact of modern business organization easily validated by casual observation. While it may not be true for all industries, there is ample evidence to suggest that, at least in industries based on natural resources, joint-venture firms are an increasingly popular form of corporate organization. This claim is probably nowhere truer than it is in the aluminum industry, particularly in its upstream stages of production. The joint-venture form of organization differs in important ways from the traditional firm's or corporation's and affects an industry's behavior and performance. So far, researchers in economics and business management have come up with only a few, limited theories and empirical observations pertaining to the implications of the joint venture, and apart from some work published in the U.S. antitrust literature concerning the legality and competitive significance of joint ventures, and some work on the management of joint ventures, the field is somewhat of a vacuum.

Even the definition of joint venture is unclear, but, for my purposes, I define it as the organizational and legal entity created when two or more *separate* groups jointly participate as co-owners of a producing organization. I must further emphasize that each joint venturer continues to exist as a going concern independent of the joint-venture firm. Thus mergers and acquisitions are not joint ventures. Joseph Brodley, an academic lawyer, also adds the specification of *continuity*—the joint venture exists throughout a series of transactions, usually for a significant period of time.[1] Legally and organizationally, most joint ventures take advantage of two forms of business association that are similar in principle across national legal systems: partnership and incorporation. Partnership implies that each participant owes a fiduciary duty to the other partner(s). The advantages of incorporation include a limited liability of the parent companies to third parties, an indefinite life, and a familiar framework for financing and control.

In some countries, corporate law reserves the use of the expression *joint venture* to describe a very specific type of jointly owned enterprise, and like *partnership* and *corporation,* is the legal classification for a particular type of commercial institution. In this book, joint ventures in the aluminum industry are more broadly defined. Their partners can include basic aluminum firms (as previously defined), firms from other industries, financial institutions, such as banks and life insurance offices, governments, or state-owned enterprises. Furthermore, the joint-venture contract, explicit or implicit, can take a variety of forms. The application of this broad concept of joint venture to the upstream aluminum industry in 1979 produced the list of sixty-four joint ventures presented and described in Appendix D.

Because I am analyzing only the aluminum industry, my findings apply to other industries only to the extent that the same forces and effects are at work in them. Within the upstream aluminum industry itself, there are approximately sixty joint ventures. In 1979, they accounted for 66 percent of the world's bauxite capacity, 51 percent of its alumina capacity, and 35 percent of its primary capacity. In 1965, by comparison, the respective proportions were merely 15 percent, 13 percent, and 16 percent. The steady upward trends are clearly shown in Figure 4.1. In the last decade or so, the majority of *new* capacity at each stage of production has come in the joint-venture form of organization. In two major upstream aluminum nations, Australia and Guinea, joint-venture organizations constitute the entire industry. The growth in joint ventures is quite staggering, and

Percentage of Capacity
Owned by Joint-
Venture Organizations*

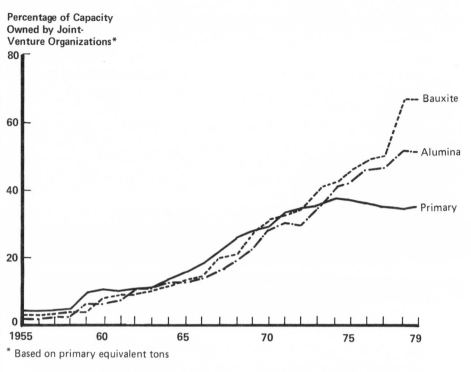

* Based on primary equivalent tons

Figure 4.1 Trends in the proportions of bauxite, alumina, and primary capacities owned by joint-venture organizations. *Source:* Data described in Appendixes A and D. See Stuckey, "Vertical Integration and Joint Ventures in the International Aluminum Industry," p. 235, for details.

according to firms' announced plans for the future, the trend will continue.

Production and exchange in the modern capitalist economy usually result from the market-coordinated behavior of individual firms or corporations. The predominance of this arrangement is presumably attributable to its superior efficiency vis-à-vis alternative institutional arrangements, in the context of the prevailing social, legal, and political framework. In Chapter 3, I summarized the inherent strengths of the individual firm as an organizing institution, but in certain business situations, the joint-venture firm is more efficient, at least from the points of view of the partners, because the joint enterprise allows some of the economically important relationships between the otherwise separate partners to be internalized by one organization. The partners can gain because the new organization provides a medium through which their relationships can be managed for greater mutual benefit.

The easiest case of this to see, and a most important one, occurs when a joint venture replaces an arm's-length market as the mechanism for exchanging some good or service between partners. When two independent firms perceive a potential for a mutually advantageous exchange relationship, but the market for the good or service involved is significantly imperfect, or even nonexistent, and particularly if the exchange relationship is by desire or necessity long term, then the two firms may find it advantageous to internalize the exchange relationship. The good or service involved, or the volume involved, may represent only a part of each firm's business, and hence merger or acquisition may seem an unnecessarily extreme response. Merger may also be undesirable for a variety of other reasons, such as management's desire to retain a corporate identity, and the risk of antitrust prosecution. In any case, a jointly owned enterprise allows circumvention of the unreliable market, and if both joint equity (or separately secured debt) and an appropriate contract are provided, some reasonable minimum of cooperation is ensured. In this way, the chances that the potential mutual advantages will be realized can be maximized, and the natural conflict in bilateral exchange relationships can be minimized. This is of course just a version of the argument used to explain vertical integration in the upstream aluminum industry, but the argument for joint ventures made here does not apply only to *vertical* market relationships.

In the aluminum industry, the reasons for creating joint ventures to avoid market failure arise in three areas. First, as I have already discussed, the markets for the aluminum industry's intermediate products, particularly bauxite and alumina, are subject to failure. Second, technical know-how and management expertise are not easily exchanged via markets to the satisfaction of both supplier and buyer; joint ventures can provide a vehicle for such transactions. Third, the combination of the aluminum industry's high barriers to entry and exit with the incompleteness of capital markets may mean that the average cost of capital for a large project may be lowered if a joint venture, rather than an operation wholly owned by an individual firm, is organized.

Another class of interfirm relationships that might be handled better within the context of a joint-venture organization is the management of oligopolistic mutual interdependence. A joint venture offers the opportunity for cooperative and collusive behavior between an industry's going firms, during both planning and operation. In the aluminum industry, joint-venture management committee meetings provide a (presently) legal occasion for "competitors" to air ideas about the future, particularly the timing and location of expansions to capacity and determination of the group's optimal pricing policy. Joint ventures between the industry's going firms may also have the anticompetitive effect of blocking opportunities for entry by new firms, by, for example, ensuring that all substantial bauxite reserves are under the control of going firms. Joint ventures allow the cost of this insurance against entry to be spread across the going firms, an arrangement that guards against interfirm misunderstandings and inequities.

The final type of relationship that can apparently be mediated more successfully within a joint venture than "at arm's length" is the relationship between an overseas firm and a host country's government. Many governments, particularly of small or economically underdeveloped nations, insist on local participation in projects involving multinational enterprises as a means of protecting national sovereignty and ensuring "a fair slice of the pie." This is the explanation for a number of joint ventures between the aluminum majors and national governments.

Most actual joint ventures are motivated by a mixture of these reasons, but for analytical purposes it is best to treat each separately. Unfortunately the nature of the reasons and the data concerning them defy formal multivariate statistical tests as a means of assessing the relative importance of each explanation, but the available descriptive information is used to get as close to this objective as possible. (Some of the specific features of individual joint ventures are included along with the list of joint ventures presented in Appendix D.)

Economies of Scale and Shared-Output Joint Ventures

The argument of this section revolves around three characteristics of the aluminum industry that have already been described thoroughly, namely, the existence of substantial economies of scale, the differences in minimum efficient scales between the stages of production, and the strong motivations to achieve complete integration. Firms often find it difficult simultaneously to achieve or maintain balanced, complete integration and technical efficiency through minimum efficient scale (MES) plants. Joint ventures can offer an attractive solution to the problem.

The first point to establish is that individual firms have an incentive to be integrated vertically. By now, of course, it should be clear that for the bauxite and alumina markets, very strong incentives to do so exist, but so far, I have not explained why firms should want to integrate across the primary market. Briefly, they do so to increase the security of outlets (for sellers of primary) and supplies (for buyers) during ups and downs in the aluminum business cycle. The primary market does not clear reliably through price, and demand-side rationing (during booms) and supply-side rationing (during slumps) occur as a means of resolving problems of excess demand and supply, respectively. Additionally, some aluminum consumer products, such as foil, are successfully differentiated and earn above-normal profits, and the producers of primary have an incentive to integrate into final manufacture of these goods to internalize the gains.

It is clear that the bauxite, alumina, and primary markets can fail. Assume, however, for purposes of this analysis, that all of the other markets upon which aluminum firms trade are perfectly competitive, complete, and efficient. In particular, assume that the markets for capital, technology, managerial and technical personnel, and intangible assets such as culture-specific knowledge, all have these properties. The assumption will be relaxed shortly.

When economies of scale are large, the firm wishing to add capacity faces the classic dilemma: either build an MES plant, achieve low unit costs, but confront the problem of quickly finding voluminous new outlets; or build a small, high unit cost plant, the output of which can be marketed relatively easily. Long-run average cost curves in this industry rise quite steeply below MES, so the second option is not often practical at all. Ignoring for a moment the differences in MES's across the stages of production, and taking the bauxite MES as the overall MES for the industry, the first option would add about 5 percent to the world's capacity. In a growing industry this may not appear to be a problem, as long as the additions to capacity coincide with demand growth. But in an oligopolistic industry like aluminum, the individual firm cannot risk such orderly additions to capacity, because it means that the firm "voted" by the group to make the next addition to capacity wins an immediate addition to its market share. Furthermore, an ambitious potential entrant can always take it upon itself to make the next addition to capacity, causing the going-firm oligopolists to lose out as a group. Consequently, in a growing oligopolistic industry with imperfect internal collusion and potential entrants, each individual firm has an incentive to add capacity continually. So the important parameter is not just the ratio of MES to two or three years of demand growth, but that ratio *times* the sum of the number of going firms plus the number of potential entrants intending to enter. If several firms add MES capacities at roughly the same time, either prices or capacity utilization, or both, must decline, unattractive circumstances not uncommon in the aluminum industry.

But joint ventures can help avoid such predicaments. A series of appropriately timed joint ventures allows the simultaneous achievement of (1) efficient-scale plants, (2) capacity growth commensurate with demand growth on an *industry* level, (3) capacity growth commensurate with growth of outlets of a *firm* level, and (4) approximate maintenance of the status quo for market shares. This argument offers a plausible (and partial) explanation for the "explosion" of joint ventures shown in Figure 4.1. During the last fifteen years or so, the trends in the variables upon which the argument rests have been quite strongly in the directions that should encourage joint ventures.

First, MES's in bauxite, alumina, and primary have grown substantially, largely because of infrastructure indivisibilities in the relatively undeveloped countries into which the industry has pushed. Second, the industry's growth rate has dropped markedly, particularly during the 1970s. Third, the number of firms in the industry has increased. Each of these trends would have made the management of MES capacity additions more difficult. (The effect of the increase in the number of firms upon oligopoly management is pursued later.)

Recognition of the differences in MES's across the stages of production complicates the analysis, but goes a considerable way in explaining the actual pattern of joint venture activity. At the present time, it is approximated that a new plant at each stage has the following MES (in tons of primary equivalent): bauxite 1,000,000; alumina 400,000; primary 150,000; and the MES in fabrication is typically much smaller. In 1979, plants of these sizes would have added 5.4 percent, 2.6 percent, 1.1 percent, and generally less than 0.5 percent, respectively, to the world's capacity. The implication is that an individual firm can easily add an efficient-scale fabrication plant, and maybe even a smelter, to world markets, but such plants must rely upon arm's-length inputs. Otherwise, the firm must add one mine, and, say, two refineries, six smelters, and numerous downstream plants to avoid arm's-length markets and to achieve MES in all stages of production.

One solution to this predicament is to develop mines, refineries, and, probably, smelters as joint ventures. By recognizing the differences in MES's, one would predict that joint ventures will increase in significance upstream through the stages of production. The firms establish independent downstream plants, and secure integrated, low-cost inputs by participating in large upstream joint ventures. If this occurs, one would also expect the number of partners in a joint venture to be correlated positively with the MES of the relevant stage of production.

Most of these predictions are upheld strongly by the evidence. Figure 4.1 showed that the proportion of capacity in joint ventures is greatest in bauxite, somewhat less in alumina, and much less in primary. Joint ventures in fabrication are most probably even less significant. Furthermore, the majority of the substantial joint ventures listed in Appendix D involve the sharing of outputs (and sometimes inputs) across at least some of the partners, and sharing rules are typically part of the joint venture contract.

If one looks only at shared-output joint ventures, the evidence on the more specific predictions for bauxite, alumina, and primary, based on averages computed for each stage of production, is quite convincing. Empirically, the number of partners in a joint venture correlates strongly with the MES of the stage of production at which it occurs. Bauxite joint ventures average 4.30 partners; alumina joint ventures, 3.10 partners; and primary joint ventures, 2.35 partners. Moreover, the average capacity of the joint ventures at each stage is similar to the (independent) estimates of MES's recorded above: 800,000; 534,000; and 146,000 tons of bauxite, alumina, and primary, respectively. On average, the joint venture plants are much larger than other plants: 160 percent larger in the case of bauxite, 80 percent in alumina, and 60 percent in primary. Furthermore, shared-output joint ventures are relatively more important in bauxite and alumina than in primary, composing 25 percent of both bauxite and alumina capacity, and only 19 percent of primary capacity.

The joint-venture solution to the dilemma posed by vertical integration and economies of scale is obviously appealing to the de novo firm, but it can also be attractive to the going firms, even the majors, by allowing the addition of relatively small chunks of capacity here and there along the vertical chain, and here and there across locations. Recall that technical complementarity between plants severely limits spatial and temporal adjustments for the established firms, and that joint ventures can add to flexibility. It can then be shown that several characteristics of existing joint ventures can often be explained by the argument involving economies of scale and vertical integration. As indicated, the number of partners is one such characteristic, but the identity of the partners, and their equity shares (and hence output shares), can also be explained. There seems no way of using industry-wide summary measures to verify this claim, but a careful case-by-case analysis shows that a firm's involvement in a joint venture, and its output share, often fits neatly (in time and space) with its corporate-wide vertical structure.

The net effect of the shared-output joint ventures is a quite amazing international network of joint-venture plants and interplant flows. Price and quantity decisions are to a large extent made inside the joint ventures, or just outside the front or back door between the partners. Strictly arm's-length transactions are kept to a minimum.

There are two types of joint ventures that arise as vehicles for vertical integration and that differ in fundamental ways. One type, which can be called vertical-*link* joint ventures, occurs when two or more firms operating at nonadjacent stages of production form a joint venture to "plug the vertical integration gap." The other type, vertical-*extension* joint ventures, occurs when two or more firms operating at the same stage of production form a joint venture to take them both in the same vertical direction.

Vertical-extension joint ventures are straightforward; they almost always involve several firms pushing upstream to secure in-house supplies of primary, alumina, or bauxite. At least one of the partners in this kind of joint venture could not have supported independently an operation the size of the joint venture, given its timing and location, without medium-term reliance upon arm's-length sales or a very rapid growth in downstream facilities. There is considerable evidence that indicates that such joint ventures have been motivated at least partially as a means of simultaneously achieving upstream integration and economies of scale. For example, the first such joint venture was the Ormet Corporation, formed as a fifty-fifty partnership between the U.S. copper producers Olin Mathieson Chemical Corporation and Revere Copper and Brass Corporation. After several years as a downstream aluminum fabricator, Olin announced in 1955 its intention to establish its own integrated alumina-primary operation, but only a year later it announced a larger joint-venture operation instead. "These facilities represent a major upward revision of the original Olin Mathieson aluminum program . . . They will provide the Corporation with a greatly increased supply of metal, *at a significantly lower cost per ton*, and will place the Corporation in an advantageous position to meet the expanding need of its aluminum fabricating facilities" [emphasis mine].[2]

The same applies even to the aluminum majors. For example, when the Reynolds-Kaiser-Anaconda Alpart joint venture was announced in 1966, the usually tight-lipped Reynolds was reported to have given the following explanation.

Why did Reynolds Metals Co., the largest participant in the new three-way alumina project in Jamaica, go along with a joint venture?

Richard S. Reynolds, Jr., chairman of Reynolds, the second largest U.S. aluminum producer, told Iron Age exclusively that it was simple economics.

"Some of our people had their pride hurt a little and wanted us to expand on our own, which we could have done. But we looked over the figures of the three-way deal, and the costs were so much better, that we decided not to let our pride get the better of us."

"The size of the plant," he continued, "makes it considerably more efficient to operate." [3]

Neither Reynolds or Kaiser could have absorbed internally the entire alumina output of the joint venture; when it came on-stream in 1970, either one would have required an expansion in its primary capacity of about 45 percent to maintain the alumina-primary balance it had at the time. For the third partner, Anaconda, Alpart was its first move into bauxite and alumina, and its equity (and hence its share of the output) neatly matched its primary capacity.

As a final illustration, the Intalco Aluminum Corporation smelting joint venture between the Howmet Corporation (PUK's U.S. subsidiary) and the Alumax Corporation was heavily influenced by economies of scale and integration. PUK wanted a primary source within the United States to support its downstream operations there, a strategy emanating from the transport costs and the tariff (then 5.5 percent) for shipping metal from Europe to the United States, and its desire to counter the North American invasion of the European Economic Community. Alumax, on the other hand, then the aluminum arm of the metals firm American Metal Climax Corporation (now Amax) was just a downstream producer and required an in-house supply of primary metal. In the context of a case study on Alumax, Edward Graham reports that "the Howmet Corporation . . . was interested in the possibility of backwards integration into primary aluminum production. Howmet, however, had a problem. New developments in the technology of primary reduction were resulting in new levels of scale economies . . . If Howmet were to build a plant having such a large capacity it would be unable to utilize the full output." [4]

One of the attractive features of vertical-extension joint ventures is that to a large extent the interests of the partners are the same. In particular, each partner simply wants to minimize the cost of the commodity at the joint venture's *front* door. The joint venture operates as a cost center: if the venture involves mining, then it is managed to minimize total costs; if the partners put in their own feedstocks, then it is managed to minimize value added. Within the industry such operations are known as tolling operations.

It is interesting to note that in those ventures where a feedstock is required, even if one of the partners can supply all of the feedstock, it usually does not. Instead, the other partner (or partners) arranges its own feedstock, and in so doing, avoids a potential source of conflict *within* the venture. For example, throughout the lives of the two PUK-Alumax smelting joint ventures (Intalco and Eastalco Aluminum Company), Alumax has supplied its own alumina under a long-term contract with Alcoa of Australia, even though PUK has persistently had a global surplus of alumina. Alumax still has to haggle over its alumina price, but with Alcoa, not with its joint-venture partner. In cases where feedstock homogeneity is required, feedstocks from independent sources are not physically combined but instead, one of the partners will swap its feedstock with the other partner on a ton-for-ton basis. This other partner will then supply all of the feedstock actually used, and will somehow channel the feedstock it acquires from the swap into other suitable plants.

Vertical-link joint ventures have one important inherent weakness, when compared to vertical-extension joint ventures. Their existence indicates that they generate net private benefits, but because of the vertically bilateral nature of the relationships, there is no easy way to divide the benefits up. If the joint venture operates as a cost center, and participants take delivery of their output at the plant's front door, then the benefits are ultimately divided up according to the price at which feedstock goes in at the back door. Here lies a major problem: feedstock input prices must be fully specified in the joint venture contract or be haggled over in the style of a bilateral monopoly. Because contracts are inevitably incomplete, periodic bargaining does occur, but it is not as problematic as it is with strictly arm's-length contracts. The bargaining takes place within the restricted range of terms dictated by the joint-venture contracts and according to the "good faith" encouraged by joint investment in long-lived plants. In a game-theory setting, the joint venture helps to keep the players within the neighborhood of the cooperative cell of the prisoner's dilemma game. It is worth noting that for precisely these reasons, vertical-link joint ventures are heavily contractualized, with take-or-pay clauses, rules for determining capacity utilization and expansion, and so on. All the same, however, price determination in vertical-link joint ventures is a source of conflict, and it has led to joint-venture failure in several cases.

Vertical-link joint ventures occur principally at the alumina and primary stages of production. They are rare in alumina, arising only when large arm's-length sellers of bauxite emerge: the Comalco-supplied Queensland Alumina Limited (QAL) and Eurallumina S.p.A. refineries are the only important cases. Chapter 3 described the problems Comalco encountered in slotting its large bauxite capacity into the worldwide industry via arm's-length contracts, and the first solution it tried was to integrate independently into refining. Comalco chose Gladstone, Queensland, as a site (where QAL is now located), but confronted the dilemma my analysis would have predicted. According to Donald Hibberd, Comalco's Chairman,

> the size of the initial plant envisaged for Gladstone, *to achieve immediate economy of scale, raised problems of sales outlets over a long period.* From contemplating a 240,000 t.p.a. [tons per annum] output in our earliest thinking, we moved through 360,000 tons and 480,000 tons to a firm 600,000 tons initial objective. At that stage of our development we would have had no chance of disposing of 600,000 tons of alumina a year ourselves because there was only limited free world trading in alumina . . .
>
> Comalco was a newcomer in the international scene and, for it, the answer lay in organizing a consortium of world producers, each guaranteeing to take their individual proportions of the whole output—basically for their own new require-

ments although they were free to dispose of it [emphasis mine].[5]

In fact, the joint-venture approach allowed an almost immediate doubling of capacity, followed five years later by another 100 percent increase. By then the plant represented almost 10 percent of the world's refining capacity, and scale economies were apparently yielded even on the final doubling. The other partners in QAL are majors, which were attracted to the joint venture because it allowed them to add relatively small (but very technically efficient) chunks of alumina capacity to complement their downstream growths.

Vertical-link joint ventures in primary are much more common, numbering about twenty at the present. Four outstanding characteristics apply to almost all: first, they include only two partners; second, one of the partners is a major, and it supplies the alumina; third, the venture is located in a country outside the major's home base; and fourth, the other partner is either the host country's government or a private local firm. The majors form these ventures as a means of penetrating overseas markets and tying up outlets, while the local firms are assured of supplies of alumina. But economies of scale are not so important here — instead, the joint ventures arise more as vehicles for the exchange of alumina and of intangible assets, and as vehicles for the management of relations between the multinational enterprise and the host country. But, here again the alumina input transfer price is a potentially contentious issue.

Joint Ventures and Intangible Asset Markets

The theme running throughout this book is that "organizations are a means of achieving the benefit of collective action in situations in which the price system fails."[6] When aluminum's intermediate product markets fail, the organizational response is vertical integration by the aluminum firms, quite often via joint ventures. Analogous logic applied to several other inputs to the aluminum production process gives rise to the second major explanation for the occurrence of joint ventures. The inputs are technological know-how, production management know-how, and what I will call nation-specific knowledge. The firms that possess these intangible assets and the firms that require their services can trade them in arm's-length markets, but such markets experience a number of problems. One way of reducing the problems is to trade the assets implicitly within a joint-venture operation that employs the assets. In this way the transactions costs and risks associated with the trade can be curtailed.

Consider, first of all, the assets of technological know-how and production management know-how. These include the capacity to design and construct a plant with the optimal technology, to operate the plant with technical efficiency, and sometimes to modify the plant optimally when unexpected events occur. There is no doubt that the services of these assets are important inputs into the aluminum production process, particularly in refining, smelting, and some specialized downstream activities. Basic processes in the production of aluminum, such as the Bayer process for refining and the Hall-Heroult process for smelting, are well known, but in any given situation the processes are modified according to the characteristics of the feedstocks and the desired outputs, the relative costs of other inputs, such as power, caustic soda, and carbon, and so on. This means that the optimal design of a particular plant is far from being a known constant. Furthermore, the efficiency of an individual plant improves over time as its operators become more experienced, but the starting point on the curve and the subsequent rate of decline in unit costs depend upon the previous experience of the operators.

The technical facts of production suggest several important properties of these know-how assets. First, know-how beyond what might be called textbook knowledge of aluminum's technology tends to be concentrated within the industry itself. Second, the know-how is embedded in individuals and firms, its quantity and quality depending largely upon the extent of the possessor's experience in the industry and the resources he has devoted to research and development of technology. Third, although individual engineers and technicians employed by aluminum firms possess know-how assets, the know-how assets possessed by a mature firm probably exceed the sum of the assets possessed by the individual technical employees of the firm, because implementation of knowledge about aluminum production is a team effort, involving professionals such as chemical engineers, mechanical engineers, and metallurgists, as well as practical professionals such as construction engineers and plant supervisors. An experienced team has already invested in the overhead costs of developing communication mechanisms, scheduling schemes, and so forth and can apply the skills and techniques of its individual members more quickly and efficiently.

It is fairly obvious who the potential buyers and sellers of the services provided by such assets are: the sellers are the mature aluminum firms, particularly the majors, and the buyers are the de novo firms. Each of the majors has quite extensive research and development, engineering, and construction divisions, and several senior executives head these operations. The skills possessed by members of these groups is a valuable and durable asset, and the majors have the normal economic incentive to use the asset to earn a return. They do this of course in their internal operations, but they can also hire out the asset to small or new firms, which thereby avoid the time and fixed costs involved in developing their own know-how team. By so doing, the majors can further exploit the economies of scale that typically occur in know-how development and implementation operations in mature industries such as aluminum.[7] The majors could well have the opportunity of pricing their know-how services at above marginal cost if they collude and avoid competition, because the minimum cost at which a new firm can internally develop comparable substitute services would likely be considerably greater than the major's marginal cost; but, as long as the majors keep their price below the new firm's minimum cost, or offer a superior service, or both, the new firm also gains from hiring a know-how team.

If the majors can produce know-how services at low marginal cost, and if there are opportunities for growth in the industry where the services can profitably be used, it might be argued that the majors will seize those opportunities themselves rather than just supply one of the inputs, because by selling know-how services, the majors are fostering entry and lowering their own market shares. This argument often does apply in reality, but in recent years a number of potential entrants have arisen which possess their own specialist input or an asset unavailable to the majors. Such entrants are mainly private or state-owned firms in underdeveloped countries that have their government's backing. They have the prime asset of local nationality. The majors are prohibited from setting up their own operation in the country, but at least they can sell their know-how services if a plant is to be built. If the majors supply the services via a joint-venture arrangement, they will have a long-run involvement in the management of the operation, which can be advantageous in the management of their oligopoly.

The majority of the inexperienced new entrants into the aluminum industry over the past several decades have realized the advantages, and even the necessity, of acquiring know-how services from established aluminum firms. The importance of such services is shown by the experience of Revere Copper and Brass as it independently expanded its operations in refining and smelting in the early 1970s. Revere was a small aluminum producer with a 50 percent interest in the Ormet refinery-smelter joint venture, and in the late 1960s, an optimistic time for the aluminum industry, Revere decided to invest $240 million in an independent, balanced upstream operation that included mining and refining in Jamaica and smelting in Alabama. With the benefit of hindsight, a *Forbes* journalist pointed out that

> when companies like Amax, Howmet and even Anaconda decided to integrate into aluminum, they called in experts like Pechiney and Alcoa to show them the ropes. But Revere . . . decided to go it alone. Pride, as they say, goeth before a fall . . .
>
> Competitors say that both the Scottsboro smelter and rolling mill and the Maggotty alumina refinery were too small, too inefficient and fundamentally too badly designed to have ever paid off. As one analyst puts it, "They underinvested in Scottsboro, and at Maggotty they thought they could leave out one step of the process, and when they started it up, the whole thing fell on the floor." [8]

Revere has subsequently attempted to take in a partner and expand or sell off the operation altogether, but its experience indicates the importance of the know-how input. It also indicates the danger associated with a balanced small-scale operation and illustrates how a joint venture from the outset could have allowed integration on an efficient scale.

Revere's mistakes aside, there are two principal means by which a new firm and a mature firm can trade know-how assets. The first is an arm's-length contract for know-how services, and the second is a joint venture where at least part of the mature firm's input to the joint venture is its skill and experience. Both of these methods are in fact used quite often in the aluminum industry. Contracts have the normal advantages that all arm's-length transactions have in free-market economies, but here they also have serious disadvantages. One is contractual incompleteness, this time due as much to measurability problems as to incomplete or insufficient contingency clauses. If a firm is to design an optimal plant, construct it, and successfully commission it, it is extremely difficult to specify in contractual terms exactly what is expected of the supplier. Uncertainty undoubtedly exists. For example, the supplier will not be sure how well the design will perform after it is constructed, and during the several years of construction, the costs of materials might well change. Technological advances or exogenous factors such as antipollution legislation may also occur during the period of the contract, which will itself often inhibit optimal adjustment for such developments. A second disadvantage of contracts for know-how is that if the parties disagree, after the event, about the performance of the supplier under contract, it may be difficult for an outside arbitrator to establish accurately what has transpired. When ex ante contractual incompleteness and ex post assessment problems are combined, the opportunity exists for strategic misrepresentations, because both parties have an incentive to interpret contractual and assessment ambiguities to their own advantage. For example, the supplier may use disguised shortcuts in construction to cut costs, while the buyer may refuse full remuneration because of some claim regarding the plant's actual performance relative to that promised by the supplier. Whatever the specific circumstances, the parties to contracts for know-how may well expose themselves to heavy transactions costs or financial risks.

Contractual incompleteness and opportunities for strategic

misrepresentation probably exist in most commercial contracts, but the magnitude of their effects in know-how contracts in the aluminum industry is potentially great. This is partly because it is so difficult to measure an intangible good, such as a service, and partly because of the enormous amounts of capital involved in plants such as refineries and smelters. It is probably impossible to harmonize fully the interests of the parties to such a contract, but considerable progress can be made in this direction if the parties internalize the transaction within a joint venture.

The major advantage of this arrangement is that if the supplier of know-how has permanent equity in the plant, then he has an incentive to optimize its design and performance. The supplier can be compensated for his input with cash or a cash-free equity allocation. This does not necessarily solve the whole problem, because although the joint venturers as a group would like to see know-how employed up to the point where its marginal cost equals its marginal value product, the partner supplying the know-how has a dual interest in the quantity of know-how used. It will recommend a higher "technology input" than might be optimal for the joint venture. However, there is no doubt that if the return on such an investment in technology comes in the form of a future stream of profits, the partner putting in the technology has a strong incentive to perform efficiently.

The other major type of intangible asset often required in the aluminum industry but intrinsically difficult to buy and sell at arm's length is what I call nation-specific knowledge. The need for the services of this asset typically arises when an established firm decides to set up operations in a country where the firm has had limited previous experience. Local firms or groups possess specialized information on the country's economy, politics, customs, and so on, information that is costly and time consuming for the multinational enterprise to gather. This information is more accessible and is synthesized and used more efficiently within the relatively cooperative atmosphere of a joint venture. Again, the supplier of the information then has an incentive to perform honestly and reliably, because its payment comes as future profits.

That multinationals value such information and often acquire it by taking in local partners is not specific to the aluminum industry. In a survey of ninety-nine U.S. multinationals having overseas manufacturing joint ventures with local partners, John Stopford and Louis Wells found that the local partner's contribution of nation-specific knowledge was, on average, regarded by the multinational as distinctly the most important of the local partner's contributions to the joint venture at the time of incorporation. On a scale of 6 ("very important") to 0 ("no importance whatsoever"), the mean score for nation-specific knowledge was 4.83.[9]

There are many examples in the aluminum industry where the opportunity to combine the services of partners' intangible assets was a major motivation behind the formation of a joint venture, a claim given empirical support later on. In most cases, the joint venture's role as a vehicle for vertical integration, or as a means of overcoming local equity participation regulations, was also important. One interesting case where the role of vertical integration was absent and the combination of intangible assets was crucial was in the formation of the Hindustan Aluminium Corporation (Hindalco). Hindalco was one of the first joint ventures; it was formed in India in the late 1950s by the local Birla organization (73 percent equity) and Kaiser (27 percent). Kaiser "provided the joint venture with all the necessary know-how, technical assistance, and training. Part of Kaiser's share was obtained against cash payment, and the remainder was acquired in exchange for its know-how and technical assistance."[10] For its part, the Birla organization contributed local knowledge and contacts, Indian nationality, and access to Indian bauxite.

Although Kaiser and Birla had assets that could profitably be combined, at least one of the parties had to be aware that the potential existed. In a world of incomplete information, the identification of attractive joint-venture opportunities often seems to result as much from past informal associations and coincidence as from formal search procedures. The Kaiser-Birla link is a case in point. George Woods, a former president of the World Bank, had been a personal friend of the Birla family and a financial adviser to the Kaiser Corporation. He introduced Edgar Kaiser to the Birla family, thinking that an association could be fruitful, and the formation of Hindalco was the result of the negotiations conducted at the top level. Quite a number of joint ventures in the aluminum industry had similar sorts of origins.

The rather unusual 73:27 split in ownership is not coincidental (it was originally 74:26). Although Kaiser was only interested in a minority interest, with little cash and management input, the Indian Companies Act of 1956 specified that certain major corporate decisions had to have a three-quarter majority. Hence Kaiser's 26 percent was sufficient to veto major decisions with which it did not agree. Here again is evidence that the shares in joint-venture ownership result from rational and strategic causes.

The national bauxite company of Guinea, Office des Bauxites de Kindia (OBK), provides an unusual example of a joint operation where technical and production management know-how was a vital input from one of the partners. OBK is wholly state owned and thus is not a joint venture in the strict sense, but effectively it is. The other "partner" is the Soviet Union, and the terms of the deal were as follows:[11] the Soviet Union would be responsible for design, construction, operations management, and the training of local employees, plus a $113 million loan to finance the scheme; while OBK would deliver 40 percent of the mines' annual output to the Soviet Union, over a twelve-year period, as a direct loan repayment, and an additional 50 percent to the Soviet Union under a fixed-price contract. OBK is a typical example of a production operation in the aluminum industry where the major inputs (a bauxite deposit, technical and production management know-how, and capital) and output (semiprocessed bauxite) are organized as a package within the joint venture, conventional arm's-length markets being almost totally avoided.

The use of a joint venture as a nonmarket means of packaging inputs and outputs in small-numbers exchange situations is further illustrated by the recent formation of the Dubai Aluminium Company (Dubal). Dubal will smelt primary from alumina in a new Persian Gulf smelter, but the complex planned also includes a power plant (based on dry gas), a desalination plant, and an anode plant. Eighty percent of the company is owned by the government of the Dubai Emirite and 20 percent by Alusmelter Holdings, Limited, 40 percent of which is held by Alcan, 40 percent by National Southwire Aluminium (the U.S.-based National Steel-Southwire Corporation's aluminum joint venture), and 20 percent still to be allocated.

Dubal will use arm's-length alumina from Alcoa of Australia, and is largely being financed with debt by international financial institutions, but the joint-venture package replaces most other arm's-length markets. The Dubai government will supply the gas and in return will take 20 percent of both the metal produced and the desalinated water. National Southwire is providing the smelter technology and will receive 40 percent of the metal. Alcan will take the remaining 40 percent of the metal; other aspects of Alcan's involvement are unclear. Obviously, the major "trade" being made within this joint venture is Middle Eastern energy for Western technology and outlets.[12]

The Availability and Cost of Capital

Probably the most popular general explanation for the existence of joint ventures is that they can help relieve the capital cost penalties and quantity rationing that the capital market imposes upon projects that are highly risky, require large amounts of capital, or both. Arguments of this type appear frequently in studies of joint ventures and in statements made by joint venturers themselves. For example, Paul Dixon, as chairman of the Federal Trade Commission and concerned about the anticompetitive aspects of joint ventures, granted that two of the "real functions" of joint ventures were:

1. To provide the large amounts of capital needed for the exploitation of raw material sources, particularly natural resources.
2. To supply security in a new industrial development, of borderline concern to the major business of the corporate partners, where considerable financial risk is involved.[13]

Similarly, Comalco's chairman, Donald Hibberd, had pointed out that two of the main characteristics of consortium joint ventures are:

Sharing of Risks: By this means there is a pooling of all the usual commercial risks which are normally associated with large scale entrepreneurial action . . .

Access to Capital Markets: The individual credit standing of each participant, and the established sources of finance of each of them, facilitate the very large capital raisings associated with some of these new processing plants, particularly in the case of alumina refining.[14]

These and other similar statements are presented as factual descriptions of the real world and, strictly speaking, are empirical propositions. I have not found any attempts to explain them more fully, let alone to rationalize them theoretically. There is no doubt that the aluminum industry's upstream projects require large amounts of capital, and furthermore, that they are quite risky in the sense that they involve durable and specific assets, the return on which is highly sensitive to the ups and downs of the aluminum business generally and to other project-specific factors such as technical efficiency, expropriation, resource taxes, and so on. But, such explanations cannot alone carry the arguments of Dixon, Hibberd, and others; it must also be shown that the capital markets prefer projects to be developed as joint ventures rather than as single-firm ventures. Given two projects identical in every respect except that one is a joint venture and the other is a single-firm venture, why might investors value the joint venture more highly?

To focus solely on the financial aspects of the question, consider the following hypothetical situation. The opportunity to develop an alumina refinery in a bauxite-rich Third World country has been identified. Imagine that for strictly technical reasons, the plant has a unique optimal design, size, and so on. Assume that, with the exception of capital, all of the other goods and services involved in the project (bauxite, alumina, labor, technical know-how, and so forth) are bought or sold (as the case may be) on perfectly competitive markets. The local government has no regulations regarding local equity participation (although there is always the chance that the government will expropriate the refinery). Thus, for the purpose of analysis, all of the nonfinancial or real reasons for joint ventures discussed in this chapter are neutralized. To retain balance, also assume away the nonfinancial internal inefficiency disadvantages of joint ventures.

Given this idealized situation, how will the opportunity to invest in the refinery be evaluated, and will its evaluation depend upon how and by whom it is financed and owned? Whether or not the project is a "goer" depends ultimately upon how its risk and return characteristics compare, from the individual investor's point of view, with those of alternative investments (given limited wealth and a relatively boundless investment opportunity set). But there is a strong tradition in economics that such comparisons can and should be made independently of the actual firm (or firms) considering the project's adoption. The implication of this tradition is that, given no real economies or diseconomies associated with the joint-venture form of the project's execution, the refinery's value is independent of its corporate organization.

The proposition that a project's value is *financially* independent of the firm considering its adoption was first proven rigorously by Jack Hirshleifer. He demonstrated that in a riskless world with perfect capital markets and firms that are intent upon maximizing their current market values, each project should be evaluated as if it were a mini-firm financed via a special and distinct security. The evaluation criterion is the net present value of the project calculated using the riskless rate of interest, a market-determined rate independent of any particular firm (or firms).[15]

The Effect of Risk

Clearly Hirshleifer's assumptions are unrealistic and therefore suggest opportunities to disprove the firm-independence result. The assumption of a riskless world is the obvious candidate for relaxation, but it turns out that even in a risky world the project's value is independent of the firm. This is known as the risk-independence principle. To illustrate, let V_A be the market value of, say, Alcoa, V_{AR} the market value of Alcoa after it has undertaken the refinery project, and V_R the market value of the refinery if set up as a new and independent firm. The risk-independence principle states that $V_{AR} = V_A + V_R$. The principle also implies that if Alcoa and, say, Kaiser develop the refinery as a joint venture, defining V_K as the market value of Kaiser and $V_{K'}$ and $V_{A'}$ as the market values of the firms after the refinery joint venture has been undertaken, then $V_{A'} + V_{K'} = V_A + V_K + V_R$.

Risk-independence is a general property of perfect and complete capital markets.[16] In a Markowitz-Sharpe-Lintner world of investors and security markets, any imperfect correlation between the returns on two securities can have diversification value for a risk-sensitive investor, but the firm receives no reward for undertaking the diversification on behalf of the investor. As long as each investment project carries its own securities, and the securities are continuously and costlessly tradable, the individual investor can just as easily undertake his own, "home-made" diversification by choosing the portfolio of basic securities that best suits his preferences. All that matters about a security, or ultimately the project to which it gives title, are the magnitude, timing, and nondiversifiable (or β) risk of its cash flows. These characteristics alone determine whether or not a project is a "goer," although the appropriate procedure for making this evaluation is complicated.[17]

So, in the case of an Alcoa-Kaiser refinery joint venture, the nondiversifiable risk of the refinery is not altered relative to that of the refinery's being financed as an independent firm. Even if the future cash flows of Alcoa, Kaiser, and the refinery are not perfectly correlated, and even if the parent companies were to accept liability for the refinery under the joint-venture form of organization, the *internal* pooling of risks would be of no advantage. If such pooling was attractive to the individual investor, he would simply buy shares in Alcoa, Kaiser, and the independent refinery in the appropriate proportions.

But even if the capital market did reward internal diversification, say for reasons concerning transactions costs, a joint venture between Alcoa and Kaiser would hardly represent much of a diversification. The major risk associated with a refinery is what could be called aluminum industry risk, the risk attached to ups and downs in the industry, resulting from its being over and under capacity, from increases in the price of energy, and so on. Joint ventures between aluminum firms offer very little escape from this risk, simply because they each have independent cash flows highly correlated with the overall industry's ups and downs. On the other hand, the project-specific risks associated with the refinery (such as the risk of expropriation) could feasibly be diversified away internally via joint ventures between the widely multinational aluminum firms. It is precisely these sorts of risks, however, that can easily be diversified away by the individual investor who holds stocks in twenty or thirty different companies.

If a joint venture were to arise to spread financial risk, one would expect it to be undertaken between firms with independent cash flows that are not highly correlated. But this is not what actually occurs. The vast majority of the aluminum industry's joint ventures that involve large amounts of capital and that occur in "risky" Third World countries are partnerships between aluminum firms. Furthermore, many of these firms are largely single-business organizations, and firms from outside the aluminum industry are rarely significantly involved in them. Major projects, such as Queensland Alumina, Alpart, Eurallumina, Boke, and Trombetas, support this claim, so both theory and evidence suggest that joint ventures do not serve an important financial purpose in the spreading of risk. The inference is that the economic feasibility of my hypothetical alumina refinery is independent of its ownership structure. Theoretically, then, a project's net present value is independent of the firm (or firms) that undertake it. In other words, the cost of capital for the refinery will be the same whether it is organized as a joint-venture consortium or as a new and independent firm.

The Separation of Ownership and Control

There are, however, at least two other assumptions necessary to obtain the theoretical risk-independence result, although probably they are not supported by reality. Their relaxation can be shown to lead to some financial advantages for joint ventures vis-à-vis single-firm ventures. First, the theory assumes that the capital markets discipline firms to an extent that dictates that the firm is intent solely upon maximizing its market value. This is the equivalent in a dynamic and uncertain world to maximizing profits, and as William Baumol, Robin Marris, and many others have argued, it may not be an accurate description of the real world. If the capital markets allow the managers of aluminum firms room to pursue their own interests, the managers will arrange some degree of internal diversification as a means of reducing the risk of corporate and personal professional failure. The Markowitz model of portfolio choice shows that this can be achieved by grouping together a number of businesses with imperfectly correlated rates of return, where personal risk rather than β risk is the relevant measure of risk. If the aluminum firms behave in this fashion, one would expect to observe internal diversification of two broad types: product-market diversification and geographical diversification. Under these circumstances the advantage that joint ventures offer is that they make lumpy businesses more divisible for investment purposes. For example, in bauxite mining, efficient-scale plants are large, and no single aluminum firm is large enough to support wholly owned mines in every major bauxite-source nation, but joint ventures in bauxite allow the individual firm to have an interest in many mines.

A suitable way of testing this hypothesis is to examine the extent to which the aluminum firms are internally diversified across product and geographical markets. Tables 4.1 and 4.2 show this for the six aluminum majors. Most of the other significant firms in the industry are divisions of firms that are involved heavily in other industries as well. In terms of product markets, diversification divides the majors into two groups. Alcoa, Alcan, and Reynolds are aluminum specialists, having 0 percent of their sales from nonaluminum businesses, while Kaiser, Alusuisse, and especially PUK are multiproduct firms, each having chemicals as their other major interest, and having, respectively, 32, 22, and 75 percent of their sales from nonaluminum businesses. The internal diversification hypothesis suggests that the three specialists should be relatively more diversified geographically in aluminum as a means of insuring against their product specialization.

This prediction is tested in Tables 4.1 and 4.2, but before examining that evidence, another distinction between the majors must be noted. The internal diversification hypothesis relies upon a separation of ownership from management control. If there is no separation, owner-managers can diversify their portfolios easily by investing in other stocks and bonds and have no great need for diversifying within their firm. Reynolds is distinguished from the other five majors by not having a sharp separation, for it has always been partially managed and owned by the Reynolds family. In the late 1970s the firm's six-person executive committee was composed of three Reynolds family members, one who was the chairman and chief executive officer and the other two who were executive vice presidents. This suggests that Reynolds will not be as concerned about internal diversification, and at least as far as product diversification is concerned, that suggestion is upheld. The same logic applies to geographical diversification, and hence in this way Reynolds may be more like the product diversifiers (Kaiser, PUK, and Alusuisse) than like the other product specialists (Alcoa and Alcan).

Table 4.1 presents evidence for the bauxite, alumina, and primary stages of production and the extent to which the six firms' capacities are located in different countries; it also shows the extent to which joint ventures are involved in those capacities. Table 4.2 shows the number of countries in which these firms are active. Alcoa and Kaiser are the extreme cases. Alcoa gets its bauxite from seven different countries (of which four are major); 58 percent of its bauxite capacity is in joint ventures. All of Kaiser's bauxite capacity is in Jamaica, and only 15 percent of it is in joint ventures. (In Table 4.1 the majors' operations in Jamaica that have recently become owned jointly with Jamaica are not counted as joint ventures, because the majors have recently been forced into joint ownership with the Jamaican government. Their exclusion amounts to my crude attempt at multivariate analysis.)

If all of the comparisons in Table 4.1 were as clear-cut as this one, the evidence would strongly support the hypothesis that joint ventures are formed as a means to internal diversification. They are not all as clear-cut, but there are some systematic relationships. First, Alcoa and Alcan, the product specialists with a potential ownership-control separation, do tend to have a higher degree of international diversification in their aluminum operations than the other four firms. This is especially apparent when they are compared to Reynolds and Kaiser, because these four firms are based in the same region and therefore have many other things in common. Alcoa and Alcan have substantial operations in numerous countries, while Kaiser and Reynolds (in particular) are heavily dependent upon Jamaica and the United States. Second, Alcoa and Alcan depend more upon joint ventures than do Kaiser and Reynolds (but this is surely also due to other factors apart from the role joint ventures play in enabling geographical portfolio diversification, as I discuss later). All the same, the patterns are consistent with the argument that Kaiser's product diversification and Reynolds's family control allow those firms to escape from the need for geographical diversification. The evidence is weaker when PUK and Alusuisse are introduced into the analysis. These two firms are in most cases less diversified geographically than Alcoa and Alcan, as would be expected, considering their product diversification. But, they are involved in more joint ventures than we would expect, suggesting that other forces are probably also at work.

Overall, the data tend to support the hypothesis that internal diversification is related to the separation of ownership and control, and that product and geographical diversification are substitutes for achieving corporate-wide diversification. However, the evidence is not as supportive of the argument that joint ventures play an integral role in internal diversification by allowing the divisibility of geographical investment opportunities. The data in Tables 4.1 and 4.2 do indicate a loose link between joint-venture activity and geographical diversification, but that link can also be explained by other factors. One thing is certain: internal diversification is not the predominant reason for joint ventures, because if it was, the link shown in Tables 4.1 and 4.2 would be much stronger.

The Effect of Capital Structure

The second assumption made in obtaining the risk-independence result — that firms are financed entirely by equity, or alternatively, that capital structure, dividends, and so on, are irrelevant to firm valuation — requires examination. Ever since the famous Franco Modigliani and Merton Miller papers indicated the irrelevance of capital structure and dividend policy to firm valuation, many studies, often conflicting, have been done on this topic. Confusion still reigns, and although a summary of those studies now would take me too far afield, observation and theory suggest to me that capital structure and dividends can and often do matter.[18] Assuming this is so, Stewart Myers has shown

Table 4.1 Geographical diversification of the six aluminum majors, 1978

Countries[a]	Alcoa % of firm's capacity	Alcoa % in joint ventures	Alcan % of firm's capacity	Alcan % in joint ventures	Reynolds % of firm's capacity	Reynolds % in joint ventures	Kaiser % of firm's capacity	Kaiser % in joint ventures	PUK % of firm's capacity	PUK % in joint ventures	Alusuisse % of firm's capacity	Alusuisse % in joint ventures
Bauxite sources												
Australia	44	100	0	—	0	—	0	—	0	—	60	100
Guinea	12	100	34	100	0	—	0	—	41	100	6	100
Jamaica	10	0	38	0	68	26	100	15	0	—	0	—
Surinam	22	—	0	—	0	—	0	—	0	—	0	—
Guyana	0	—	0	—	0	—	0	—	0	—	0	—
Greece	0	—	0	—	0	—	0	—	4	100	0	—
France	0	—	7	0	0	—	0	—	56	1	6	0
Other	12	17	21	29	32	0	0	—	0	—	28	0
Total	100	58	100	40	100	18	100	15	100	45	100	67
Alumina refining												
Australia	44	100	13	100	0	—	25	100	18	100	55	100
United States and Canada	31	0	31	0	74	0	60	0	0	—	16	100
Jamaica	7	—	27	0	16	100	16	100	0	—	0	—
Japan	0	—	21	100	0	—	0	—	0	—	0	—
Germany	0	0	0	—	10	100	0	—	0	—	25	0
Surinam	16	—	0	—	0	—	0	—	0	—	0	—
France	0	—	0	—	0	—	0	—	53	0	0	—
Other	2	100	8	63	0	—	0	—	29	100	4	100
Total	100	46	100	39	100	26	100	40	100	47	100	75

Primary smelting

United States and Canada	78	0	42	0	90	0	64	0	18	100	25	100
Japan	0	—	17	100	0	100	0	—	0	—	0	0
Germany	0	100	0	—	3	—	7	100	0	—	26	100
Norway	9	—	15	100	0	—	0	—	0	—	9	—
France	0	—	0	—	0	—	0	—	38	0	0	—
United Kingdom	0	—	6	0	0	—	11	100	0	—	8	—
Italy	5	100	2	100	0	—	0	—	0	—	0	100
Australia	0	—	0	—	0	—	0	—	0	—	0	—
Netherlands	0	—	6	100	0	—	0	—	16	100	0	—
Spain	0	—	5	100	0	—	0	—	8	100	0	—
India	0	—	3	100	0	—	0	—	0	—	0	—
Brazil	3	100	0	0	0	—	0	—	0	—	0	—
Other	5	0	4	100	7	100	18	100	20	25	32	42
Total	100	17	100	48	100	10	100	36	100	47	100	52

Source: Data described in Appendixes A and D.

Note: Alcoa's, Alcan's, Reynolds's, and Kaiser's previously wholly owned Jamaican operations are assumed not to be joint ventures in this table.

a. The countries listed individually are the major producers of each commodity, collectively accounting for the following shares of the Western world's output in 1978: bauxite, 84 percent; alumina, 86 percent; and primary aluminum, 86 percent.

Table 4.2   Number of countries in which the six aluminum majors were active in 1978.

	Number of countries			
Firm	Bauxite mines	Alumina refineries	Primary aluminum smelters	Total
Alcoa	7	5	6	18
Alcan	6	6	9	21
Reynolds	3	3	6	12
Kaiser	1	3	5	9
PUK	3	4	7	14
Alusuisse	6	4	8	18

Source: Data described in Appendixes A and D.

that the net present value of a project may vary according to the firm undertaking it.[19] From a mathematical programming formulation, he shows that a marginal investment unit in some project j should be adopted by a market-value maximizing firm if:

$$APV_j = A_j + \sum_{t=0}^{T} [Z_{jt}\lambda_t^F + c_{jt}\lambda_t^c] > 0,$$

where

APV_j = adjusted present value of a marginal investment in project j;

A_j = change in the market value of the firm resulting from adding the marginal unit of project j to the firm;

Z_{jt} = change in the debt capacity of the firm at time t resulting from adding the marginal unit of project j to the firm;

C_{jt} = change in expected net after-tax cash inflow or outflow at time t resulting from adding the marginal unit of project j to the firm;

λ_t^F = change in the market value of the firm resulting from relaxing the debt capacity constraint by one unit at time t;

λ_t^c = change in the market value of the firm resulting from a

unit change in issued stock or a unit change in dividend payout; and
$t = 0, 1, \ldots, T$.

If capital structure and dividend policy are irrelevant, then the criterion reduces to

$$APV_j = A_j > 0,$$

A_j being equal to the conventional "base case" net present value. But if the firm faces a ceiling on its debt-equity ratio (or alternatively, if its interest rate on debt goes up as its debt-equity ratio increases), and if the cost of debt is tax deductible, and if the adoption of an additional unit of the project expands the firm's debt capacity, then adoption of that unit of the project may increase the value of the firm by the present value of the tax shields generated by the interest on the incremental debt financing. Using the Myers criterion, this effect is measured by $Z_{jt} \lambda_t^F$. Notice that neither Z_{jt} or λ_t^F is necessarily constant as extra units of the project are evaluated.

To turn to the cash flow effects: a firm's sources and uses of funds have to be equal, so a project's incremental cash flows (typically negative in the early years) have to be balanced by matching flows of financing. If the marginal investment in the project necessitates a stock issue, then transactions costs will be incurred and the value of the firm will decrease. If the marginal investment necessitates a change in dividend payout (presumably a cut), and if investors care about changes in dividends because of their informational content or because they are taxed at the personal tax rate, then the value of the firm may go up or down. In Myers's equation, these effects are captured by $C_{jt} \lambda_t^c$, where once again they need not be constant across continual marginal additions to the project.

There are a number of "ifs" in the Myers model, but acceptance of the empirical significance of some of them suggests that the financial organization of an alumina refiner may not be irrelevant to its value. In the context of the Alcoa-Kaiser case, it is possible, for example, that

$$V_{A'} + V_{K'} > V_{AR} + V_K.$$

That is, the sum of the market values of Alcoa and Kaiser after undertaking the joint venture may be greater than that of the value of Alcoa if it had independently undertaken the refinery project, plus the (unaltered) value of Kaiser. This result could arise if the financial structure and cash status of Alcoa would not allow Alcoa to finance the entire project without (at worst) a dangerous increase in leverage, a share issue, and a dividend cut. On the other hand, financing for half of the project might necessitate only one or two of these policies, with Kaiser also requiring only a relatively modest financial rearrangement.

Even if this sort of reasoning is theoretically valid, its relevance is empirically questionable. For example, how large are Z_{jt}, C_{jt}, λ_t^F, and λ_t^c for the typical aluminum firm and the typical new project? Clearly, a proper answer to this question is not possible for someone outside the firms, but a few empirical observations throw a little light on the issues. First, there is no doubt that most upstream projects require large amounts of capital, relative to individual firms' total market values or retained earnings. Second, the aluminum firms are highly leveraged, relative to industry-wide averages. In 1976, the four North American majors had ratios of long-term debt to total long-term liabilities ranging from 40 to 46 percent, while the two European majors had ratios of over 50 percent. Although the relevance of interindustry comparisons of debt ratios lies at the heart of the problem of corporate capital structure, many analysts would argue that the aluminum firms ride hard up against their debt ceilings.

One possible explanation for the existence of these debt ceilings is that the financial institutions that arrange debt finance experience monitoring costs that are an increasing function of leverage, and when the ceiling is reached, marginal monitoring costs exceed the benefits of an additional unit of debt. Monitoring costs are usually referred to as agency costs, which arise because debt holders find it difficult and expensive to monitor and police the behavior of a firm's management after they have taken on the firm's debt instruments. When the original terms of a debt contract are agreed upon, the debt holders must obviously be satisfied; it is possible, however, that the terms of the contract will not be tight enough to prevent the firm's managers from subsequently adopting policies that jeopardize the interests of the bondholders and enhance the interests of the shareholders (or even the managers themselves). Debt indentures attempt to prevent such reallocations of wealth, but the point is that they fail to do so completely—another case of contractual incompleteness.[20]

If agency costs inhibit leverage, then an advantage of a joint venture is that it represents a formally separate company and its financial management can be less expensively monitored by financial institutions. As a condition of the debt contract, the financial institutions that arrange the debt may require that one of its representatives be part of the joint venture's board or executive committee, and because the joint venture is separated from its parent companies, the financial institutions can write more precise contracts and can more accurately observe compliance with them. These sorts of financial arrangements are known as project financing and are used for most of the aluminum industry's joint ventures; it has been observed that they are highly leveraged.[21] The large size of these projects may also encourage leverage if there are economies of scale in agency costs, a plausible hypothesis.

The Case of Queensland Alumina Limited

The theory proposed suggests two possible financial advantages for firms undertaking joint ventures. First, if managers pursue internal diversification for their own protection, then joint ventures can be useful to an aluminum firm by allowing it to diversify into countries by "taking a slice" of a number of efficient-scale plants. Internal diversification certainly does seem to occur, and an interfirm analysis provides some evidence that joint ventures are an integral part of the process. Second, joint ventures for large projects with high own-risk may also be preferred by the capital markets, because they allow the sponsoring firms to maintain conventional financial structures and policies and because their behavior can be monitored less expensively by outsiders. This second possibility cannot be denied; although it is difficult to test empirically, my assessment is that aluminum firms find that the capital markets prefer joint ventures principally because investors are aware of the *real* economies joint ventures offer. In particular, investors realize that joint ventures serve as vehicles for efficient vertical coordination, improved oligopolistic coordination, and efficient intangible asset exchange. In practical terms, if a large mine, refinery, or smelter is developed as a joint venture, it is more likely to be constructed at minimum efficient scale, it is more likely to operate at or near capacity over time, and it is more likely to be well designed and well run. Investors' recognition of these real economies lowers the cost of capital, eases capital rationing, or both, and this is what the aluminum firms observe. Thus the reason for undertaking a joint venture lies more in *real* economies than in *financial* economies.

Good support for this conclusion comes from an examination of the financing history of two major joint ventures, Queensland Alumina Limited (QAL) and New Zealand Aluminium Smelters Limited (NZAS), both Comalco-inspired projects. With its Weipa bauxite deposit under development in the late 1950s, Comalco realized the need for integrated processing facilities, and the company was on the lookout for refining and smelting opportunities. The first development program Comalco attempted to float involved a 360,000-ton refinery located at the mine, and a 120,000-ton hydroelectric power plant and smelter complex in New Zealand. The New Zealand government contributed approximately $100 million via government-guaranteed bonds for the hydro power project, but this left about $300 million for Comalco to finance independently. Comalco approached its U.S. investment bankers, but the financing was not available because, among other reasons, "a new overseas industry was being considered, one without a cost/profit history, which had to be attractive in comparison with U.S. domestic investment either by reason of return or security; . . . projections were based on 100 percent capacity operations, but 80–85 percent capacity operations would have been more realistic in the light of the history of the aluminium industry."[22] These reasons are quite consistent with the theoretical propositions I have presented. The project did not compare favorably with other investment opportunities, particularly when its risk-return characteristics were adjusted for the capacity utilization implications of reliance upon open-market sales of primary aluminum. The project was not a "goer" for real economic reasons.

Comalco needed to create a development strategy with more appeal to the capital markets. The solution was to harness the real economies offered by joint ventures. First, the QAL refining consortium was organized, a move that attracted finance because it promised lower unit costs through economies of scale (initially 600,000 tons per year, two-thirds larger than the originally proposed refinery) and an assured outlet via the joint-venture partners. As Comalco's chairman Donald Hibberd subsequently explained,

> raising the sort of capital needed for alumina refining (Gladstone at its initial stage of 600,000 tons per annum cost $120 million), presented difficulties. The plant itself is never seen by lenders as adequate security. So the credit standing and marketing arrangements entered into by members of the consortium really become the security on which debt money was raised. The way to guarantee the sale of the plant's output and thus the economic viability of the project was to have a collection of alumina customers, with high credit rating in world finance, captive as participants in the venture.[23]

Admittedly Hibberd stresses the partners' credit ratings, but he also emphasizes that the marketing arrangements were vital. Investors realized that the QAL joint-venture contract amounted to pseudo – vertical integration, and that vertical integration was the most efficient form of vertical coordination in upstream aluminum. QAL is now the world's largest refinery, it is one of the most efficient, and its average rate of capacity utilization has been far above the industry's average.

Meanwhile, Comalco was also attempting to get a smelter project under way. The major problem with the original New Zealand proposal had been the insecurity of arm's-length sales. One potential solution was a fabricating joint venture with Mitsui in Japan as an outlet for New Zealand primary, but this never came to fruition, presumably because Japan's MITI responded to pressure from Japan's going aluminum firms. Comalco had options with the New Zealand government on power for a smelter, but the chairman of Comalco Maurice Mawby explained in a 1966 letter to New Zealand's prime minister,

> funds can be obtained only if the project is supported by firm commitments, extending over the term of the loan, that the

resulting products will be taken or paid for by substantial customers. By this means the lenders are assured that the companies operating the facilities will have the cash flow necessary to pay interest and repay their loans . . . the key to succeed with lending institutions will be the firmness of the underlying long-term commitments, which Comalco and others can make to take or pay for the output of the Bluff smelter. Not only will these commitments directly affect the availability of finance for the smelter itself, but they will have an equal bearing upon the raising of loans for the construction of additional facilities at Gladstone and Weipa.[24]

Here again we see evidence of the inferiority, at least from the individual firm's point of view, of reliance upon open markets in this industry, and, of more immediate relevance, the ability of the capital markets to recognize the inferiority. Comalco searched the world for suitable joint-venture partners and eventually secured the interest of Showa Denko and Sumitomo of Japan. Subsequently, finance was made available, and a joint-venture contract was negotiated over a two-year period, culminating in the formation of NZAS in 1969.

Comalco's experience with QAL and NZAS clearly indicates that the real economies available in joint ventures had to be exploited as a means of hurdling capital availability barriers. But QAL and NZAS also provide a little evidence that joint ventures are not totally neutral in a strictly financial sense. QAL was financed almost entirely by debt, the borrower being QAL itself. In effect, each partner was facing the same cost of capital through the "take or pay" clause in the joint-venture contract. In contrast, each participant in NZAS arranged its own share of the financing and had to meet its own (apparently different) cost of capital.

The original QAL partners, Alcan, PUK, Kaiser, and Conzinc Riotinto of Australia Limited, were all large, mature, Western metal-mining companies, with similar financial structures and strategies. Comalco, the initiator of the project, was not financially involved for the first several years of QAL, though it was no coincidence that QAL's two parent companies, Kaiser and Conzinc Riotinto, were heavily involved. Presumably, investors, through the investment bankers, viewed as acceptable the addition of each partner's share of the QAL debt to its already outstanding debt. As far as I am aware, there were no covenants on the QAL debt over the partners' assets outside QAL, but the "take or pay" clauses effectively tapped into each partner's corporate-wide cash generation. Indeed, the "take or pay" clauses may have had the effect of granting priority to each partner's QAL debt over some of its non-QAL debt. The reason is that during industry slumps, the "take or pay" clauses strongly encouraged the QAL partners to cut capacity utilization in other plants and to maintain a high output rate from QAL.[25]

But in the NZAS case, Hibberd explained that

> there was a simple reason for the three participants' proceeding individually in their financing. We would not have been able to find a foreign source sufficient to cover the total amount needed — mainly because we found we could not borrow on behalf of the Japanese. This was due partly to Japanese Government restrictions and partly to Japanese external credit not being acceptable in Europe at the time. Thus each participant was responsible for finding its own share of the finance based on its own credit supported by a "take or pay" contract.[26]

Capital market imperfections, and probably the high debt ratios of the Japanese firms, excluded the Japanese firms from obtaining Western credit. But Comalco, investing in a project identical to the project for which the Japanese firms required finance, was granted access to Western credit. So here is an actual example of a project's being "held constant" and the availability of finance being a function of the identity of the investing firm. This refutes the firm-independence result.

The Management of Oligopolistic Rivalry and Entry

The classic problem confronting the firms in an oligopolistic industry is to achieve individual and collective rationality. Individual rationality requires that the individual firm perform as well as it can for itself, given the constraints imposed upon it. Collective rationality requires that the group-imposed constraints be managed to optimize the group's performance. The major thrust of studies of oligopolies has been to identify the factors that explain how successful a group of oligopolists will be in achieving collective rationality, or, put another way, how well they manage strategic interdependence. In more concrete terms, this amounts to the group's ability to define and maintain the collectively optimal set of competitive strategies, and to adjust the set following exogenous disturbances. Given this context, I want to examine the hypothesis that joint ventures can improve the group's ability to achieve, or at least approach, collective rationality.

In the aluminum industry, the major strategic variables that require collective rationality are capacity additions, capacity utilization rates, and price. The performance of the individual firm depends upon its own strategy across these variables, the strategies of the other going firms in the group, and, in the longer run, the strategies of potential entrants. Consider first the effect of joint ventures on the ability of the going firms to achieve collective rationality.

The group's profit-maximizing policy will generally be a monopolist policy. This is fine in theory, but in a changing world where information is incomplete and where explicit collusion is often illegal, the selection of and agreement upon collectively optimal price and output via tacit coordination is problematic. Even if this were possible, the agreement would have to be policed and recalcitrant firms punished. Again, the availability of certain kinds of information is vital. Joint-venture linkages between the industry's going firms provide them with ideal opportunities to collate and process the same information, to reach agreements, and possibly even to police them. Tacit coordination runs a poor second to a joint-venture's management committee meeting in some out-of-the-way country as a means to control rivalry within the oligopoly.

Joint ventures can also assist collusion in another way, apart from just offering an oligopoly the opportunity for explicit communication. Partners in a joint plant expose themselves to the same set of plant-specific factors, such as the plant's technology, its cost structure, its location, expropriation, and exchange risks, and so on. The effect is to homogenize the firms' commercial environments. In particular, they will be affected similarly by changes in the state of the world, and they will be more likely to adjust their competitive strategies in the same directions. This can assist oligopolistic coordination by promoting a consensus on collective rationality.

These general observations can be put on a more rigorous footing by turning to some predictions from several explicit theories of oligopolistic collusion. In a game theory context, Michael Spence derives several factors that impinge upon the ability of a group of oligopolists to maintain collective rationality, factors that have implications for joint ventures.[27] Spence suggests that an industry in which each firm has diversified into other industries will have less difficulty tacitly colluding than an industry containing single-product firms. Technically, this is because diversified firms have higher security levels (that is, they are less "minimax minded"), which reduces the set of competitive outcomes sustainable as reaction equilibria. Nontechnically, diversification means that temporary breakdowns of coordination in the industry are less disastrous for the firms involved, and hence their competitive strategy can be anything from middle-of-the-road to aggressive and does not need to be conservative. Many of the firms in the aluminum industry are aluminum specialists, or at most, modestly diversified. The three largest firms (Alcoa, Alcan, and Reynolds) have only minor interests outside the industry. If Spence's result is general, then the inference is that the aluminum firms have trouble with tacit collusion because of the wide set of possible outcomes resulting from the extreme "minimax" behavior typical of nondiversified firms. Table 4.1 demonstrated that Alcoa and Alcan have relatively high propensities to participate in joint ventures, a fact consistent with the theoretical prediction.

Spence also examines the effects of competitive response lags on tacit collusion, and although the theoretical results are somewhat ambiguous, he concludes that tacit collusion fails conspicuously in areas of strategic interaction where the response lags are long. In the aluminum industry this result is directly applicable to capacity additions, where there can be long lags before discovery of a competitor's pipeline capacity and before implementation of a response. Private rationality under these circumstances leads to cheating on the tacit group agreement on capacity. The aluminum firms seem to respond to this problem in two ways.

First, they are very open with the financial media about their plans for capacity additions. Second, they use joint-venture planning meetings to test the industry's reaction to the idea of, say, a new bauxite mine in Brazil.

Another implication of Spence's model is that tacit collusion becomes more difficult when atypical performance by firms can be due to exogenous randomness as well as cheating. This problem relates to a firm's own performance as well as to the observable performance of its competitors. The problem is analogous to the concept of moral hazard in insurance, resulting from an inability to disentangle the contribution of nature to the final observed outcome from that of people's decisions. The firm is not sure how to react when it observes performance that does not jibe with the group's tacit agreement. Of course, in the aluminum business, there are many exogenous factors that can produce enough of a disturbance to set off a chain of reactions. Joint ventures (among other institutions, such as industry associations) can help solve these problems by getting at their source; they provide the information and the opportunity to analyze it jointly that can separate causes from effects.

Almarin Phillips, in his well-known theory of interfirm organization, argues that "interfirm organization must become more formal, better planned, and better co-ordinated if the efficiency of simple oligopoly is to be maintained with a larger number of firms in the group." [28] This proposition runs throughout studies of oligopoly and needs no elaboration here, but it offers a convincing, if partial, explanation for the upward trend in joint-venture activity in the aluminum industry. Figure 4.1 showed that between 1955 and 1979, the proportion of the world's total capacity occurring as joint ventures increased for all three upstream stages of production from an average of 3 percent to 51 percent; at the same time, the number of significant separate firms increased from eleven to thirty. Tacit collusion among thirty firms would obviously be more difficult than among eleven firms. So the firms, particularly the majors, may have encouraged joint ventures as a way of avoiding a breakdown in collusion.

Phillips also proposes that as the value systems of firms become more unlike each other, it becomes increasingly necessary for the firms to formalize collusive arrangements. This might also help explain the upward trend in joint ventures, for certainly the nationality and cultural context of today's aluminum firms are much more diverse than they used to be. In the 1950s, the North American and Western European firms controlled about 95 percent of the industry, but today there are substantial producers in Japan, Australia, Brazil, Spain, and other countries. I pointed out earlier that joint ventures are a very successful means of homogenizing interests.

A similar proposition derives from recent studies of strategic groups within an industry.[29] For example, Michael Porter argues that many industries can be seen to consist of several groups of firms, the delineations dependent upon strategic similarities within groups and differences between groups. The ability of the overall industry to achieve collective rationality via tacit coordination declines (ceteris paribus) as the number and size symmetry of groups increases, as intergroup differences in strategies become greater, and as the identities of groups' final customers become more alike. In the aluminum business, the increase in the number of firms has also meant an increase in the number of strategic groups and greater equality in the size of the groups. In the 1950s, one group, the fully integrated majors, dominated the industry, but today, several groups can be identified: the six majors, the diversifiers from other natural-resource based industries (especially copper, steel, and oil), the Japanese firms, and the state-controlled firms. As might be expected, these groups differ significantly along some important strategic lines, particularly in their vertical structure and degree of multinationality. According to the theory of strategic groups, these differences should have inhibited tacit coordination, but joint ventures between members from different groups may serve to improve coordination.

Thus, there is no doubt theoretically that joint ventures can improve the management of oligopolistic rivalry, but proving it empirically is another matter. A first step can be made by showing that the structure of joint-venture interrelationships provides the *opportunity* for the hypothesized behavior. Beginning with the majors strategic group, Figure 4.2 shows that of the fifteen possible bilateral linkages between the six firms, eight

THE ALUMINUM INDUSTRY

	ALCOA (USA)	ALCAN (Canada)	Kaiser (USA)	Reynolds (USA)	PUK (France)	Alusuisse (Switz.)
Alusuisse					Friguia	
PUK	CBG	CBG QAL	QAL			
Reynolds		MRN	Alpart			
Kaiser		QAL				
ALCAN	CBG					
ALCOA						

CBG   = Cie des Bauxites de Guinea — bauxite (Guinea)
QAL   = Queensland Alumina Ltd. — alumina (Australia)
MRN   = Mineracao Rio do Norte — bauxite (Brazil)
Alpart = Alumina Partners of Jamaica — bauxite and alumina (Jamaica)
Friguia = Friguia consortium — bauxite and alumina (Guinea)

Figure 4.2 Joint-venture linkages in bauxite and alumina among the six aluminum majors. (With one minor exception — Volta Aluminum, 90 percent of which is owned by Kaiser, 10 percent by Reynolds — the majors have no joint ventures in primary aluminum.)

occur via joint ventures. Each major is involved with at least one other major, while five are involved with at least two. Alcan is involved with all of the other majors except Alusuisse. Of the eight linkages that exist, only one (Alcan and PUK) occurs in more than one joint venture. These patterns would seem to offer the opportunity to the majors for quite systematic explicit coordination within this, the dominant strategic group.

Turning to joint venture links between the majors and the other strategic groups, Figure 4.3 shows that of the seventy-eight possible bilateral links between the majors and the diversifiers strategic group, twenty-three joint ventures presently exist. In terms of size and strategic interdependence, the majors and the diversifiers are clearly the dominant groups, so this quite high rate of bilateral connections is consistent with the hypothesis that joint ventures serve as a vehicle for collusion. The diversifiers listed in Figure 4.3 are the principal members of this group, and each of them is linked with at least one of the majors.

	ALCOA	ALCAN	Kaiser	Reynolds	PUK	Alusuisse
Anaconda		Aughinish	Alpart	Alpart		
Amax					Intalco Eastalco	
CVRD		MRN		MRN		
Elkem-Spiger-Verket	Mosal					
Gove Alumina					Newcastle	Gove
Grangesburg		Granges				
Martin Marietta	CBG	CBG			CBG	
National Steel		Dubai				
Noranda					Friguia	Friguia
Phelps Dodge						Conalco
Revere						Ormet
Riotinto Zinc		QAL	Comalco Anglesey		QAL	
Shell		MRN Aughinish		MRN		

Figure 4.3 Joint-venture linkages among the six majors and the thirteen principal members of the diversifiers strategic group. Entries are the names of the joint-venture firms — see Appendix D for details.

Virtually all of the state-controlled firms involved in the industry also have a joint venture with one of the majors, but with two obvious exceptions, their strategic roles in the industry are insignificant, because in an industry-wide strategic sense, they are controlled by their multinational major partner. The two exceptions are the West German VAW and the Italian Ente Partecipazioni Finanziamento Industria Manifatturiera (EFIM). They are among the largest of the second-tier firms, they are multinationals, they have interests in a substantial number of countries and plants, and they are fully integrated. These features distinguish them from the other state-controlled firms, and not surprisingly, they are also distinguished by a much higher rate of joint-venture formation with the majors. VAW is linked with every major except Kaiser, while EFIM is in a joint venture with Alcoa, Alcan, and PUK.

The final strategic group, the Japanese firms, has in the past been distinguished from the other groups by being largely domestically orientated, unintegrated into bauxite, and independent of the majors. Alcan's 50-percent purchase of Nippon Light Metal in 1955 is the only important exception. However, more recently this has changed, in most cases via joint ventures with overseas firms. At present, Mitsubishi is the only one of the five Japanese firms that is not involved with overseas aluminum firms in joint ventures. So here again, joint ventures are providing the opportunity for explicit communication between strategic groups.

With the exception of the majors, joint-venture linkages between firms within the same strategic group are relatively uncommon. Possibly, this is because strategic interdependence within these groups is not great, particularly among the diversifiers and the state-controlled groups. The Japanese firms would certainly experience mutual interdependence, but in Japan explicit communication between "competitors" is apparently quite acceptable, and sometimes even encouraged and organized by governmental bodies. If this is so, joint ventures for purposes of collusion are unnecessary.

Overall, the pattern of joint-venture connections within the industry seems to correlate quite highly with the pattern of strategic interdependence. Joint ventures are more likely to arise between firms with a great deal of mutual interdependence and less likely to arise between firms with less mutual interdependence. This empirical finding is quite consistent with the hypothesis that joint ventures serve to assist the oligopolistic group in achieving group rationality. In more practical terms, the pattern of joint ventures suggests that the majors lure the second-tier firms into joint ventures as a means of keeping a grip on their behavior while the majors themselves get together to set the rules of the game and to umpire the action.

According to studies of the anticompetitive impact of joint ventures, their ability to improve the management of oligopolistic rivalry is only part of the story.[30] They are also assumed to decrease potential competition by reducing the number of separate firms in the industry relative to the number that would have existed had the joint venturers entered the industry independently. But the aluminum industry disproves the assumption, because its joint ventures have facilitated firms' entry by allowing them to hurdle barriers to entry jointly, and they have provided an escape from the straitjacket of pure vertical integration. The effect has been a decline in concentration and an increase in potential competition, the mechanics of which have been described earlier. The crucial argument is that without joint ventures, many of the significant new entrants of the last two decades would not have entered the industry, or if they had, they would have been considerably less successful than they have been. Note that I claim only that entry, subsequent growth, and hence potential competition have been facilitated — I have already argued that the realization of the potential is rather dubious.

Table 4.3 lists fifteen joint-venture firms that have represented the means of entry for seventeen new producers. The list of new producers is restricted to include only those firms that were not already active in the relevant stage (or stages) of production when the joint venture was formed and that were (or have subsequently become) significantly involved in the industry independently of the joint venture in question. In other words, the so-called new producers do not include firms that became partners in a single joint venture but are otherwise uninvolved in the industry.

Not all of the seventeen new producers have made successful entries — in fact, five have fully or partially liquidated their interests in the industry, although in so doing, two have allowed "overnight" entry for other new producers. By 1979, the new producers controlled 22 percent of the world's bauxite capacity, 10 percent of its alumina capacity, and 11 percent of its primary capacity. It would be stretching the point too far to claim that these significant shares of capacity held by the new producers would not have arisen without joint ventures, but there is no doubt that their magnitude and the overall viability of the new producers have depended to a large extent upon the real economic benefits accruing from participation in joint ventures.

So, joint ventures seem to have allowed entry and expansion

Table 4.3 Potentially procompetitive joint ventures that facilitated the entry of new firms to the industry or to particular stages of production.

Joint-venture firm[a]	Stage(s) of production[b]	Entering firm(s)
Cie des Bauxites de Guinee	B	Harvey Aluminum
Mineracao Rio do Norte	B	Compagnie Vale do Rio Doce (CVRD)
Alpart	B and A	Anaconda
Friguia	B and A	Olin Mathieson
Gove Joint Venture	B and A	Gove Alumina
Eurallumina	A	Metallgesellschaft
Queensland Alumina	A	Comalco
Ormet	A and P	Olin Mathieson and Revere
Intalco	P	AMAX (now Alumax)
National-Southwire	P	National Steel and Southwire
Alcasa	P	Corporation Venezolana de Guayane (CVG)
Venalum	P	Group of Japanese fabricators
Leichtmetallgesellschaft	P	Metallgesellschaft
Kaiser-Preussag	P	Preussag
Anglesey Aluminium	P	British Insulated Callender's Cables

a. For further details on these joint-venture firms, see Appendix D.

b. *B* denotes bauxite, *A* denotes alumina, and *P* denotes primary aluminum.

by new firms. But strangely, many of them are partnerships with the majors, which suggests that the majors have encouraged entry. Even if the involvement of the majors with the new firms in joint ventures allows the majors to monitor and partially control their behavior, the outcome still appears to be a second-best situation from the point of view of the majors. Why then, for the last several decades, have the majors allowed such a high rate of entry? The answer is that, even though the structural barriers to entry into the industry have been high, several factors made entry inevitable. In the United States, as Mertin Peck explains in detail, the government provided "considerable assistance" to the three entrants of the 1950s and at the same time restricted any retaliatory behavior by the going firms.[31] A second factor was that large firms in other metal industries, particularly copper, perceived a long-run threat from aluminum as a substitute metal and decided to enter the industry. Their considerable financial resources and experience in similar industries made them viable entrants. More recently, though for slightly different reasons, the cash-rich oil companies have become powerful entrants. Third, during the 1960s aluminum took the place of steel as a means by which underdeveloped nations could achieve "industrial" status, and the governments of these nations were willing to subsidize local firms' entry.

For these and other reasons, the tight aluminum oligopoly could not prevent entry, so the majors adopted the strategy of maintaining control over raw materials and technology and "sold" them to the entrants via joint ventures with them. The joint ventures also helped to minimize the negative impacts of entry and of decreased concentration upon collective rationality.

National Sovereignty

Many governments of countries host to multinational aluminum firms believe that their country's interests are better served by local-foreign joint ventures than by wholly foreign-owned ventures. Consequently, local or state-owned firms participate in many aluminum firms.

The reasons why host governments see advantages in joint ventures have been reported and reviewed widely in studies of the multinational firm and do not need repetition here.[32] The only point worth making is that in many ways the problem that host countries have with multinational enterprises boils down to one of contracting. If complete contracts could be written, and if they could be enforced according to international law, then there would seem to be no need for joint ventures. If it were mutually advantageous to both parties for the multinational to set up local operations, then an initial bargain would be struck according to relative bargaining strengths and encapsulated in a once-for-all contract. The contract would specify in what proportions the "surplus" was to be divided up.

The reasons why such contracts do not exist and why incomplete contracts can give rise to heavy bargaining costs and risks are the same in principle here as they are for other small-numbers bargaining situations, and as should be apparent by now, one way to curtail bargaining problems is to internalize the relationship within a joint venture. This does not remove the fundamental problem of how to slice the pie, but it allows both parties access to similar information and it provides the organizational machinery to cut bargaining costs.

Overall Empirical Evidence

How can the relative importance of each of the theoretical explanations for joint-venture formation that has arisen be empirically assessed, and how can one explain interfirm differences in joint-venture participation rates? Problems with measurement and data make formal testing extremely difficult, if not impossible, but useful comparisons can be made by first using individual joint ventures, and then individual firms, as the unit of observation.

Motivation for Joint-Venture Formation

In assessing theories of joint-venture formation, it is useful to classify the joint ventures that have actually been formed in the industry according to observable characteristics that relate closely to those predicted by the theory. The results are presented in Table 4.4. The first column of the table lists eight observable characteristics of a joint venture that have a number of fairly direct implications for what might have motivated the firms in question to form the partnership. Each of the joint ventures listed in Appendix D was studied closely for the partnership characteristics exhibited at the time of its formation. The scores are disaggregated because the implications of the theory differ somewhat from one stage of production to another. Within each stage of production, three statistics are presented: first, the number of joint ventures that on formation had the partnership characteristic; second, this number as a percentage of the total number of joint ventures at that stage of production; and third, the characterized joint ventures as a percentage of the capacity of all of the joint ventures at that stage of production. Nineteen bauxite, twenty-two alumina, and forty-five primary joint ventures were characterized (including double counting for

Table 4.4 Characteristics and distribution of joint-venture partnerships for bauxite, alumina, and primary.

Characteristics of partnership[a]	Bauxite joint ventures			Alumina joint ventures			Primary joint ventures		
	Number	% of total	% of capacity[b]	Number	% of total	% of capacity[b]	Number	% of total	% of capacity[b]
Upstream vertical extension	8	42	53	7	32	41	13	29	36
Vertical link	n.a.	n.a.	n.a.	6	27	35	19	42	47
Technological asymmetry	15	79	77	14	64	68	36	80	75
Local-foreign	14	74	67	17	77	83	35	78	77
Major-major	5	26	33	4	18	30	3	7	7
Major–second tier	9	47	64	7	32	46	9	20	27
Second tier–second tier	3	16	23	3	14	11	2	4	6
Major-outsider	11	58	53	9	41	42	29	64	60
Undetermined	1	5	1	2	9	2	2	4	3

Source: Appendix D.

Note: Includes all joint ventures listed in Appendix D: 19 in bauxite, 22 in alumina, and 45 in primary.

a. The partnership characteristics are defined as follows: *upstream vertical extension*—at least two partners moving upstream together; *vertical link*—at least one partner a net supplier of input and at least one partner a net taker of output; *technological asymmetry*—at least one partner with previous experience at this stage of production and at least one without; *local-foreign*—at least one partner based in the country in which the joint venture was established and one partner not; *major-major*—at least two of the six majors involved; *major–second tier*—at least one of the partners a major and at least one a second-tier firm; *second tier–second tier*—at least two second-tier firms involved; *major-outsider*—at least one partner a major and at least one a firm or state authority not otherwise involved in the industry; and *undetermined*—does not appear to have any of these features.

b. Capacity at 1979, or at termination of the joint venture, in primary equivalents.

c. N.a. = not applicable.

multistage joint ventures). Notice that the total number of joint ventures in the categories do not equal these numbers, nor do the percentages total one hundred: this reflects the fact that most joint ventures showed more than one of the partnership characteristics.

The first two characteristics listed in the table, "upstream vertical extension" and "vertical link," include those joint ventures whose formations apparently were motivated at least partially by the desire to use them as vehicles for vertical integration. In the upstream vertical extension cases, at least two of the partners had the opportunity to benefit from making a less-than-MES addition to upstream capacity, but in an MES plant. Overall, about one-third of the joint ventures provided this opportunity, and, as the theory predicted, the effect is related to the MES of a stage of production. As the table indicates, over 40 percent of bauxite joint ventures showed this characteristic, but only 32 percent of alumina and 29 percent of primary joint ventures did. Another interesting result is that when measured as a percentage of total joint-venture capacity, ventures with an upstream vertical extension component are considerably larger than other joint ventures.

Joint ventures having vertical link aspects are those in which one or more partners supply the feedstock and the other partners share in the output. By definition they do not occur in bauxite, but 27 percent of alumina joint ventures and 42 percent of primary joint ventures had this characteristic. Once again these joint ventures tend to be larger than the others. Taking the vertical extension and vertical link characteristics together, about 50 percent of the joint ventures showed either or both, indicating that joint ventures are important vehicles for vertical integration. The importance of this role relative to the others within a particular joint venture is not measurable, but my assessment is that it is often a major factor *when* it arises.

The third partnership characteristic is technological asymmetry, and the joint ventures exhibiting it were those in which at least one partner had previous firsthand experience at the relevant stage of production and at least one had none. Joint ventures formed because of technological asymmetry substitute for the markets for technological and production management know-how. The majority of joint ventures had this characteristic, up to 80 percent in the case of primary joint ventures. This implies that the intangible-asset exchange role of joint ventures is very important (in fact, more important than I expected). However, there is a strong possibility that the measure overemphasizes the role, because all the measure does is monitor the *possibility* of the role, and not its actuality or importance. But by the same token we must conclude that many joint ventures have effectively involved an exchange of such intangible assets, and in some cases, other evidence indicates that it was a major factor behind their formation.

The local-foreign category includes those joint ventures in which at least one partner was indigenous to the country of incorporation and at least one was not. It was of course a simple matter to identify the joint ventures with this characteristic, but it is a characteristic that could be capturing many motivations to form joint ventures. However, the evidence is clear that, consistently across the stages of production, about three-quarters of the joint ventures are multinational. Earlier, I suggested two reasons for forming local-foreign partnerships: first, they provide an efficient medium for the exchange of nation-specific knowledge, and second, they allow host nations to protect local interests. The table does not differentiate between these two reasons, but other evidence indicates that the latter is probably the most important. In many cases local participation is, in effect, mandatory.

The next four partnership characteristics revolve around the identity of the partners, classified as major firms, second-tier firms and outsiders (all other firms and state-owned authorities). These four characteristics describe joint ventures that are based on firms' desires for collusive opportunities. The results complement those presented earlier. The table shows that the majors do not combine with each other in many joint ventures, but not surprisingly, when they do, they do so relatively more often in bauxite and alumina, the stages where coordination on expansion is most vital. Major second tier partnerships are much more common, and again they are more common in bauxite (47 percent) than in alumina (32 percent) or primary (20 percent). This concurs with the earlier observation that the second-tier firms are bound up securely with the majors in the upstream stages of production. Second tier–second tier partnerships are shown to be infrequent, as alluded to earlier, but major-outsider partnerships are common, as would be expected for "vertical link" and "local-foreign" reasons. They do not affect oligopolistic collusion.

The final line of Table 4.4 includes those joint ventures that do not have any of the listed characteristics. There are only two, one in Brazil (Companhia Brasileira de Aluminio) and one in Italy (Alumetal), which arose when the Italian state firm EFIM was forced to "bail out" Montedison S.p.A.'s ailing aluminum business. Brasileira de Aluminio is a partnership between the state and a private company. The fact that only two of the sixty-four joint ventures listed in Appendix D are not at all explained by the earlier theory is reassuring.

It will have been noticed that none of the characteristics in Table 4.4 relates directly to the cost-of-capital hypothesis for joint ventures. No observable variables are available to check this hypothesis, so the results presented in this section should be seen as neither a confirmation nor refutation of it.

Interfirm Differences

The analysis of the likely motives behind the formation of the sixty-four joint ventures in Appendix D has obvious applications to interfirm differences in joint-venture activity and for the identities of the firms that form joint ventures. For example, if a small and technically inexperienced primary producer based in a bauxite-poor nation were to decide to integrate upstream, one could predict that it would probably enter an overseas joint venture in partnership with at least a major firm and a representative of the host nation. The major firm would supply the technology and the opportunity to build an MES plant and would play the role of "big brother" for the oligopoly, while the host nation would insist on local participation to protect local interests. It seems impossible to describe concisely and then compare the joint-venture behavior of individual firms to demonstrate that such predicted outcomes do actually occur systematically, largely because of the large number of variables involved and the difficulty of measuring some of them; nevertheless, close firm-by-firm analysis does show that the predictions do occur, although of course the fit is imperfect because each firm has its own special characteristics that affect its joint-venture activity.

So, pragmatism dictates that this conclusion be presented in largely unsubstantiated form, at least for the numerous nonmajor firms in the industry. In the case of the six major firms, however, interfirm differences in joint-venture activity can be examined concisely, because since the early 1960s, the period when most joint ventures have been formed, most of the factors behind joint-venture formation have been very similar for the majors. They have had complete and reasonably balanced integration, they have been of similar sizes and have therefore had similar abilities to absorb MES capacity additions, they have all had extensive technical experience, they probably have had similar motives to form joint ventures to help their management of the oligopoly, and if the capital markets prefer joint ventures to new, independent firms for financial reasons, then the majors have probably all been affected similarly by those markets. The only kind of motivation for forming joint ventures upon which the majors could differ significantly is that concerning foreign projects. If the majors differ in their propensities to participate in joint ventures, one would expect to find that the differences relate to the extent to which they are involved in projects outside their home countries.

One reason for a link between joint ventures and foreign projects — namely, internal geographical diversification — has already been considered, and some evidence was found to support it, but here more detail is necessary. First it has to be established that there is such a link, and this is achieved in Tables 4.5 and 4.6. Table 4.5 compares the three upstream stages of production in terms of the percentage of each firm's capacity outside its home country and the percentage of its capacity produced in joint ventures. Table 4.6 presents similar information, based on number of operations rather than capacity.[33] The firms do differ somewhat in their propensities to form joint ventures: in Table 4.5 the range is from Reynold's 10 percent of primary capacity in joint ventures to Kaiser's 100 percent of

Table 4.5 Joint-venture activity and multinationalism for the six major firms, 1979: (capacity in percentages, based on primary equivalents).

Joint-venture activity	Firm						Average	Simple Correlation
	Alcoa	Alcan	Reynolds	Kaiser	PUK	Alusuisse		
Bauxite								
Capacity outside home country	96	100	85	100	44	100	88 ⎫	r = 0.77
Capacity in joint ventures	68	84	68	.100	45	67	72 ⎬	
Alumina								
Capacity outside home country	69	69	26	40	47	100	59 ⎫	r = 0.89
Capacity in joint ventures	53	77	26	40	47	75	53 ⎬	
Primary								
Capacity outside home country	22	58	24	36	62	89	49 ⎫	r = 0.90
Capacity in joint ventures	17	48	10	36	47	52	35 ⎬	

Source: Data described in Appendixes A and D.

Table 4.6 Joint-venture activity and multinationalism for the six major firms, 1979: number of operations.

Joint-venture activity	Firm						Average	Simple correlation
	Alcoa	Alcan	Reynolds	Kaiser	PUK	Alusuisse		
Bauxite								
Total number of operations	7	6	4	2	5	6	5.0 ⎤	
Operations outside home country	6	6	3	2	3	6	4.3 ⎬	$r = 0.76$
Joint ventures	4	4	2	2	4	4	3.3 ⎦	
Alumina								
Total number of operations	5	6	3	3	4	4	4.2 ⎤	
Operations outside home country	4	5	2	2	3	4	3.3 ⎬	$r = 0.95$
Joint ventures	3	4	2	2	3	3	2.8 ⎦	
Primary								
Total number of operations	6	9	6	5	8	9	7.2 ⎤	
Operations outside home country	5	8	5	4	7	8	6.2 ⎬	$r = 0.54$
Joint ventures	4	6	4	4	7	4	4.8 ⎦	

Source: Data described in Appendixes A and D.

bauxite capacity in joint ventures; in Table 4.6 the range is from
PUK's seven joint ventures out of eight operations in primary to
Alusuisse's four out of nine in primary. The main difference
between these data and those presented in Tables 4.1 and 4.2,
where the internal-diversification hypothesis was tested, is that
here are included those foreign operations created originally as
wholly owned subsidiaries but that, at the "request" of host
governments, have subsequently become foreign-local joint ventures. The difference is not insignificant, particularly in bauxite
and alumina operations.

The tables also show that there is a strong positive correlation
between joint-venture formation and multinationalism. That is,
as a firm depends more on foreign operations, it also depends
more upon joint ventures. In statistical terms the simple correlations between the six relevant pairs of data are high, except
perhaps for the $r = 0.54$ for primary when measured by number
of operations. It is likely, in fact, that multinationalism leads to
joint-venture formation. The attitudes of host nations undoubtedly play an important role in such links, but there are other
factors as well. One is that even the majors tend not to be able to
absorb MES additions in foreign locations: for bauxite, the
majors have been forced by virtue of the global location of
deposits to go outside their home countries into infrastructure-
poor nations where MES's are large, while for primary, the
majors have not been able to increase their local downstream
operations overnight to absorb an MES smelter in a foreign
venture. For alumina, both of these influences have been at
work. Of course another factor behind the link is that foreign
joint ventures are usually perceived by the majors as being more
risky in terms of corporate survival, so if managers value internal
diversification, they use joint ventures to make their international investment opportunities more divisible and hence expand the feasible portfolio set. More direct evidence for this has
already been analyzed, but the effect is still visible in the data of
Tables 4.5 and 4.6.

The Limits of Joint Ventures

If joint ventures have all of the advantages claimed, why do they
not pervade the entire industry? A few very brief comments are

needed to clear-up this doubt. Joint ventures have inherent internal inefficiencies that usually more than counter their advantages. I have argued that the advantages arise when the internalization of a relationship between two or more groups improves the relationship relative to an arm's-length arrangement — the organization replaces the market. But the internal management of the joint-venture organization can be difficult; when compared with the conventional firm, the joint venture scores poorly in internal management efficiency.

The conventional firm usually has a fairly clear-cut set of goals, and even allowing for the alleged problems associated with the separation of ownership and control, the participants have a relatively uniform view of the goals. Relative, that is, to the joint venture, where the partners are ultimately self-interested and where their self-interests can fairly easily be diametrically opposed to each other. A joint venture has the essential features of the prisoner's dilemma game: by virtue of its existence it must offer all partners mutual benefits, but each partner will often see the possibility of furthering its interest at the expense of the other(s). This probably occurs to some extent in a conventional firm as well, but there ultimate authority rests with the chief executive or the board. In a joint venture there is no such single, ultimate authority.

This would not be such a great problem if only major issues, such as transfer pricing, ended up over a bargaining table between the joint ventures. But apparently many day-to-day decisions in joint ventures fail to be handled within the joint venture and ultimately must be resolved between the joint venturers. As one joint-venture manager hired from outside the parent firms expressed with considerable feeling, "Joint ventures are for the birds. I spend half my life on the telex to New York trying to get authority for decisions which in most firms wouldn't get past middle-management. Differences in partners' internal and external reporting requirements produce an unbelievable volume of paper work." [34]

In the language of internal-organization theory, this sort of inefficiency arises not only because of the ambiguity of ultimate authority, but also because the joint-venture organization does not gain as much as the conventional firm from the development of internal information channels and codes. In his *Limits of*

Organization, Kenneth Arrow argues that the major advantage of the organization is that such channels and codes, combined with authority, allow highly efficient processing of the costly and imperfect information required for decision making in an uncertain world.[35] But in the joint venture, a system of channels and codes has to be developed that is consistent with efficient communication within the joint venture and between the joint venture and its owners. The problem expands as the original channels and codes within the parent firms become less alike.

One prediction here is that joint ventures between firms from countries with different commercial, legal, and social cultures will face the greatest difficulties in communications. An illustration is the Gove joint venture between Switzerland's Alusuisse and Australia's Gove Alumina Limited. Executives from both parent firms explained in interviews that one of the main reasons why the venture was so heavily contractualized, and why the contract took more than two years to write, was that the cultural differences between the two partners meant that very little could be taken for granted. The norms of business behavior and the legal traditions were not necessarily consistent between the two.

Given that joint ventures suffer from some inherent weaknesses relative to conventional firms, it is clear that they will be formed only when the gains from internalizing certain relationships exceed the costs. The costs usually exceed the gains, but judging by the number of joint ventures formed in the aluminum industry during the last decade or so, apparently the inequality has often swung the other way in aluminum. The evidence also indicates that most of aluminum's joint ventures have been successful, at least to the extent that few of them have been dissolved.

Conclusions

Joint-venture firms have arisen frequently in the aluminum industry since the early 1960s to the point where they will soon account for half of the industry's capacity in bauxite, alumina, and primary. The theory and evidence indicate that joint ventures occur when they can manage relationships between otherwise independent economic agents more efficiently than can alternative institutions such as arm's-length markets and tacit communications. The fact that joint ventures have been formed and have survived shows that they yield net private benefits, but there has been some suggestion that their net impact upon social welfare is negative.

The first reason I advanced to explain joint-venture formation was that in the upstream aluminum industry, participation in joint ventures can make it easier for the individual firm to simultaneously achieve balanced vertical integration, low unit costs through MES plants, and sufficient markets for their final output in the short run. The private advantages that accrue here would also seem to accrue to society, at least potentially. Chapter 2 argued that vertical integration in this industry can improve performance by promoting technical efficiency and reducing transactions costs, so if joint ventures facilitate integration, they are socially desirable. Similarly, if they lead to the building of more efficient-scaled plants, then society can gain.

To the extent that joint ventures are a more efficient means than the alternatives of organizing the intangible assets used in aluminum projects such as technical know-how and nation-specific knowledge, society can again benefit from them. Intangible assets are difficult to transact at arm's length, because of contractual incompleteness and the risks of strategic misrepresentation, but when they are exchanged implicitly within a joint venture, transactions costs and risks may be reduced, and this improves the industry's performance. The evidence indicates that aluminum's joint ventures often do involve the trading of these intangible assets.

Nevertheless, set against these positive impacts of joint ventures upon the industry's performance is the negative one that, quite likely, joint ventures improve the management of oligopolistic rivalry. The number and pattern of partnerships between the firms with moderate or great mutual interdependence clearly indicates the potential for explicit communication among firms in the industry, and it would be irrational of the firms not to take advantage of the potential to more nearly achieve collective rationality. Yet even if this does occur, it is a mistake to presume that performance unambiguously declines as collective rationality is approached.

To the extent that collective rationality leads to a monopoly policy for the industry, with a restricted output and high prices, the familiar negative impact upon allocative efficiency results. But in a dynamic analysis of the aluminum industry's performance, efficiency also depends upon how the rate of output changes as the level of demand changes. The demand for aluminum end-products fluctuates considerably as a result of variables exogenous to the industry, and because several years can elapse between the decision to expand capacity and the actual expansion, the industry has difficulty matching capacity with demand. Maximum performance would result if capacity could be adjusted so that all plants were fully utilized, with price equal to marginal cost.

What tends to occur, however, are waves of under- and over-capacity, and no matter how competitively the firms respond to these waves, society loses. Idle capacity during slumps is wasteful of resources, while excess demand indicates that too few resources have been allocated to the industry. Under these circumstances the private performance of the firms also suffers relative to the ideal, and while performance from society's point of view and the individual firm's point of view do not correspond exactly, a closer matching of capacity to demand would generally be to the advantage of both society and the individual firms.

Joint ventures can be important in assisting the industry in matching capacity to demand. By improving oligopolistic coordination, the aggressive capacity-addition policies typical of boom times in this industry can be moderated. The explicit communication in joint ventures should allow the firms to come to an agreement on the expected optimal capacity in, say, five-years' time and to decide how the implied additions should be spread across the firms. Furthermore, joint ventures make it possible for individual firms to add relatively small chunks of capacity — hence each firm can share in the industry's growth while aggregate capacity grows at a collectively optimal rate. If it is true that joint ventures foster collective rationality in this way, then it is probable that the capacity growth rate decided upon will be the monopoly rate, but the resulting welfare loss could well be less than the loss that would result from the over-expansion associated with unchecked oligopolistic rivalry.

Joint ventures probably also affect the industry's performance via their effects on entry. The evidence indicates that most of the successful new entrants into the industry over the last decade or two have relied heavily upon participation in joint ventures as part of their entry and growth strategies. Many of these firms would either have not entered or have failed if the opportunities for joint ventures had not been available. The significant decline in concentration of firms that has resulted should have improved the industry's allocative performance. The fact that entry and joint-venture growth are highly correlated over time belies the proposition popular in studies of joint ventures that they impede entry.

The many joint ventures between the multinational aluminum firms and host governments or private, local firms seem to be initiated by the host country because joint ventures are the best means by which a government can protect and promote the interests of (ultimately) its constituency. Presumably, the societies of such host nations benefit because many of the industry's joint ventures are foreign-local partnerships. The multinationals are often forced to accept local partners, but there is some evidence that they too benefit from foreign joint ventures because geographical diversification results within the firm. Large foreign joint-venture projects usually involve several multinationals and local interests.

Joint ventures, it is clear, are formed because of a combination of the factors discussed. The social desirability of any particular joint venture therefore depends upon the relative strengths of the motives involved and the welfare effects associated with each of the motives. Public policy authorities in a position to control joint-venture formation should therefore examine proposals on a case-by-case basis, because in most instances there will be both positive and negative impacts upon the industry's performance.

5 Downstream Vertical Integration

Vertical integration in the aluminum industry extends beyond the integration of mining, refining, and smelting. The operations of most firms also embrace the production of fabricated aluminum products, such as sheet, foil, and tubing, meaning that these products, rather than primary metal, constitute the majority of arm's-length sales. Why do aluminum producers opt for this pattern of behavior, and what are the implications for economic welfare?

My analysis of these issues is restricted to the U.S. industry because I examine only those primary producers and independent manufacturers that produce fabricated aluminum products in the United States. This does not represent much of a restriction, though, because all of the majors are active in the United States and bring with them the implications of the highly international nature of the three upstream stages, including, in practical terms, significant amounts of foreign metal (principally from Canada). The flows of metal into the United States are largely intracorporate transfers by the integrated producers; trade in fabrications, however, is very limited. Here I discuss what the primary producers do with the metal they produce in or import to the large U.S. market.

Before investigating this, it is necessary to clearly define the terms used here to describe the downstream industry, because there is some ambiguity in the terminology popularly employed (refer to the downstream flow-chart in Figure 1.2).On the upstream side, the expression *primary metal* (or just *primary*) is used to describe all of the products primary aluminum smelters produce, which include a variety of alloys and shapes (such a sheet ingot, casting ingot, and extrusion billet). *Secondary metal* (or just *secondary*) includes all of the alloys and shapes that secondary aluminum smelters produce; together, primary and secondary are referred to as *metal*. On the downstream side, the entire collection of semifabricated and fabricated products is referred to as *fabrications* or *fabricated products*. Fabrications can be either *castings* or *wrought products*. Castings are produced by foundries and include sand, permanent molds, dies, and other forms. Wrought products include all other fabrications, including sheets, plates, foils, extrusions, welded tubes, rolled and continuous-cast rods and bars, bare wire, aluminum cables steel-reinforced (ACSR), and bare cables, insulated and covered wires and cables, forgings and impacts, and powders. (In the United States, *mill products* is often used as a synonym for wrought products.) There is a general connection between the type of metal and the type of fabricated products: most secondary flows into castings, and most castings are made from secondary, while most primary flows into wrought products, and most wrought products are made from primary; however, the two streams are not economically independent. Finally, all products made from fabrications are referred to as *manufactured products,* including, for example, window frames, cans, and automobile transmission housings.

With the terminology defined, downstream integration in the United States can now be described. Table 5.1 presents the proportions of gross U.S. wrought products shipments made by U.S. primary producers from 1946 through 1979. The data clearly indicate that downstream integration is high, the U.S. primary producers being responsible for 76 percent of wrought products shipments in 1979. However, for two reasons this understates the extent to which integrated primary producers use their own primary for in-house wrought products production in the United States. First, it excludes the wrought products shipments of those integrated producers that do not produce primary within the United States but obtain it from imports or

Table 5.1 U.S. primary producers' share of gross U.S. wrought products shipments, 1946, 1950, 1957, and 1965–1979.

Year	Percentage share
1946	90
1950	85
1957	76
1965	64.9
1966	65.2
1967	68.6
1968	67.7
1969	67.7
1970	70.1
1971	69.3
1972	73.7
1973	76.0
1974	77.6
1975	76.6
1976	76.5
1977	77.0
1978	76.1
1979	75.9

Source: M. J. Peck, *Competition in the Aluminum Industry 1945–1958* (Cambridge, Mass.: Harvard University Press, 1961), p. 98, for 1946, 1950, and 1957; U.S. Department of Commerce, "Aluminum Ingot and Mill Products," *Current Industrial Reports,* issues from 1965 through 1979.

from swaps with domestic producers. The two important cases in point are Alcan, which ships its primary across the border from Canada to feed its U.S. fabrication plants, and VAW, which swaps its German-produced primary for North American producers' primary. Alcan's and VAW's downstream operations in the United States are therefore effectively integrated, and by the late 1970s this meant that the actual degree of downstream integration in the United States was about 85 percent, 10 percent higher than is indicated in Table 5.1. Second, about 10 percent of the metal used in wrought products is secondary aluminum. This means that the wrought products which the primary producers fabricate are really closer to 94 percent $(85/[100 - 10] \times 100/1)$ of the primary used in wrought products.

Another fact obvious from Table 5.1 is that the extent of downstream integration into wrought products has followed two distinct trends since World War II. From the end of the war to about 1960 there was a marked decline in the degree of integration, while since the mid-1960s it has steadily increased again. The inclusion of Alcan and VAW would accentuate the upward trend since 1965, because at that time they had only minor operations in the United States, perhaps 1 or 2 percent of the market, whereas they now have about 10 percent. The implication is that integration has always been high but that it has varied considerably over time. Both of these facts must be explained.

Another interesting feature of U.S. downstream integration is that its degree varies substantially across fabricated products. This is shown in Table 5.2, where the U.S. primary producers' shares of 1978 shipments of the various fabrications are listed. They peak at 87 percent for sheet and plate and range down to

Table 5.2 Gross U.S. shipments of fabricated products and U.S. primary producers' shares, 1978.

Fabricated product[a]	Gross shipments (tons)	Percentage share of U.S. primary producers
Sheet and plate	3,090,400	86.6
Extruded products	1,147,800	45.6
Castings	902,900	5.0[b]
Foil	397,600	84.2
Rolled and continuous-cast rod and bar	246,000	87.5
Insulated and covered wire and cable	185,900	60.5
ACSR[c] and bare cable	177,000	92.7
Forgings and impacts	1,161,900	73.5
Powder	1,161,700	64.4
Welded tube	1,150,100	41.1
Bare wire	1,146,300	62.3

Source: U.S. Department of Commerce "Aluminum Ingot and Mill Products," *Current Industrial Reports,* Summary for 1978; Aluminum Association, *Aluminum Statistical Review, 1978* (Washington, D.C.), for castings.

a. Alcan's and VAW's shipments are again excluded. Their inclusion would increase the sheet and plate share in particular.

b. Estimated.

c. ACSR denotes aluminum cable, steel-reinforced.

an estimated 5 percent for castings. (Notice that there does not appear to be a systematic relationship between degree of integration and size of market.) So here is another empirical fact to be explained.

Nothing yet has been said about further downstream integration from fabrication to final product manufacture, because here integration is much less important, the majority of fabrications being sold at arm's length to a large number of manufacturers that use fabricated aluminum products in a multitude of applications. However, sometimes the nature of the manufacturing stage does influence the integration behavior of fabricators, and these influences are accounted for.

Four partial explanations for downstream integration can be identified. First, primary producers integrate downstream to develop markets for new aluminum applications. Second, integration allows the primary producers to practice price discrimination on primary. Third, integration improves the ability of firms, from their private points of view, to adjust to exogenous short-run shifts in final demand. Fourth, in certain product lines, notably household foil, product differentiation rents are available and are able to be gained by primary producers. Their internalization requires integration downstream to the marketing of a branded consumer product.

Development of New End-Use Markets

The application of Stigler's life-cycle theory to downstream integration that was presented in Chapter 2 yielded the finding that during the aluminum industry's first fifty or so years of large-scale operation, the primary producers integrated downstream as a means of finding new applications for the metal and to demonstrate to potential user industries that such applications were economical.

What role has new end-use market development played in downstream integration since World War II? There is no doubt that, earlier, Alcoa was forced downstream in the United States for these reasons, but were the postwar producers such as Kaiser and Reynolds similarly motivated? Do the same forces explain today's high degree of integration, or have other forces taken over? Also, was it in society's interests for the primary producers to use downstream integration to develop markets? The analysis is divided into two rough time periods: from 1945 to the early 1960s, and from the mid-1960s to the present. This division coincides approximately with a change from a period of high growth and many new end-product applications to a period of moderate growth through relatively mature product lines.

From World War II to the Early 1960s

A useful starting point is a 1956 study by E. Raymond Corey into the development of markets for new manufacturing input materials, based on a case-by-case investigation of examples from the aluminum, fibrous glass, and plastics industries. Corey found that adoption of new materials in applications where ultimately they were recognized as clearly being superior to the traditional materials was typically a slow process. The materials producers were forced to play a very active role:

> to develop the markets for materials, the materials producer has found it necessary to undertake marketing programs of great breadth and complexity at two market levels. He has had to work extensively with his immediate customers, the end-product fabricators, to build an industry which will make and supply the new product to end users. In addition, he has had to undertake long-range promotional programs in the end-product market to create demand for the product among consumers and industrial purchasers.[1]

Potential users of the new materials were typically not interested in either undertaking design and development work or commercialization of a new product, even if it had already been developed. One reason for this was their investment in durable assets specific to the production of the existing products, such as machines and accumulated know-how. This source of reluctance was especially strong for manufacturers with dominant market positions in traditional product lines. Another reason was that the perceived risk associated with a new product was greater than the risk associated with established products, a condition that could be sufficient to prevent risk-averse decision makers from adopting a new product even if its prospects appear promising.

Consequently, new end-use design and development work was undertaken by the materials producers, who had no vested interest in traditional products and who were already exposed to aluminum-industry risks. Often, small manufacturers with relatively weak market positions were the first to try the new products. For example, the widespread use of aluminum in van trailers by the 1950s came only after twenty years of effort by Alcoa: an Alcoa engineer had developed the basic design, Alcoa engineers had been involved heavily in designing individual models, and three small, little-known trailer manufacturers were the first to enter production (subsequently becoming major members of the trailer-building industry). A vital step in the successful penetration of the trailer market was the educational effort Alcoa representatives made to trailer fleet operators, aimed at persuading them to specify aluminum when ordering new trailers.

Alcoa's experience with aluminum windows was similar. Alcoa first tried to persuade three major manufacturers of steel windows to also produce aluminum windows of a type Alcoa had already developed, but this approach met with little success. The emphasis was then directed toward industrial architects in an effort to create a demand for aluminum at the end-user level, and eventually several small steel-window manufacturers began to make and sell aluminum windows. They became a great success. Corey also details Alcan's pioneering development of aluminum cans as a substitute for tin-plated cans, a development very similar to Alcoa's for trailers and windows.

Corey's investigations of these and several other aluminum end-product developments during the decade following World War II indicate consistently that during this high-growth period the aluminum producers were forced to undertake two vital functions if new end-uses were to be found for the metal: technical design and development work, and potential end-user education. Usually, however, the producers did not enter end-product manufacturing, at least on a large or lasting scale, but instead put considerable effort into encouraging independent manufacturers to make aluminum products. That is, the development of most new applications for aluminum did not necessitate integration into end-product manufacturing. This finding is consistent with Merton Peck's estimate that only 15 percent of primary output in the late 1950s was consumed by vertically integrated end-product manufacturers; an estimate for the 1970s is 14 percent, indicating that the degree of integration into manufacturing has not changed significantly. About half of this integration is due to the efforts of primary producers to earn differentiation rents on several established consumer products, a subject examined later on.[2]

But this does not establish whether or not it was necessary for the aluminum majors to integrate into fabrications for the development of new end-use markets. One argument suggesting that it was necessary stems from the fact that new-product manufacturers typically required special fabrications as inputs rather than simple ingot, and the special fabrications were generally not available. In their design and development work in the period following World War II, the majors introduced many new alloys and shapes, and the performance of many end-products was found to depend crucially upon their being made from the correct fabrications. There are several reasons why the majors were motivated to supply these specialized fabrications.

Apart from the majors' integrating forward, there were logically two other procedures that could have evolved to supply manufacturers with the specialized fabrications. First, the majors could have relied upon their end-user educational programs to pull the new fabrications through independent fabricators, just as the new products were pulled through the manufacturers. Second, the manufacturers could have integrated backward into fabrication and purchased ingot from the majors. The circumstances under which these two alternatives can arise have recently been analyzed by Michael Porter and Michael Spence.[3] They consider a situation where downstream manufacturers demand specially tailored inputs, but find that the input industry only provides a standardized or "compromise" input. The standardized input has a wide variety of applications, but in some, the end-product is distinctly inferior to what would be possible if a specialized input were used. Porter and Spence do not consider the possibility that a firm further upstream (in the case of aluminum, a primary producer) would integrate forward to produce specialized inputs, but they do identify factors that influence whether independent suppliers of specialized inputs will arise, or whether the manufacturers will integrate backward to produce specialized inputs, or whether the standardized input will prevail.

One clear and obvious result is that as the difference between the performances of the standardized input and a specialized input increases, the more likely it is that the specialized input will be produced. I have pointed out already that this difference can be very significant for aluminum fabrications. However, as the size of the end-product market declines relative to the level of fixed costs involved in the production of the specialized input, the less likely it is that the specialized input will be produced. Independent specialized-input producers will not arise if the manufacturers' derived demand curve for the input lies entirely below the independent's average cost curve, though the manufacturer may still integrate backward if the "losses" on the production of the input are more than compensated for by the profits on the final product. But, as Corey's research showed, quite definitely, the aluminum producers had great difficulty persuading manufacturers to switch to aluminum, let alone persuading them to produce fabrications as well.

It is quite possible therefore that producers of primary were forced to accept losses on specialized fabrications as the only way to develop new markets. Of course those that were ultimately successful would easily have recouped early losses, but there is evidence that a number of new-product initiatives were failures. In any case, the expected losses and risks on specialized fabrications probably were not as great for the primary producers as they were for the independents, because the primary producers would benefit from the economies of producing many kinds of specialized fabrications. For them, the additional fixed costs associated with the marginal specialized fabrication may have been relatively small because their existing investment in fabricating plant and equipment was heavy.

Another reason why the majors integrated into fabrications as part of their market development programs was to ensure that they, as individual firms, would receive the maximum share of the returns accruing to the originator of a successful new application. The development of new product applications involved an up-front investment in research and development, marketing effort, and possibly some operating losses on fabrication, investments made only if the forecast profits, appropriately discounted, were sufficiently large. Integration into fabrications, particularly into specialized fabrications, ensured that, at least in the short-to-medium-run, the new-product originator would maximize its share of the metal used in the new product. It took time for competitors, both the other majors and the independent fabricators, to develop a close substitute fabrication to offer to the independent manufacturers. During the intervening period, the originator of the new product had the opportunity to gain a high market share, or a price above cost, or both. The encouragement of independent fabricators would, in contrast, have not ensured that the metal was obtained from the originator of the new product.

Corey was convinced from his study that sometimes it was necessary for the aluminum producers to maintain involvement in new applications, even after they were established successfully, to guard against a decline in end-product quality standards. They could not achieve this directly, because typically, manufacturing was undertaken by independents, but they used two indirect methods. One was to establish end-product quality standards: for example, the Alcoa-backed Aluminum Window Manufacturers Association supported a system of standard sizes and specifications through an emblem that stamped "Quality Approved" on Alcoa's products. The other approach was to retain control of fabrication, and therefore the quality of inputs. This also encouraged a continual technical liaison between the aluminum producer and manufacturers, with the benefit that manufacturers were more likely to remain loyal to the original supplier.

These arguments plus Corey's research indicate that forward integration was associated with market development, so it may seem surprising that the extent of forward integration by the primary producers actually declined during the postwar period (recall Table 5.1). The decline was owing largely to Alcan's strategy of selling Canadian metal at arm's length into the

United States, a strategy that proved to be misconceived. In contrast, the other primary producers were very active in fabrications during the period from 1946 to the early 1960s. So, with the exception of Alcan, the behavior of the primary producers was consistent with the market development explanation for forward integration.

To the extent that integration into fabrication was necessary for market development, was it socially desirable? With one or two minor qualifications, the answer is yes. When the majors produced specialized fabrications because independent fabricators were unwilling to, since the market was too small to cover fixed costs, society gained where the resulting new products were successful. New-product failures caused resources to be wasted, but of course situations after the fact cannot be used to evaluate decisions made before they occur. The aluminum producers obviously would not have bothered with new products that would fail if they had forecast failure, and there does not appear to be any reason why their forecasts would have been biased systematically.

Integration into semifabrication motivated by the maximization of individual returns to new-product development was, in Peck's opinion, socially desirable. Peck recognized that some degree of vertical integration into fabrication was required for the level and type of sales engineering carried on by the primary producers, and he reasoned that

> these [sales effort] expenditures have facilitated a better allocation in the relative use of the different metals. Aluminum has become relatively cheaper than other metals since the war. As a result, a large-scale shift towards aluminum, facilitated by these marketing efforts, has occurred. Even without the relative price change, the efficient operation of markets presupposes knowledge by the participants, and this knowledge is effectively distributed by the kind of selling described above.
>
> At the same time, there is little danger of overselling to the businessmen buyers. In many products like aluminum windows or trailers, sales efforts were ineffective until the relative price of aluminum declined to make aluminum clearly the most desirable material.[4]

From the Mid-1960s to the Present

Both the theory, and the evidence from the postwar period, indicate that forward integration into fabrications, and sometimes into final-product manufacture, was associated with the development of new end-use markets. From about 1946 to, say, 1964, U.S. fabricated-product shipments grew by a compounded annual rate of 8.0 percent, and many new products and applications were developed. But since 1964 that growth rate has been 5.8 percent, and the moderate excess here above economy-wide output growth has resulted much more from market penetration from established products than from new-product developments. One major exception to this generalization is the two-piece aluminum beverage can.

In recent years only a small fraction of the primary producers' fabricated output has gone into relatively new end-products. Most fabrications have been available for years, they are virtually the same from one producer to another, and they are classified by a standardized system of alloy numbers, thicknesses, lengths, and so on. If end-use market development was the major reason for downstream integration, as the primary producers often infer, the degree of integration should have been on the decline for some time. This, of course, is the opposite of what Table 5.1 showed—that the primary producers' share of wrought products shipments increased steadily from 65 percent in 1965 to 78 percent in 1979.

The cross-sectional data on integration by fabricated-product type can also be used to test the hypothesis that integration is caused by market development. One would expect to find that integration is highest in those fabrications that are used in new, high-growth applications. Integration data are available only for the broad classes of fabrications listed in Table 5.2, and not for specific fabrications, but it is reasonable to suggest that if market development is still important in integration, then the degree of integration into a fabricated-product type should be correlated positively with the product type's growth rate. Using data on integration percentages and growth rates by product type, two forms of models were used to test this prediction:

$$VI\%_i = f(G_i), \quad \text{and}$$

$$\Delta VI\%_i = f(G_i),$$

where $VI\%_i$ is the primary producers' share of shipments of fabricated product type i (in percentages), $\Delta VI\%_i$ is the change in this share over a number of years, and G_i is the growth rate in shipments of fabricated-product type i over a number of years. Several versions of these equations were estimated, using various time periods and time-lag structures for the period 1965–1979, but all were hopelessly insignificant. This does not mean that there are no cases of specialized fabrications that fit the end-use market development hypothesis, but it does suggest that such cases are few or weak in effect. Another interpretation of the poor estimation results is that the equations are misspecified to the extent that other factors which cause forward integration have been left out, but even when this problem is removed in multivariate tests, the effect of growth is still insignificant.

As noted earlier, however, the development of aluminum beverage cans in the 1960s and 1970s did support the market development hypothesis. Two-piece cans were developed by Alcan in the mid-1950s, but it was not until 1963 that the market "took off," when two large breweries began marketing beer in aluminum cans. It took Reynolds's, and then Kaiser's, initiative to manufacture cans in-house before brewers and soft-drink manufacturers would switch from tin-plated cans. As mentioned earlier, the established manufacturers of tin-plated cans were not willing to switch to aluminum, though they did so as soon as end-users realized the advantages of aluminum cans. Between 1963 and 1979 aluminum shipments to the can market grew by a compounded annual rate of 19 percent, compared with a compounded annual rate of 5 percent for all other end uses. The primary producers now supply the overwhelming majority of the fabricated product (can stock) used for can manufacturing and still produce some of the cans themselves.

It appears, therefore, that forward integration, at least into fabrication, has often been a necessary part of the development of new end-use markets, and such integration is socially desirable. This was the case in the first decade or two after World War II, but since the mid-1960s the development of aluminum cans has been the only important new product that has required forward integration as a means of developing a large market. The conclusion is that forward integration to develop end-use markets is no longer important. There must be other explanations for the continually high, increasing levels of integration into primary–fabricated products.

Price Discrimination

In his study of Alcoa's upstream aluminum monopoly in the United States prior to World War II, Donald Wallace concluded that Alcoa had practiced price discrimination across several industries using primary aluminum, a strategy made possible by its downstream integration.[5] Wallace had trouble "proving" that price discrimination occurred, a task no easier now than it was then, but his conclusion is referred to regularly in subsequent theoretical work on price discrimination and forward integration. The basic theory has been well known for years: in its simplest form, a monopolist of an intermediate product can profit from charging differential prices across the using industries if the using industries have differential elasticities of demand, and if arbitrage by downstream agents is somehow prevented (or at least restricted). Leaving aside the differential elasticities condition for the moment, primary aluminum is a relatively homogeneous and durable producer-good, and hence it lacks significant self-enforcing properties preventing reselling. But integration into fabrication adds value and physically differentiates the product offered for sale, making uneconomic the transformation of a "cheap" fabrication into an "expensive" fabrication. Forward integration can also be advantageous in a country like the United States, where antitrust authorities are relatively vigilant, because it helps disguise discriminatory pricing practices.[6]

If price discrimination is possible, the monopolist's optimal strategy, assuming it sells primary to n distinct using industries, is to integrate into and control all of the using industries except the one with the most inelastic demand. The $n - 1$ transfer prices and the market price for primary are then set so as to equate the (common) marginal cost of primary production with each using industry's marginal revenue, resulting in an ordering of prices in which the open-market price is at the top, and the transfer price for the in-house using industry having the most elastic demand is at the bottom. By controlling the price-sensitive, and therefore optimally low-priced, fabrications, the primary monopolist prevents reselling on the high-priced arm's-length primary market as long as each price spread is less than the cost of converting each low-priced fabrication into the high-priced fabrication.

In the period Wallace studied, the seemingly restrictive assumptions of the simple model were sufficiently realistic: Alcoa had close to a monopoly on primary aluminum, the few different grades and shapes of metal that Alcoa produced could be converted inexpensively, and Alcoa overwhelmingly dominated some of the fabrication industries. Wallace claimed that "conditions enabling the exercise of monopolistic power to discriminate evidently exist in the aluminum industry, and the data upon prices, costs, and earnings indicate that discrimination is practiced in this industry, although they do not afford a basis for precise estimate of its range and degree."[7] The evidence Wallace was able to collect showed that Alcoa sold some fabrications, which were in intense competition with substitutes, at an effective price that was less than that charged for other semifabrications. For example, Alcoa had a monopoly on aluminum cable for the electrical industry but experienced intense competition from the traditional copper cable. The price per pound of aluminum cable sometimes even fell below the arm's-length price of the grade of metal from which it was made, an occurrence that would have required even more than just forward integration to be maintained. Similarly, Alcoa's dominance of aluminum sheet allowed it to shave its margins during periods when steel sheet was highly competitive. The existence of close substitutes of course makes own-price elasticities high. In a reexamination of Alcoa's pricing strategies prior to 1930, Martin Perry also found that the observed pattern of downstream integration was consistent with price discrimination.[8]

Before extending the basic price-discrimination model, it is convenient at this point to mention the welfare implications of price discrimination. The relevant issue is whether or not society prefers a price-discriminating monopolist to one using uniform pricing — in other words, which is the worst of the two evils?

Extensive studies have explored this question, but as Frederick Warren-Boulton concludes in a survey of it, "We cannot, therefore, make any general statement about the desirability of price discrimination. In principle the welfare effects of discrimination could be determined in any particular case, although in complex cases this may not be easy. These difficulties are enormously increased when, as would generally be the case, the public-policy choice is not really between discrimination and no discrimination, but rather between alternative methods of achieving discrimination." [9] Price discrimination can have a number of effects on various welfare parameters, including consumer surplus, output, resource allocation, income distribution, and transactions costs. There is no point in regurgitating the theoretical work here, because I see no manageable way of empirically applying it to the primary aluminum market, but my intuitive judgment inclines me toward Robert Bork's assessment that "if horizontal monopoly [in primary aluminum] is legal, there should be no objection to price discrimination, and hence none to vertical integration employed to effect discrimination." [10] That is to say that if public-policy authorities are concerned about welfare losses arising from market power in primary aluminum, they would best pursue the source of the power (collusion among the primary producers) rather than worry about price discrimination.

Modifications of the Basic Theory

Several changes have occurred in the structure of the aluminum industry since World War II that make theoretical predictions on price discrimination and forward integration more difficult (and that would, incidentally, make welfare assessments even more obtuse). One change concentrated in the 1940s and 1950s was the rapid growth in the number of alloys available and the corresponding increase in the extent to which fabrications became specific according to their applications and composition. Each alloy contains small but precise quantities of other metals, has unique properties of corrosion resistance, conductivity, and workability, is identified by an alpha-numeric code, and is technically suited to only a limited range of applications. [11]

The implication is that price discrimination would have become easier to achieve without the need for forward integration. If primary producers made alloyed metal rather than virgin metal available for sale from smelters, then price discrimination could be practiced without forward integration to the extent that the following factors hold: the costs of converting low-priced alloys into high-priced alloys are greater than the price differentials; the declines in performance from substituting low-priced alloys for high-priced alloys are greater than the price differentials; and there are systematic links between alloy types and final-market segments. Apparently a thorough assessment of these factors would be a very involved exercise, because they vary considerably across alloys and uses. However, discussions with several industry experts have led me to the tentative conclusion that although the alloying system certainly would prevent reselling in some particular cases, it probably would not allow the sort of sophisticated price-discrimination scheme that forward integration would allow.

The second important change that has occurred in the U.S. industry since World War II is the dissolution of Alcoa's virtual monopoly on the supply of primary aluminum through the entry of new producers. As Table 5.3 details, the change has been quite dramatic, beginning with the creation of Reynolds and Kaiser in 1946 and the severance of Alcan from Alcoa in 1950. Alcoa's share of the market (domestic capacity plus imports) fell to 40 percent by 1950, and then declined slowly to be 28 percent in 1979. Even the combined share of the six international majors has slipped, from 100 percent in 1950 to 80 percent in 1979. The number of nonmajor producers grew from zero in 1950 to six in 1979.

The clear theoretical implication of the decline in concentration is that the likelihood that price discrimination will occur has declined. To the extent that the primary producers are competitive, and ignoring short-term excess demand or supply, the price of all aluminum products (metal and fabrications) should approach their marginal costs of production. Under competitive supply, price discrimination is eliminated along with all pricing strategies that involve prices above minimum costs. So, the issue is the extent to which the decline in concentration has increased competitive pricing.

Table 5.3 Capacities and shares of U.S. primary producers and primary imports, and concentration ratios, 1950, 1960, 1970, and 1979.

Firm	1950 Capacity (tons)	1950 Share (%)	1960 Capacity (tons)	1960 Share (%)	1970 Capacity (tons)	1970 Share (%)	1979 Capacity (tons)	1979 Share (%)
Alcoa	335,000	40.4	723,000	31.2	1,202,000	29.6	1,542,000	27.6
Reynolds	216,000	26.1	636,000	27.4	952,000	23.5	1,043,000	18.7
Kaiser	117,000	14.1	553,000	23.9	643,000	15.9	657,000	11.8
Conalco	—[a]	—	—	—	—	—	319,000	5.7
Olin Mathieson	—	—	108,000	4.7	133,000	3.3	—	—
Anaconda	—	—	54,000	2.3	159,000	3.9	272,000	4.9
Alumax	—	—	—	—	119,000	2.9	198,000	3.5
Howmet	—	—	—	—	119,000	2.9	198,000	3.5
Martin Marietta	—	—	49,000	2.1	163,000	4.0	190,000	3.4
Revere	—	—	55,000	2.4	83,000	2.0	184,000	3.3
National Southwire	—	—	—	—	163,000	4.0	163,000	2.9
Noranda	—	—	—	—	—	—	130,000	2.3
Imports	161,000	19.4	140,000	6.0	318,000	7.8	688,000	12.3
Total	829,000	100.0	2,318,000	100.0	4,054,000	100.0	5,584,000	100.0
C6[b]		100.0		88.5		79.7		79.6

Source: Aluminum Association, *Aluminum Statistical Review 1979*, (Washington D.C.: Aluminum Association, 1980).

a. Dash indicates that the firm was nonoperative at this time.

b. The sum of the share of the six majors: Alcoa, Reynolds, Kaiser, Alcan, PUK (Howmet), and Alusuisse (Conalco). Assumes all of the imports come from subsidiaries of the majors — in fact, the vast majority have always come from Alcan and, to a lesser extent, Reynolds.

This issue has arisen throughout this book, and the general
conclusion is that the degree of competition must have increased
but that competition is still imperfect. My earlier analysis has
indicated that the structure of the international industry, including concentration, strategic-group conformation, and joint-venture patterns, suggests high mutual-dependence recognition and
tacit collusion, particularly within the majors' strategic group.
Subsequent analysis indicates that pricing dynamics on the primary and fabrications markets follow the price-leadership
model, further evidence of tacit collusion. The combination of
these results with the fact that the primary producers continue to
be integrated heavily into fabrication indicates that price discrimination through forward integration is still possible.

If mutual recognition of dependence among all of the North
American primary producers is high, or, in modern parlance, if
they are all in one strategic group, then one would expect that
they would cooperate on the exploitation of any price-discrimination opportunities. One would observe a tendency for them all
to follow similar policies for price discrimination via forward
integration, with collectively and individually high degrees of
integration into fabrications having elastic demands, and low
degrees of integration into fabrications having inelastic demands. This prediction can be empirically tested, but first it is
necessary to consider whether other forms of behavior within
the primary producers' oligopoly would produce different forward integration policies.

I have suggested in earlier chapters that the North American
primary producers, when seen in an international context, come
from two strategic groups rather than one. The majors constitute six of North America's eleven producers, the other five
being second-tier producers. It is possible that recognition between firms of their mutual dependence is higher within each of
these groups than between them, and this may have implications
for price discrimination and forward integration. An analytically
convenient, though rather extreme, assumption is that the
majors collude perfectly and behave as a monopoly while the
second-tier firms behave as a competitive fringe. Using a general
model with very similar specifications, Martin Perry derived
some interesting predictions relating to price discrimination

through forward integration.[12] On the assumption that the competitive-fringe firms suffer a cost disadvantage on primary production, or collectively have an upward-sloping supply curve, or both, there is a range of outcomes that involve the monopolist group's integrating into and controlling some downstream industries. The monopolist group first integrates into the industry with the most elastic demand and charges continually increasing prices to industries with successively less elastic demands, until the industry is reached for which the monopolist group's optimal price is above the price that induces supply from the competitive fringe. For all industries with more elastic demands than the "cut-off" industry, the monopolist group practices price discrimination in a manner identical to that of the monopolist in the simple model described earlier. All of the other industries having relatively inelastic demands receive primary at a single price (the market price) from the competitive fringe, and from the monopolist group if the competitive fringe cannot meet all of the demand at that price. The suppliers of the industries with inelastic demands are indifferent to selling primary to independent fabricators or integrating themselves, unless they have motives not accounted for by the model.

The extent of forward integration for purposes of price discrimination depends crucially upon the supply curve of the competitive fringe. It must lie above the majors' marginal cost curves for at least part of the relevant range of quantities, to allow the monopolist group to control the low-priced elastic-demand industries. As the supply curve shifts up, the number of fabrications the monopolist group controls increases (the maximum being $n - 1$), and as it shifts down, the number decreases (the minimum being 0, at which point the entire industry is competitive). Where the "cut-off" industry falls on the 0 to $n - 1$ range depends on several parameters, but it is quite plausible for aluminum that it takes on an intermediate value. The fact that the second-tier primary producers exist and hold 20 percent of the market indicates that they are not totally uncompetitive on cost, but they are probably higher-cost producers than the majors. The smelters they are involved in have an average capacity 16 percent smaller than the majors' North American smelters, their cumulative production volume and hence experience is vastly less, they all rely upon the majors for bauxite and alumina through joint ventures or long-term contracts, and they probably have an average power-cost disadvantage.

If the "cut-off" industry does fall between 0 and $n - 1$, then Perry's model provides several predictions. First, the majors should dominate those fabrications having elastic demands, at the exclusion of both the second-tier primary producers and the independent semifabricators. Second, the majors should not be as heavily integrated into fabrications with inelastic demands, leaving them to independents supplied by the second-tier primary producers. However, it would not be inconsistent with the model to find some integration, by either the majors or the second tier, into the inelastic-demand industries, if there are other advantages to doing so.

Empirical Evidence

The theory indicates that the present structure of the North American smelting industry could produce a range of forward integration patterns consistent with price discrimination's being a motive for integration. But whichever the case, it is necessary that differences exist in the elasticities of downstream demand curves. Empirical testing requires the identification of the downstream demand curves, and this is a major problem, because aluminum is used in more applications than probably any other metal. Strictly speaking, each end-use has its own demand curve.

The available data allow a breakdown of the fabrications market along two lines, and fortunately they are quite useful in testing for price discrimination.[13] One breakdown is by end-use sector, which classifies ingot and fabrications shipments into seven consuming sectors: building and construction, transportation, consumer durables, electrical, machinery and equipment, containers and packaging, and "other." Although these are aggregates of numerous individual markets, it is economically valid to consider that each sector has its own (composite) derived demand curve for aluminum. In any case, there is a strong practical justification for this approach, and it is that long-run elasticity estimates are available at this level of disaggregation from a large-scale econometric model of the aluminum industry developed over a number of years by the Charles River Associates (CRA).[14] The advantages of the CRA elasticity estimates are that the sectoral demand functions were estimated simultaneously with price and other equations, thus helping to avoid biases, and they are long-run estimates, making them appropriate for the analysis of price discrimination. Aluminum shipments are also broken down by fabricated-product type, as described in Table 5.2. Breaking them down by product type and end-use sector simultaneously is also possible, allowing the link between the two to be observed.

These data are best employed to calculate weighted average elasticities of demand for each fabricated product from CRA's estimates of end-use sector elasticities. The seven end-use sector elasticities are presented in Table 5.4. The estimates for transportation, machinery and equipment, and consumer durables come directly from the CRA demand equations, because they have constant elasticities, owing to their being estimated in logarithmic form. The estimates for building and construction, and electrical come from linear equations; they equal the product of their price coefficients and the ratios of their average prices and average quantities. The averages are arithmetic, based upon annual prices and quantities from 1960 to 1973 as used in the CRA model. The final two elasticity estimates, those for containers and packing, and "other," are subjective. The price terms in the CRA demand equations for these sectors were statistically insignificant. In containers and packaging, the effect of price was overwhelmed by a strong upward trend in shipments associated with the introduction of aluminum cans, although other analysis indicated that price effects were important. The importance of price in this sector, where substitutes are strong, is stressed in trade publications and has been confirmed through my personal communication with aluminum marketers. Accordingly, I estimate the elasticity of demand at −2.0. In contrast, the insignificance of the price term in the "other" sector is probably a reliable indication of the insensitivity of demand to price. The industries involved typically use only small amounts of aluminum in specialized applications, mostly for defense purposes. Demand is therefore likely to be inelastic, so I have adopted an estimate of −0.5. Notice in Table 5.4 that both of the subjective elasticity

Table 5.4 Estimated long-run elasticities of demand by end-use sector and by product type, 1960 to 1973 averages.

Product / Market	Elasticity
End-use sector	
Transportation	−2.49
Building and construction	−2.30
Containers and packing	−2.00
Machinery and equipment	−1.16
Consumer durables	−0.587
Other	−0.500
Electrical	−0.383
Product type	
Plate	−2.01
Extrusions	−1.84
Foil	−1.82
Sheet	−1.80
Forgings and impacts	−1.70
Bare wire	−1.34
Castings	−1.33
Rolled and continuous-cast rod and bar	−1.24
Welded tube	−0.791
Powder	−0.500
Aluminum cable steel-reinforced and bare cable	−0.383
Insulated and covered wire and cable	−0.383

Source: Based on data from Charles River Associates, *Cartelization in the World Aluminum-Bauxite Market: Economic Analysis and Policy Implications* (Cambridge, Mass.: Charles River Associates, 1976); and Aluminum Association, *Aluminum Statistical Review* (Washington D.C.: Aluminum Association, 1965–1975 issues).

estimates fall well within the range of elasticities produced by the CRA model, meaning that they do not have a large impact upon the weighted average elasticities of most product types. The only exceptions are foil and powder.

Table 5.4 also presents the elasticities by product type, the weights coming from the aggregate of net shipments from 1960 through 1973 of products by end-use sectors. The major and important implication of both sets of elasticity estimates is that even at this modest level of disaggregation there appear to be quite substantial differences in elasticities of demand. By product type they range from −2.01 for plate to −0.383 for electrical cable and wire. To the extent that the estimates are accurate, there is an opportunity for the primary producers to gain from price discrimination. Notice, that ironically, the electrical market has the most inelastic demand, the reverse of the situation that existed in the 1920s.

The price discrimination theory of forward integration can now be tested against the evidence. What one expects to observe depends upon which of the two extreme models of the structure of the primary-producing industry presented above is the more accurate description. If the Perry model of a monopolist group and a competitive fringe is accurate, one would expect the majors and the second-tier firms to have different forward integration strategies across product types. If, at the other extreme, all of the primary producers belong to a tight oligopoly, then they will all have similar forward integration strategies across product types. Precise selection of the better model is limited by the absence of data measuring the degree of forward integration by individual firms, or by the two groups. However, the data available indicate that the two groups have quite similar forward integration strategies.

Support for this conclusion is given in Table 5.5, where product-type elasticities of demand are compared with the number of majors and the number of second-tier firms integrated into each product type. Although the data are out of date, being for 1969, at least they are comparable temporally with the period over which the elasticities were estimated (1960 through 1973). Also, the data measure only the *number* of firms from each group active in each product type, and not the *extent* of their participation. However, comparison of the number of participating majors with the number of second-tier firms indicates that the two groups have similar participation rates across the product types: the simple correlation 0.857 and the rank-order correlation 0.867 are significantly positive. It therefore seems reasonable to describe the North American primary producers as one strategic group, at least as far as forward integration by product type is concerned.

There is a significant positive correlation between the number of firms participating in a product type and its (absolute) elasticity of demand. Simple correlations of elasticity with the number

Table 5.5 Product-type comparisons of elasticities and numbers of integrated majors and second-tier firms, 1969.

Product type	Absolute elasticity	Numbers of participating firms	
		Majors (out of 6)	Second-tier (out of 6)
Plate	2.01	6	6
Extrusions	1.84	4	5
Foil	1.82	4	4
Sheet	1.80	6	6
Forgings and impacts	1.70	3	2
Bare wire	1.34	4	2
Castings	1.33	1	0
Rolled and continuous-cast rod and bar	1.24	4	3
Welded tube	0.791	3	2
Powder	0.500	3	0
Aluminum cable steel-reinforced and bare cable	0.383	4	2
Insulated and covered wire and cable	0.383	4	2

Source: Elasticities from Table 5.4. Numbers of participating firms from Metals Week, *Aluminum: Profile of an Industry,* (New York: Metals Week, 1969), p. 52.

of majors and second-tier firms are 0.354 and 0.689, respectively; rank-order correlations are 0.460 and 0.718, respectively.[15] This is precisely the pattern predicted by the price discrimination theory of forward integration. However, now that it has been shown that all of the primary producers can be grouped together, a much better test can be performed on this theory. It uses data on the primary producers' shares of gross shipments by product types. Annual averages of the integrated group's shares of each product type's shipments from 1969 through 1976 are compared with (absolute) demand elasticities in Table 5.6.[16]

Again the predicted positive correlation is evident between elasticity and degree of forward integration, but here it is not statistically significant. The simple correlation is 0.122; the rank-order correlation, 0.219. The low value of the correlation

Table 5.6 Product-type comparisons of elasticities and integrated producers' shares of gross shipments, 1969–1976.

Product type	Absolute elasticity	Share of integrated producers (%)
Plate	2.01	90.0[a]
Extrusions	1.84	46.0
Foil	1.82	83.1
Sheet	1.80	82.8[a]
Forgings and impacts	1.70	72.3
Bare wire	1.34	52.1
Castings	1.33	5.0
Rolled and continuous-cast rod and bar	1.24	74.2
Welded tube	0.791	45.5
Powder	0.500	68.9
Aluminum cable steel-reinforced and bare cable	0.383	86.7
Insulated and covered wire and cable	0.383	56.7

Source: Elasticities from Table 5.4. Integration percentages from U.S. Department of Commerce, "Aluminum Ingot and Mill Products," *Current Industrial Reports* 1969–1976 issues. Integration percentage for castings estimated from Metals Week, *Aluminum,* p. 64.

a. The Department of Commerce does not separate sheet and plate. The separation is based on information from Metals Week, *Aluminum: Profile of an Industry* (New York: Metals Week, 1969), p. 62.

is due principally to the inverse relationship for extrusions, castings, and aluminum cable steel-reinforced and bare cable. The simple correlation for the other nine product types is 0.716, and it is significantly different from 0 at the 95 percent level in a two-tail test. Of course removal of the exceptions to the rule is not a valid means of proving the rule, so it could be concluded that support for the price discrimination theory is weak. But such a conclusion would be premature, because the tests are biased to the extent that there are other factors influencing forward integration apart from differential elasticities of demand. In more fully specified regression tests presented later, the price-discrimination theory is upheld as a significant partial explanation for forward integration.

Stochastic Demand, Short-Run Adjustment, and Integration

The most troublesome and recurring short-run problem the aluminum industry confronts is adjustment to the stochastic nature of final aluminum demand. The derived demand curve for fabricated products is price inelastic in the short run, but it is sensitive to changes in production rates in using industries and to a lesser extent to changes in the prices of substitutes. Thus the demand curve shifts in and out as a result of forces largely exogenous to the aluminum industry. On the other hand, the short-run "supply curve" for aluminum metal is also inelastic. If the aluminum market consisted of a large number of competitive buyers and sellers, the clear qualitative prediction would be that market clearing would produce a highly dynamic price. But this is certainly not what is observed. List and even transactions prices are relatively stable, because there are not a lot of competitive suppliers but an oligopolistic group within which mutual interdependence is well recognized. This does not offer an escape from shifting final demand, but it does offer the opportunity to employ other adjustment devices in addition to price. As a result, the aluminum producers rely heavily upon nonprice rationing and adjustments to inventories and order backlogs as means of eliminating excess supply or demand.

This description of short-term adjustment in the U.S. aluminum industry is well supported by previous studies, but there is one important structural component in the short-term adjustment process that has been neglected in the previous work: the role that the vertical integration of smelting and fabrication plays in allowing the primary producers to employ the best combination of price and nonprice adjustment mechanisms in the face of stochastic final demand. The principal reason why a high degree of downstream integration has persisted in this industry as it has matured is that it permits a relatively smooth adjustment to demand shifts without large price variations.

Demand, Supply, and Adjustment in the Short Run

The most succinct way to describe the short-run equilibrating process in the aluminum metal market as background to the rationing-integration hypothesis is to use the results of the Charles River Associates' model. Besides sectoral demand equations, the CRA model contains an equation for total U.S. nondefense aluminum consumption, demand equations for the European Economic Community, Japan, and the rest of the non-Communist world, and equations for costs of production, scrap supply, capacity, and list and transactions prices.

The own-price variable used in the demand section of the U.S. component of the model was the London Metals Exchange price in U.S. cents, the best available proxy for the transactions price. The best estimated aggregate demand equation provided the following elasticity estimates: (1) the own-price long-run elasticity of demand is -0.942, and the short-run elasticity is -0.0146; (2) the only statistically significant substitute price is that of copper, implying a long-run cross-elasticity of 0.202 and a short-run cross-elasticity of 0.00224; and (3) the elasticity of demand with respect to an index of activity in major end-use industries is 1.21, indicating that aluminum consumption rises and falls by about 20 percent more than industrial production. The end-use sector equations produced similar elasticities, with short-run own-price elasticities ranging from -0.100 (for consumer durables) to -0.621 (for transportation) and generally high elasticities of sector activity. The CRA model therefore fully supports the assertion that the demand curve for aluminum metal is inelastic in the short run and shifts in and out with the level of industrial activity.[17]

✔The two basic sources of the supply of metal, primary and secondary aluminum, respond differently to market conditions. The smelting industry for secondary is relatively competitive, with about ninety plants in the United States and C4 (the four largest firms) and C8 (the eight largest firms) concentration ratios of 50 percent and 70 percent, respectively. The short-run supply curve for secondary is therefore probably close to the sum of the secondary producers' marginal cost curves, but they are rather steep in the short run because they depend heavily upon the price of aluminum scrap. The reason for this is that the supply of scrap is inelastic in the short run, simply because the stock of scrap is largely predetermined. About 70 percent of scrap is new scrap, a by-product of fabrication and manufacturing, and its supply depends more upon the output rate in these downstream operations than upon the price of scrap itself. The CRA model estimates that the short-run elasticity of supply of new scrap is only 0.313. The supply of old scrap is similarly inelastic in the short run, estimated at 0.219 by CRA, presumably because the marginal cost of gathering old scrap is steep at about the typical rate of scrap recovery.

So, even though the smelting industry for secondary is competitive, and although secondary is a very good substitute for primary in many applications, the secondary industry does not have a strong disciplining effect upon the pricing behavior of primary producers. This is not just because of the inelasticity of the short-run secondary supply curve, but also because secondary production represents only about 20 percent of the total aluminum supply in the United States. Thus, a 5 percent increase in secondary supply would represent only about a 1 percent increase in total supply. It would be expected, incidentally, that the role of the secondary industry would strengthen as the stock of old metal increased relative to current production, but this effect has so far been very weak: the share of secondary production in the total aluminum supply in the United States rose only from an average of 19.2 percent during the 1950s to 19.7 percent during the 1960s and 20.8 percent in the 1970s.

The inelasticity and predictability of the supply of secondary is therefore accounted for easily by the primary producers in the derivation of their optimal short-run price and supply policies, but the primary producers are still left with the brunt of the adjustment burden when exogenous events shift the demand curve. The fact that the primary-producing industry is an oligopoly suggests that marginal-cost pricing is unlikely to be used as the principal rationing mechanism (and there is plenty of evidence cited later to support this suggestion), but the oligopolists cannot escape the need to adjust the supply or price of primary when demand (net of secondary supply) departs significantly from the existing level of primary smelting capacity. What, then, are the adjustment mechanisms that primary producers use?

Previous studies, particularly those of Peck and the Council on Wage and Price Stability, have produced the definite conclusion that primary producers have a strong aversion to using price as a rationing device. They have always employed a price-leadership system based on list prices, which are based securely upon the long-run average costs of primary production. The CRA model contains an equation explaining the list price, and even though a variety of explanatory variables such as capacity utilization and substitutes prices was tried, the only significant variables (apart from a dummy variable for the Korean War period) were a cost-of-production index and the list price lagged one period. The CRA equation explains 96 percent of the variation in the list price between 1948 and 1973 and indicates that the list price is effectively a function of the last three or four years' costs of production. The primary producers have shown a remarkable ability to maintain transactions prices within the neighborhood of the list price, and indeed, it was this phenomenon that prompted the Council on Wage and Price Stability (CWPS) to thoroughly investigate price formation in the industry.[18]

The reluctance of the primary producers to use price as a major rationing device seems to be due to the following factors. Demand is highly inelastic in the short run; hence, quite substantial variations in price would often be required for market clearing. The inelasticity of the supply of secondary obviously compounds this problem. Widely fluctuating prices are in turn seen as highly disadvantageous to "the industry's interests," that is, the interests of the integrated primary producers. That is so for two reasons: first, unstable prices may encourage long-run substitution out of aluminum, and second, unstable prices make oligopolistic coordination of general pricing policies more difficult.

The long-run substitution argument is popular within the industry and it rests upon the long-run elasticity of demand with respect to the absolute level of aluminum prices and what can be called the long-run elasticity of demand with respect to the level of price variability. The industry's argument is well captured by an extract from the CWPS report.

Representatives of the aluminum producers also maintain that a target [list] pricing system offers several important social advantages compared to the flexible, marginal cost pricing which would occur in a competitive industry. In a written comment to the Director of the Council's staff concerning a draft of this study, the Chief Executive Officer of one firm stated that he did not believe that setting the price so high as to clear the market during periods of "shortage" was a responsible or desirable policy. He also rejected the notion that flexible pricing in a cyclical and capital intensive industry such as aluminum was desirable. He further maintained that buyers would not expand their use of aluminum if they experienced the pricing variability implicit in the academic model of competitive behavior.

The firms maintain that their pricing system allows for long-range planning by their customers as well as themselves. They believe that stable prices for aluminum are an advantage that allows greater use of aluminum in new markets as a substitute for other materials.[19]

There certainly is evidence that the long-run elasticity of demand with respect to absolute prices is relatively high. The CRA estimate of long-run elasticity was close to unity, where "long run" amounted to an inverted-V lag structure over the present and previous four years' prices, peaking at the price two years past. If anything, this estimate is probably low: an earlier version of the CRA model produced an estimate of -3.35, while for the early postwar period Peck provides a time series estimate of -1.15 and a cross-sectional estimate of -1.818.[20] Further, it will be recalled from the previous section that CRA's estimates of long-run elasticity in several end-use sectors were quite high, notably -2.49 for transportation and -2.30 for building and construction, two of the sectors having the largest volumes.

There is, therefore a case for holding prices firm during periods of short-run excess demand to prevent long-run substitution out of aluminum, but this does not imply that prices should be kept firm during periods of excess supply — indeed, long-run substitution should encourage price cuts. The evidence on price flexibility downward versus upward is rather mixed, but the CRA econometric investigations suggest that transactions prices depart from list prices by a greater proportion during periods of excess supply (when prices are discounted) than during periods of excess demand (when they are premiums). This is what one would expect, and it is also consistent with the remarks of the aluminum executive quoted in the CWPS report. However, it is quite likely that there is an asymmetry in the effect of long-run elasticity upon price variations. For one thing, price cuts are discouraged by other factors; for another, it is plausible that long-run elasticity is greater during periods of excess demand than during periods of excess supply. As I argued earlier, the substitution of, for example, copper for aluminum by the using manufacturers often involves investment in new plant, and according to the empirically well-supported accelerator theories of investment, investment in plant is highly correlated with the growth rate in the demand. High growth rates in the demands for final manufacturers will often coincide with excess demand for aluminum, and hence users of aluminum will more often be making plant investment decisions during periods of excess demand in the aluminum industry than during periods of excess supply. Hence, price cuts during periods of excess supply may have a smaller effect on long-run demand growth than proportional price increases during periods of excess demand. In any case, nonprice forms of rationing should be more common in sectors with relatively elastic long-run demands; this is empirically tested below.

The other part of the long-run substitution argument is that price instability per se has a negative impact upon long-run demand growth. The executive quoted above stressed this, and it is easy to see that if manufacturers have risk-averse objective functions and form expectations of the variance of future prices by observation of past prices, then, other things being equal, price instability will be negatively related to demand growth. A thorough analysis of this hypothesis is too lengthy to undertake here, but it seems clear that one of the vital parameters again is the elasticity of demand. The future price of aluminum is, by definition, relatively unimportant for a buyer with an inelastic derived demand, because his optimal plans are not very sensitive to it, and hence it seems that he would also be relatively insensitive to a wide range of prices around the expected price. He realizes that even if the future price diverges from its expected value, the commitment he makes now about future input combinations and capacity, based on the expected price, will be fairly close to optimal. On the other hand, the buyer with an elastic derived demand realizes that the plant that is to end up being optimal in terms of input ratios and capacity depends crucially upon the realized aluminum price. The downside risks associated with a poor price forecast will be weighted heavily because of his risk aversion, and for this reason he may choose an input material with a low variance around its expected price. The implication is that as the variance of aluminum prices increases relative to the variance of prices for substitute materials, price-sensitive buyers will move out of aluminum. Long-run substitution owing to price variability is thus most important in elastic demand sectors. The empirical implication is therefore qualitatively the same as above—namely, that price rationing across end-use sectors should become less important as a sector's long-run elasticity of demand increases (in absolute terms). So once again, the degree of integration should be positively related to the elasticity of demand.

The second reason why fluctuating prices are avoided when possible is that they make oligopolistic coordination of general pricing policies more difficult. In the static model employed in the previous section on price discrimination, it became clear that the collectively optimal pricing policy for the primary-producing oligopoly is rather complicated, involving differential prices across ingot, wrought, and cast products. The implementation of the collectively optimal policy would be difficult enough in a world with stable demand, especially given the recent decline in the concentration of firms in the industry, but clearly, if prices were widely used to achieve short-run equality in supply and demand, then collusion on the long-run pricing policy would be much more difficult. The reader requiring detailed theoretical and empirical verification of the negative impact of randomness in demand upon price collusion should consult a recent paper by Michael Spence.[21]

The importance of holding the line on price on this industry is even greater than in most because of the high proportion (approximately 40 percent) of fixed costs at the smelting stage and the steepness of the marginal-cost curve near capacity. Price cuts during periods of excess capacity are a very tempting means of maintaining volume to cover fixed costs, while price increases during periods of excess demand are similarly tempting, because marginal costs rise fast when plants are pushed beyond capacity, and the short-run opportunity to expand capacity is virtually nil. This means that even if supply conditions were competitive, the short-run elasticity of supply would be low. So if pricing discipline breaks, supply-side factors as well as demand-side factors would lead to dramatic price fluctuations. This did, in fact, occur to a limited extent in 1972, when for the first time in the industry's history significant excess capacity coincided with the arrival of a number of new primary suppliers. Discounting at a rate of 25 percent on list price was widespread for one or two years, and finally the U.S. list price received one of its very rare cuts when Kaiser (the principal price leader during the 1970s) dropped its price by 14 percent (followed six days later by the other North American heavyweights, Alcoa, Alcan, and Reynolds).

There are other factors that encourage a stable price policy and a suitably dynamic inventory and quantity rationing policy. In a paper exploring the costs to an oligopoly of a stable price policy in the face of fluctuating demand, Michael Spence shows that there are three major factors that determine the difference between the present value of profits for the oligopoly when the group adopts an optimal combination of price changes and inventory adjustments, and when it adopts an expected optimal fixed price and leaves inventory to absorb the remaining excess demands or supplies.[22] The difference is the cost of a stable price policy, and the cost declines as (1) the elasticity of demand declines, (2) the elasticity decreases as demand strengthens, and (3) the cost of carrying inventory declines. Earlier analysis speculated that, for aluminum, the elasticity does not decrease as demand strengthens. But, as has already been made clear, demand is inelastic in the short run, and furthermore, inventory carrying costs are not high. The cost of carrying primary metal in inventory has many components; certainly ingots, billets, and other shapes do not suffer significantly from physical deterioration, they do not become technologically inferior, they are easily stacked and stored in a physical sense, and they have a relatively high value per unit of storage space. Furthermore, their financial carrying costs do not appear so high when compared to the cost of shutting down and restarting smelting pots. Taken together, these factors suggest that a stable price policy should be relatively cheap in the aluminum industry, so the application of the Spence model to aluminum supports the expectation and observation that prices tend to be stable.

The theory and evidence on the pricing of primary aluminum therefore both indicate strongly that price is not used as a major short-term rationing device. Obviously, inventory adjustments, quantity rationing, and production-rate changes must assume a large equilibrating role, given the volatility of final demand. Considerable amounts of empirical evidence on high rates of inventory change and quantity rationing are available in previous studies, particularly in those of Peck and the CWPS.

Nonprice Adjustment and Primary–Fabricated Products Integration

It can now be established that the integration of primary smelting and fabrication can be privately advantageous because the market for primary aluminum does not usually clear through price when confronted with final demand variations. The general version of this proposition has been suspected by economists for a long time and has been firmly believed by many businessmen, but only recently have some rigorous theoretical models been developed that describe and support it. The analysis that follows begins by demonstrating the problems that arise in a market like the primary metal market when there is price rigidity and stochastic demand; it then goes on to describe the advantages that vertical integration has over other coordination mechanisms (such as long-term contracts) as a means of overcoming the problems.

For the moment, ignore the existence of long-term contracts and imagine that spot markets and vertical integration are the only mechanisms available for coordinating transactions between primary producers and fabricators. In this world one can employ the results of several recent models of this sort of situation that show that spot markets are problematic and that there can be strong incentives for a firm to integrate. The models are those of Dennis Carlton, the one I concentrate on, and of Jerry Green and I. Bernhardt.[23]

The three models have rather similar specifications and results, so not much understanding is lost by concentrating on

Carlton's model. To adapt his general specifications to the aluminum industry, assume that it consists of three stages (primary smelting, fabrication, and final consumption), three groups of economic agents (primary producers, fabricators, and consumers) and two markets (primary and fabrications). Both markets are competitive, so the expected profits of primary producers and fabricators are zero. The level of consumer demand is stochastic, and consumers' utilities are a negative function of price and a positive function of the probability of obtaining fabrications when they desire them. Prices on both markets are set before each market period on the basis of expected demand, but they cannot be adjusted during the market period. Fabrications can be produced instantaneously, but the quantity of primary available during a market period must be determined before the market opens because of a production lag.

This is far from a full description of the model's specifications, but it is sufficient to make obvious one implication: supply and demand on the two markets will not in general be equal, because consumer demand will equal the preproduced stock of primary only by coincidence. If disequilibrium occurs, someone suffers, because if there is excess supply, primary producers are left with unsold metal, and if there is excess demand, then some consumers go home empty-handed and some fabricators lose potential sales. The existence of inventories would clearly "soften" the degree of rationing, but if inventory carrying costs are positive, the qualitative results remain the same. The problem for the overall industry is that, with long-run competitive forces keeping expected profits at zero, the cost of unsold primary (assumed to be worthless) must be absorbed somewhere in the system. When vertical integration is banned, the primary producers must absorb the cost in the first instance, but to stay in business in the long run they must pass the cost on. The result is that the competitive equilibrium price of primary (p) exceeds its cost of production (c), and the difference ($p - c$) is "the cost of uncertainty." To reiterate, the difference arises because in the long run the revenue that primary producers earn on the metal they manage to sell must compensate not only for the cost of producing that metal but also for the cost of producing unsold metal. Ultimately, the consumers bear the cost of uncertainty.

Not surprisingly, the wedge between the cost of producing primary and its competitive equilibrium price alerts the entrepreneurial fabricator to the possibility of cutting costs and uncertainty of supply by integrating upstream to produce the primary in house (assuming for the moment that long-term contracts are banned). The attraction of upstream integration is that the fabricator assures himself of having the necessary input to make a more profitable sale, if demand should materialize, but offsetting this saving is the potential risk that he will be left with unsold primary, produced in house at cost c, if demand happens to be weak. By producing primary himself, the fabricator bears the risk of unsold primary, but when he relies on the primary market for metal, the primary producers are the ones who bear this risk. The extent to which fabricators integrate back to smelting depends upon the effect of this tradeoff on their expected profits. If it is favorable, they will produce primary up to the point where expected profits begin to decline. The equilibrium degree of vertical integration is an empirical question, but within the confines of Carlton's particular model at least, partial integration occurs over a wide range of parameter values. If partial integration occurs, then the remaining arm's-length primary market becomes thinner and therefore "riskier," and the surviving primary-producing specialists are forced to further increase the price of primary relative to its cost of production. An understanding of this result gives rise to an alternative way of expressing why integration occurs: fabricators base their decisions to integrate on the *marginal,* not average, probability of needing an additional ton of metal. The market price of primary is based on the *average* probability of not being able to sell a ton of primary, but because the integrated fabricator will use in-house metal first, he is concerned only about the probability of being able to sell the marginal ton.

A point of detail on Carlton's model is that it is aimed at explaining upstream integration by independent fabricators, and historically this has often occurred in the aluminum industry, but the model does not allow for downstream integration by the primary producers, and this has also occurred very frequently. Nevertheless, this does not invalidate the use of Carlton's model in the aluminum industry. If integration produces private gains, then the direction of the integration does not really matter. Much of the integration that has occurred in the United States in the last several decades has occurred via the merger of existing firms. Typically, a primary producer acquires an independent fabricator, and this is reported in the financial press as downstream integration by the primary producer, but this seems to be little more than a matter of words. If Carlton's model is applicable, the suggestion is that the acquired independent receives the gain through the terms of the acquisition, a result that would be consistent, coincidentally, with the general empirical finding of studies on mergers that acquired firms tend to receive the lion's share of any gains arising through acquisitions.

Another point of detail is that the firms in Carlton's model are competitive in the sense that they drive each other's expected rate of return down to the normal level. Although this is probably not an accurate description of the behavior of the primary aluminum producers, it does not follow that the implications of Carlton's model cannot be applied to the aluminum industry. Carlton uses a competitive structure because he wants to show that even if firms are competitive, uncertainty can cause equilibrium prices to be above the marginal cost of production, a result contrary to findings of classical analysis. The sources of the problem are sticky prices (in the case Carlton considers, due to transactions costs), but this is just part of the specification of the model. There is no reason why the price inflexibility cannot be specified as being caused by an oligopolistic group's preference for price stability, the case in the aluminum industry. Furthermore, there is no reason why the equilibrium price of primary cannot include an oligopolistic profit margin as well as the "cost of uncertainty." The downstream dynamics of Carlton's model can still be applied to the cost of uncertainty, leaving the oligopolistic profit margin intact. However, for analytical convenience it is probably best to assume that the integrated majors extract their oligopoly rents via the transfer or contract price of alumina, that price then becoming a given cost of primary production. Primary production is then seen as being a fairly competitive industry, and Carlton's results follow directly. In fact, this is becoming a more accurate description of the aluminum industry as time progresses, as I outlined in Chapters 2 and 3.

Consider now the possibility of fabricators' writing long-term contracts with primary producers as an alternative to having either of them integrate. Such contracts would ensure an outlet for the primary producer and a source of supply for the fabricator, and would hence cause Carlton's risk premium on the primary price to disappear. There would be no need for integration to occur, because the fabricator would be receiving primary at marginal production cost only.

Vertical integration and long-term contracts are thus alternative mechanisms for avoiding quantity rationing and price premiums, but as I have argued at length in Chapter 3, long-term contracts can, under certain circumstances, be relatively inefficient in performing this function. To reiterate briefly, complete contracts are impossible to write, execute, and enforce, and therefore incomplete, sequential contracts are the alternative to be compared with vertical integration. As Williamson argues, in a world of uncertainty and small-numbers trading, such contracts are expensive to operate because of the need for frequent revision and are unreliable because their incompleteness means that they only buffer rather than prevent quantity rationing. For the primary aluminum market, the Williamson theory suggests that as uncertainty and small-numbers trading problems increase, contract failure will be more likely, and the use of integration will increase. (I test this theoretical prediction empirically later on, when I discuss uncertainty and numbers of traders as variables to explain the degree of integration.)

To sum up, when stochastic demand, price rigidity, opportunism, and small-numbers trading conditions occur, as they do, to varying degrees, across the primary aluminum market, spot markets and long-term contracts may fail, and a firm may prefer to integrate vertically. When smelting and fabrication are combined within one firm, the authority and control of internal organization are brought to bear to coordinate the two stages of production. Then, when final demand unexpectedly rises or falls, the central office ensures the transmission of this information and orders that adjustments be made to production and shipment schedules, inventory levels, and so on. The outcome is the avoidance of quantity rationing for both primary and fabricating divisions, capacity-utilization rates that are jointly optimal, and in general, a minimization of transactions costs.

What are the welfare implications of downstream integration for short-run adjustments? Would society be better off if downstream integration were banned? Even within the strict confines of Carlton's model, this turns out to be a very difficult question to answer. However, Carlton is able to conclude that vertical integration provides a lower level of utility to consumers than other vertical arrangements; it causes an inefficiency in the ability of firms to absorb risk and in the case of aluminum will usually result in higher primary prices. In the case of partial integration across the primary market, the price of primary is higher than it would be if there were no integration, because the primary market is riskier. Upstream integration by independent fabricators decreases the expected number of customers per primary producer and hence reduces the ability of independent primary producers to absorb risk. They are more likely to be unable to sell all their primary and must therefore increase arm's-length primary prices to stay in business. This result relies on the model's specification that vertically integrated firms not trade freely on the primary market whenever they have an excess or deficit of primary but enter it only when they have major miscalculation. Such action is justified when transactions costs are taken into account, because a firm that has decided to have balance in house will not establish internal procedures for trading on the primary market and hence will incur administrative set-up costs whenever it trades. It is quite plausible that integrated aluminum producers enter the primary market only when they must.

In Carlton's world, there is no doubt that society is better off without integration, but if integration must occur, mergers of primary producers and fabricators are preferable to independent upstream integration by fabricators. Apparently, independent integration thins the number of independent fabricators and leaves constant the number of independent primary producers. Hence, each primary producer's expected number of customers falls, and the earlier results follow. However, if a fabricator merges with a primary producer, the ratio of fabricators to primary producers on the arm's-length market is more stable.

Empirical Tests

The purpose of the preceding analysis is not just to improve our understanding of the integration process, but also to generate propositions that can be used to test empirically how well the theory explains downstream integration. The models of Carlton, Williamson, and others provide many such propositions, but it is worth concentrating only upon those that are testable with the available data.

The first testable proposition is that the degree of integration across the primary market should increase as the number of fabricators decreases. This is an unambiguous comparative statics result of both Carlton's and Bernhardt's models. In terms of Carlton's model, the reason is that as the number of fabricators decreases (holding the number of customers constant), the customer-to-fabricator ratio increases. Each fabricator has a larger number of expected customers. This means that the probability that a fabricator will receive customers increases, which in turn increases his chances of being able to sell fabrications and of being able to use his in-house primary. With the risk of unsold in-house primary declining, the incentive to integrate and avoid the price premium on arm's-length primary increases. Put another way, a decline in the number of fabricators increases each fabricator's *marginal* probability of needing an additional ton of primary. That the degrees of integration should increase as the number of fabricators decreases is also implied by Williamson's model. As the number of fabricators decreases, small-numbers trading problems increase, and hence contract failure is more likely.

In Carlton's model, all fabricators have the same constant returns to scale technology, but in aluminum fabrication several operations offer quite significant increasing returns. In particular, sheet and plate plants have relatively large economies of scale, and hence average costs are sensitive to utilization rates. The operators of these plants therefore have a stronger incentive to achieve high capacity utilization; reliable supplies during periods of excess demand are therefore more important. Integration is, of course, one way of assuring supply, so the degree of integration across fabricated-product types should be positively related to minimum efficient scales of operation. But this relationship may be difficult to disentangle empirically from the first testable proposition, because minimum efficient scales could be negatively correlated with numbers of fabricators.

A third testable proposition is that integration across the primary market probably increases as the number of primary producers increases. More accurately, this hypothesis should state that long-term contracts, vertical integration, or both should increase as the number of primary producers increases, but because the extent of long-term contracting cannot be measured, I test the more general hypothesis. Carlton's model implies that as the number of primary producers increases, the spot market becomes more inefficient, and in his model this immediately suggests integration as the remedy, but of course contracts are always possible, and according to Williamson's paradigm, their efficiency will increase as the number of primary producers increases, because small-numbers trading problems will ease.

This problem is discussed later when I present the empirical results; here I will just outline why, in Carlton's model, the spot market's inefficiency grows with the number of primary producers. This happens because the cost of uncertainty $(p - c)$ increases as the number of primary producers increases and as the incentive to integrate to avoid the price premium strengthens. The cost of uncertainty increases along with the number of primary producers because the probability of a primary producer's being rationed increases as his expected number of customers decreases. To keep his expected profits nonnegative, he must increase the price of primary even though production costs have not changed. Carlton explains that this result arises because there are economies of scale in servicing a stochastic market that are sacrificed as the ratio of fabricators to primary producers decreases. Obviously, this ratio also decreases as the number of fabricators decreases, reinforcing the first testable proposition.

A fourth testable proposition is that the degree of integration across the primary market is affected by the number of final customers, but the direction of the effect is ambiguous. An increase in the number of customers per fabricator increases incentives to integrate for exactly the same reasons discussed for the first testable proposition, but an increase in the number of customers also tends to reduce the cost of uncertainty because, by the law of large numbers, the risks caused by the uncertainty decrease proportionately. The net effect depends upon customers' preferences for price and availability.

The final testable proposition is that the degree of integration across the primary market should increase as final demand becomes more variable. The reason for this is intuitively obvious: the cost of uncertainty in Carlton's model increases with demand variability because the probability and severity of rationing must increase. This causes spot-market failure. It also causes contract failure because, as Williamson would argue, final demand volatility increases uncertainty and increases the frequency of the need for recontracting. Spot-market and contract failure push traders toward vertical integration.

Simultaneous Testing of the Propositions

The preceeding three sections have produced three basic explanations for integration across the primary market: new-product development, price discrimination, and short-run adjustment to stochastic final demand. The purpose of this section is to test simultaneously the implications of these theories against the evidence, in an attempt to determine whether they are empirically valid and, if they are, to determine their importance relative to each other. This is approached in two ways: first, a historical account of integration at the firm level over the last several decades is given, and second, some simple cross-sectional and time-series regression models are specified and estimated.

Integration Behavior of Individual Firms

The firm with the most interesting forward integration history for the purpose at hand is Alcan of Canada. Since World War II Alcan has followed several fundamentally different forward in-

tegration strategies, and the evolution of these strategies
strongly supports the theory that forward integration is required
to avoid the effects of rationing during periods of excess
supply.[24]

Until 1950, Alcan was strategically and operationally part of
Alcoa, and was effectively Alcoa's international division. The
two companies were split formally in 1928, seemingly for reasons
of internal organization, but enjoyed a happy union until 1950.
At the time of the 1928 split they had identical shareholders, and
between 1928 and 1950 eleven shareholders held a major part of
the stock in each of the two companies. As far as primary and
fabrications were concerned, Alcoa stayed inside the United
States and Alcan stayed outside, but Alcan relied significantly
upon Alcoa as an outlet for primary, and Alcoa upon Alcan as a
source of its supply. For example, from 1947 through 1949
about 80 percent of Alcan's considerable exports of primary
from Canada to the United States went to Alcoa. In the period
from 1928 to 1950, Alcan's strategy in the U.S. market was
simply to sell primary to Alcoa's fabricating division, and given
the special relationship between the two firms, it was a quite
reliable arrangement. At the same time, Alcoa could develop
downstream operations in the United States without the need for
an in-house balance of smelting and fabricating capacities. The
effect of these arrangements was that the Alcoa-Alcan *group*
pursued a strategy of balanced integration in the U.S. market for
primary and fabricated products, even though separately their
integration was unbalanced. By the late 1940s the group produced and fabricated over 50 percent of the primary consumed
by the U.S. market, a market that at the time represented about
80 percent of the total non-Communist world's market.

The Alcoa-Alcan union suffered a severe setback in 1950,
however, when Judge John C. Knox of the U.S. District Court
(New York) concluded on the basis of the Sherman Act that
Alcoa's relationship to Alcan jeopardized the public interest, and
he ruled that joint shareholders of the firms dispose of their stock
in one or the other of the firms within ten years. At first this did
not affect adversely Alcan's position as a supplier of primary to
the U.S. market, because while Alcoa quickly reduced its dependence upon Alcan by expanding its capacity to produce primary

internally and by cutting its sales of primary to independent fabricators, Alcan found keen buyers for its primary in Kaiser, Reynolds, and independent fabricators. These buyers were eager because from 1950 to 1956 there was a continual excess demand for aluminum — U.S. capacity utilization averaged over 100 percent during this period. Alcan saw no reason to integrate forward, because as president Nathanael V. Davis explained in a congressional hearing into the plight of the independent fabricators in 1955, "In the United States we have energetically solicited the business of the rapidly growing independent (non-integrated) fabricators. We have done so in the belief that the independent fabricators would look upon us as a natural supplier, not competing with them in the United States fabricating business — and that we on our part could look to them as steady buyers in both good and bad times — in comparison with those who produce their own ingot requirements.[25] This strategy of Alcan's was the main reason for the rapid growth in the independent fabricators' share of the fabrications market, shown in Table 5.1. Between 1950 and 1957, the independents' share increased from 15 to 24 percent, and it would have grown even faster if their supply of primary had not been curtailed by quantity rationing.[26]

Unfortunately for Alcan, excess demand quickly turned into excess supply in 1957 and 1958, partly because of the entry of Anaconda, Harvey, Revere, and Olin into U.S. smelting, but largely because of a sudden macroeconomic downturn in demand. In 1958 primary capacity utilization in the U.S. slumped to 78 percent, and it stayed below 90 percent until 1963. A similar situation also prevailed in the rest of the world. Alcan soon found that its independent-fabricator customers were not the hoped-for "steady buyers in both good and bad times." The unintegrated Alcan was left with vastly more than its random share of the unsold primary of Carlton's model as the integrated firms first supplied their in-house fabricating plants and then opened their doors to Alcan's unfaithful independents. Alcan's sales and profits were affected so severely — its sales of primary to independent fabricators in 1957 were down 33 percent from its 1955 sales — that it was forced to lead the first postwar cut in U.S. list prices. As president Davis later explained, "with insufficient captive outlets for its ingot, Alcan was in a particularly vulnerable position. The resulting challenge upon Alcan, as shareholders are aware, was to bolster the firm demand load on its Canadian smelters through the expansion of fabricating activities in markets where business could be created." [27] The shift to a strategy of forward integration was signaled in the company's 1958 annual report: "The Company is placing greater emphasis on the establishment and enlargement of fabricating plants whose function it is to broaden the sales and application of aluminum products and to provide larger outlets for the Company's primary aluminum." [28]

Since then, Alcan has pursued this strategy with vigor: in the period 1951–1958 only 5 percent (by value) of additions to fixed assets went into fabricating, while during 1959–1968, this increased to 51 percent. From 1961 much of this investment went into establishing a fabricating division in the United States, Alcan Aluminum Corporation, and by 1970 it was the fourth largest aluminum fabricator in that country. The growth of this division was achieved largely via the acquisition and subsequent expansion of independent fabricators, a force behind the increase in the primary producers' share of fabrications shipments that began in the early 1960s. Alcan's management has claimed on a number of occasions that its forward integration strategy has improved capacity utilization and profits significantly, relative to the bleak 1958–1963 period, and, to the extent that the published accounts are accurate, this certainly seems to have been the case. At which stage of production the increased profits are recognized is largely an accounting matter, but a comment made in 1971 by Davis is worth repeating. "Alcan has raised its fabricating tonnage from 36% to 51% of overall sales tonnage, and its gross integrated profit on fabricating from 42% to over 60% of gross profit from aluminum operations. This increase has been achieved at some considerable cost in terms of capital expenditures and start-up expenses. *While this program has contributed to profits by providing increased outlets for metal, there has been little return on the investments made when measured solely at the fabricating level*" [emphasis mine]. [29] The interesting point is that profits increased through forward integration, but they did not appear at the fabricating level, in an accounting sense. The explanation is that integration allowed a fuller utilization of primary capacity, and hence lower unit costs of production and decreased costs of carrying inventory. This is just the sort of result predicted by Carlton's theory.

Alcan's change in downstream strategy and its search for independent fabricators suitable for acquisition were induced by the 1958–1963 period of excess supply of primary. However, the rate at which it could implement the new strategy was limited by the availability of established and viable independents, and this was due indirectly to periods of excess demand that pre-ceeded and followed the period of excess supply. In the early 1950s, Alcan's arm's-length primary had allowed independents to grow in size and number, but because nonprice mechanisms were used to ration out the then tight supply, the independents were unable to purchase as much primary as they could have used. Independents in the mid- and late 1960s were similarly afflicted when once again the cycle swung to excess demand. The long-run solution for the independents was the mirror-image of Alcan's solution: to secure in-house supplies of primary.

The substantial barriers to entry into the upstream industry would normally have prevented the independents from imple-menting this solution, but at the same time, a number of large and powerful potential entrants were deciding that the U.S. aluminum industry was a prime candidate for diversification. The potential entrants were chiefly copper producers, con-cerned that in the long run aluminum would substitute for copper, and the two European aluminum majors, concerned about the American invasion of their home markets. These firms brought with them not only access to capital and suitable techni-cal skills, but also the belief from experience that the integration of primary with fabricated products was essential. The outcome was a series of acquisitions of independent fabricators by the new entrants, followed by the establishment of new primary smelters. The new entrants were not the only ones to acquire independent fabricators, because Alcoa, Reynolds, and Kaiser also made ac-quisitions when the antitrust authorities allowed them to. The wave of acquisitions made the realization of Alcan's new down-stream strategy difficult: "because it was late to move in the U.S. . . . the independents had already been rather thoroughly picked over." [30]

The backgrounds, dates of entry into smelting, early down-stream structures, and initial downstream integration strategies of the twelve postwar entrants into the U.S. aluminum industry are summarized as follows:

Reynolds, 1946	Entered aluminum foil production in 1926, and was a major producer by 1940. Received government allocation of wartime fabrication plants as well as smelters.
Kaiser, 1946	Previously a metal manufacturer. Also received government allocation of wartime fabrication plants as well as smelters.
Anaconda, 1955	Long-time copper producer and fabricator of copper, brass, and aluminum. Initially consumed one-third of its primary in house but quickly expanded fabricating capacity through its 1958 acquisition of Cochran Foil and the construction of new plants. Was balanced downstream by 1960.
Harvey, 1958	Prewar producer of metal aluminum parts. Acquired Defence Plant Corporation extrusion plant after the war. Had government purchase contracts for primary for the first five years, so its need for integration was not as urgent.
Olin Mathieson Chemical Corporation, 1958	Managed a governmental smelter during World War II. As a diversified manufacturer was a major consumer of aluminum products. Constructed rolling mill adjacent to smelter and was immediately approximately balanced downstream.
Revere Copper and Brass, 1958	Long-time fabricator of copper, brass, and aluminum. Quick expansion of in-house aluminum fabricating capacity.
Alusuisse, 1963	Entered fabrication in the United States in 1950 through wholly owned Aluminum Foils, Inc. During the 1950s, established other fabrication operations.
Phelps Dodge, 1965	Long-time copper producer. Entered aluminum fabrication in 1963 through acquisitions and new plants. Did not own a smelter, but had aluminum bought under long-term contract from Billiton tolled by Alusuisse.

	Secured both arrangements with substantial loans to Billiton and Alusuisse, so by 1965 was effectively a primary producer. Was immediately approximately balanced downstream. Merged all downstream operations with Alusuisse in 1971 to form Conalco, Inc.
PUK, 1966	Entered fabrication in the United States in 1962 through 55% acquisition of Howe Sound Company, a leading independent fabricator.
Alumax, 1966	Started as division of Amax, a long-time copper producer. Entered aluminum fabrication in 1962 through acquisition of two sizable independents, Kawneer Company and Apex Smelting Company (whose acquisition had been attempted by Kaiser and Alcan, respectively, but prevented by the Justice Department). Acquired Hunter Engineering Company in 1963, a major independent producer of wrought products, and Johnston Foil Company in 1965.
National Steel and Southwire, 1970	National Steel entered aluminum fabrication in 1968 through 20% acquisition of Southwire, the largest independent producer of aluminum and copper rod and electrical conductor and cable. Acquired Republic Foil, Inc., and Hastings Aluminum Products, Inc., in 1968. Formed a 50-50 joint venture with Southwire for a smelter.
Noranda Mines, 1971	Entered aluminum fabrication in the United States in 1967 through acquisition of the Pacific Coast Company, a manufacturer of aluminum building products. Was previously a major independent fabricator in Canada.

There is a remarkable consistency in the histories of most of the entrants. Many were already (among other things) independent aluminum fabricators reliant upon arm's-length primary, and most made the *decision* to enter smelting during a period of excess demand and supply-side rationing. Four firms entered smelting in the mid- to late 1950s, four in the mid-1960s, and two in the early 1970s. The entry decision frequently was made at a time when independent fabricators were being rationed, accounting for the approximately two-year lag between the decision to enter and actual entry. In most cases, existing fabricating capacity was significantly below that required to consume all the primary the planned smelter would produce, so completion of the smelter was preceded by a rapid expansion of fabricating capacity, and acquisition of substantial numbers of independents, most of which had grown using Alcan's early 1950s primary, was common. The effect was to reverse the postwar trend of decreasing integration of fabricated-products firms and primary.

That primary rationing during periods of excess demand caused unintegrated fabricators to seek in-house primary is further demonstrated by comments made by individual fabricators. For example, the president of one of the first upstream integrators, Revere Copper and Brass, told a congressional hearing in 1958 that, "beginning in the early 1950's and continuing through 1955, when aluminum was in extremely short supply, Revere was required to enter a series of large, firm, long-term contracts with the aluminum producers in order to assure to Revere and its customers the essential supplies. These contracts have not involved any price concession to Revere . . . It become clear, however, that Revere would ultimately have to secure its own source of primary aluminum." [31] Similarly, the president of the most recent upstream integrator, Noranda, explained to shareholders in 1966 that, "for many years our manufacturing subsidiaries have been substantial purchasers and, in total, the largest independent users of aluminum in Canada. Having no primary aluminum production, however, we have long felt our fabricating activities to be highly vulnerable to competition from integrated producers . . . Therefore, as protection for our fabricating activities . . . your Directors, after many years' consideration, decided that Noranda should enter the primary aluminum business." [32]

The experiences of Alcan and the independent fabricators convincingly indicate that nonprice rationing on the primary market during periods of supply and demand disequilibrium has been a dominant force behind the trend toward increased integration of primary smelting and fabrication. Unintegrated firms suffered in quantity terms, and via a combination of mergers, acquisitions, and internal expansions, most firms have worked toward achieving in-house balance. The effect has been a further shrinking, proportionally, of the arm's-length primary market, a decline in the relative number of independent fabricators, and an increase in the number of primary producers. The predictions of Carlton's model have been upheld.

No evidence has yet arisen regarding the other two theoretical hypotheses concerning downstream integration — new-product development and price discrimination. The published statements and observed behavior of most of the firms discussed provide little support for the idea that new-product development is an important consideration in a firm's decision to integrate downstream. The exception is Alcan, which has often stated that new markets, as well as security of outlets, lie behind its downstream thrust. New-product development by most of the new entrants seems to have been minor. On price discrimination, the evidence is neutral. It is difficult to discern any systematic patterns between the integration strategies of individual firms and final demand elasticities, but this could well be caused by the inadequacy of the data. The price discrimination question is best tested in regression models.

Simple Regression Tests

Enough data are available to allow two tests of my forward integration theories to be made. The first test is cross-sectional and examines whether or not the theories can explain the differences in the degree of integration across the various fabricated products. The second test is time series, which examines whether or not the theories can explain changes over time in the degree of integration. The precision of both types of tests is limited by the small number of observations available, but the results are worthy of reporting. The variables are defined precisely in Appendix E along with a listing of the data and their sources.

Cross-Sectional Test. The cross-sectional model is

$$VI\%_i = f(G_i, ELAS_i, NF_i, MES_i, NM_i, VAR_i).$$

The dependent variable $VI\%_i$ is the average annual percentage of gross shipments of fabricated-product type i made by the U.S.

primary producers over the eight years 1969–1976, as listed in Table 5.6. The eight-year average evens out short-term cyclical influences and is timed to coincide with the estimates of elasticity of demand. These are averaged for the period 1960–1973, but the $VI\%$ data are not available prior to 1969. In any case, the implicit lag could be rationalized by a partial adjustment model, as explained below. The independent variables and my reasons for using them are as follows.

G_i is a measure of the growth rate in demand for fabricated-product type i. My earlier analysis suggested that the producers of primary integrate forward into those fabrications used in new-product applications as a means of fostering the products' development. If this effect were strong, one would expect a significant positive relationship between G and $VI\%$, but the earlier analysis, and the aggregate nature of the product types, indicate that this is not very likely. Several different measures of G were tried in the model, but they all gave similar results; the measure reported below is the average annual rate of growth of shipments over the years 1960–1973.

$ELAS_i$ is the absolute value of the long-run elasticity of demand for fabricated-product type i, as listed in Table 5.4. According to the price-discrimination theory of downstream integration, it should have a positive relationship with $VI\%$. A positive relationship between $ELAS$ and $VI\%$ is also expected from the long-run substitution argument, because nonprice forms of rationing are more likely as demand elasticity increases, and integration improves the management of nonprice rationing.

NF_i is the number of independent fabricators of fabricated product type i that would exist if there were no forward integration by the primary producers. Obviously this is an unobservable variable, so it is proxied by the number of plants (in hundreds) producing product type i in 1969. There is considerable variance in this proxy variable; the range is from 12 plate plants to 2,800 castings plants. From Carlton's and Williamson's models one expects NF to be related negatively to $VI\%$.

MES_i is the minimum efficient scale of operation in plants producing fabricated-product type i. It is estimated by the ratio of annual shipments in 1969 of product type i to the number of plants producing product type i in 1969, measured in units of 10^5

tons. *MES* should be related positively to *VI%*, because fabricators with high minimum efficient scales rely more heavily upon a stable supply of primary.

NM_i is the number of manufacturers (or customers) purchasing fabricated-product type i. Actual data on the number of manufacturers are not available, so a dummy variable is used, where $NM = 1$, when there is known to be a relatively small number of major manufacturers (otherwise $NM = 0$). $NM = 1$ for powder, aluminum cable steel-reinforced and bare cable, and castings. Most powder is sold on governmental contracts for defense purposes, most ACSR and bare cable is sold to power authorities and utilities, and most castings go into the automobile industry. Buyer concentration in these lines is considerably higher than in the others, where there are multitudes of buyers. Following Carlton's model, there is no expectation as to the direction of the relationship between *NM* and *VI%*.

VAR_i is the degree of variability in the demand for fabricated-product type i. A number of measures for *VAR* were tested, but the best on both theoretical and statistical grounds were based on the absolute values of the annual percentage changes in shipments. Measures of this type emphasize annual changes in the output rate from one year to the next and capture the businessman's sense of instability. The best specific measure was the sum of the squares of annual percentage changes in shipments from 1960–1973, the squaring having the effects of making all observations positive and of weighting instability in a nonlinear fashion. The nonlinear weighting has the effect of capturing the presumed risk-aversion of businessmen. The sum of the squares was divided by one thousand for estimation purposes. From the earlier theory, one would expect *VAR* to be related positively to *VI%*.

Although the model is cross-sectional, it implicitly contains a time element. The dependent variable is an average over the 1969–1976 period, while the independent variables are for 1969 or are averages over the period 1960–1973. This implies average lags of four to six years. The actual length of these lags is set by the available data, but the existence of lags of this order of magnitude is quite plausible. Vertical integration decisions are usually long-term strategic decisions, and firms take a number of years to adjust their vertical structures to changes in causal variables. In any case, the results were very similar when the minor variations in the lag-structure allowed by the data were tried. Furthermore, most of the variables were fairly stable over the full period of 1960–1976.

The model as specified has seven explanatory variables (including a constant term), and obviously, with only twelve observations, reliable estimation was problematic. The existence of some collinearity among several of the explanatory variables made the task even more difficult, but fortunately, after estimating various versions of the model by using different combinations of explanatory variables and different functional forms, it was found that the results were remarkably consistent. Seven different estimated versions of the model are summarized in Table 5.7, differing only in their combinations of explanatory variables. They are all in semilogarithmic form, with the natural logarithm of *VI%* as the dependent variable, the specification that produced the best results in terms of overall fit and the pattern of the residuals. In general, the equations are statistically strong, they are consistent with the theoretical expectations, and they are robust to the seven different specifications. Given the considerable variance in the variables (see Appendix E), the results are encouraging, even though the number of observations is small.

Apart from the constant, five of the six variables have coefficients that are always correctly signed and are usually statistically significant: *NF, NM, ELAS, MES,* and *VAR.* As the matrix of simple correlations in Table 5.8 indicates, several of these variables are somewhat collinear, but the only pair that was unstable under alternative specifications of the model was *ELAS* and *MES.* In the fourth through the seventh equations, this problem was removed by including a simple product variable, denoted as *ELAS · MES.* With this modification, the best and most reliable model is the sixth regression listed.

NF is the variable that provides most of the power in the model: its sign and size are almost invariant across equations, and it is highly significant throughout. According to Carlton's model, this indicates that the benefits of integrating smelting and fabrication are highly sensitive to the negative effect that the number

Table 5.7 Regression-equations for the integrated producers' share of gross shipments across fabricated-product types (dependent variable in all cases is the logarithm of $VI\%$).

Constant	NF	NM	ELAS	MES	ELAS · MES	G	VAR	$\overline{R}^2$
3.85[a] (20.4)	-0.109[a] (-11.4)	0.415[b] (2.13)	0.273[b] (2.17)	—	—	—	—	.939
4.11[a] (52.2)	-0.0966[a] (-11.9)	0.192 (1.36)	—	1.35[b] (2.57)	—	—	—	.947
3.94[a] (21.3)	-0.102[a] (-10.4)	0.324[c] (1.70)	0.147 (1.03)	0.964[c] (1.50)	—	—	—	.947
4.12[a] (54.4)	-0.0987[a] (-12.3)	0.241[c] (1.66)	—	—	0.689[b] (2.58)	—	—	.947
4.24[a] (25.1)	-0.103[a] (-10.4)	0.288[c] (1.81)	—	—	0.624[b] (2.19)	-0.0119 (-0.802)	—	.944
4.01[a] (39.7)	-0.0972[a] (-12.9)	0.298[b] (2.13)	—	—	0.852[a] (3.14)	—	0.127[c] (1.50)	.954
4.14[a] (24.5)	-0.102[a] (-(11.1))	0.349[b] (2.30)	—	—	0.786[b] (2.79)	-0.0127 (-0.933)	0.130[c] (1.52)	.953

Note: $\overline{R}^2$ values adjusted for degrees of freedom; t-statistics in parentheses. See Appendix E for full definitions of variables.
a. 99% significant in a one-tail test.
b. 95% significant in a one-tail test.
c. 90% significant in a one-tail test.

Table 5.8 Simple correlations among independent variables used in regression equations (in Table 5.7).

	NF	NM	ELAS	MES	ELAS · MES	G	VAR
NF	1.0						
NM	.51	1.0					
ELAS	.05	−.52	1.0				
MES	−.24	.23	.50	1.0			
ELAS · MES	−.20	−.32	—	—	1.0		
G	−.40	.13	−.59	−.14	−.24	1.0	
VAR	−.42	.34	.40	.21	.34	.21	1.0

Note: See Appendix E for detailed definitions of variables.

of fabricators has on each fabricator's expected number of customers. The result is also strong support for Williamson's argument that as the number of traders across a market declines, difficulties with contracts increase and vertical integration becomes more attractive.

Another possible explanation of this result is that as the number of fabricators of some product becomes relatively small, primary producers may have an incentive to integrate forward into that product as a means of preventing the adverse effects of monopolistic behavior at the fabrication stage. If the few fabricators treat the price of primary as fixed but collude and behave monopolistically in their own output market, a successive-monopoly distortion arises. Relative to single-stage monopoly or a joint-profit maximizing bilateral monopoly, successive monopoly causes reductions in the industry's profits and in the profits of the single-stage monopolist. Integration to remove a successive-monopoly distortion would not only improve things for the primary producers but would also increase the output rate and decrease the price of the fabricated product in question, and hence would improve the situation from society's point of view.

It will be recalled that the theory was neutral as to the direction of the relationship between $VI\%$ and NM, but the evidence consistently indicates that it is positive. NM is imperfectly represented by a dummy variable, but it appears that integration increases as final buyer concentration increases. If Carlton's model is applicable, the explanation could be that concentration on the buying side of the market increases the cost of uncertainty. But a better explanation is that when the buyers have market power, as, for example, the power authorities and electric utilities have in the aluminum cable steel-reinforced market, the aluminum producers have an incentive to control production and exclude competitive independents. By so doing, they create a bilateral oligopoly market structure rather than allow independent fabricators to give the market an oligopsony structure. Oligopsony structures are to be avoided because they allow the buyers to dominate price bargaining.

The collinearity between *ELAS* and *MES* means that one cannot be very confident about the size of their separate effects, but the evidence is convincing that they are significant and that they both have the expected positive relationship with *VI%*. *VAR* is stable in size and sign across the regressions and is significant at the 90 percent level. It also has the expected positive effect upon integration.

The only variable to perform poorly is *G*. It consistently has the incorrect sign and is statistically insignificant, but this outcome is not surprising, because earlier analysis and evidence also rejected the significance, at least for the period since the mid-1960s, of the underlying end-use market development hypothesis. This conclusion should not be interpreted as a rationalization ex post facto, because in the course of research, the earlier analysis and evidence was in fact completed before any regressions were run.

One final point about the cross-sectional model should be made. Reference to the data in Appendix E shows that one of the product types, castings, is distinguished from the other product types by having a much lower *VI%* and a much higher *NF*; it makes a large contribution to the overall variation in the data. The castings industry is also distinguished from the others by being more closely connected to the secondary industry than the primary, partly for technical reasons. It might therefore be argued that the castings industry is not comparable with the wrought products industries discussed in this chapter. The issue is whether integration between smelting and castings firms is low because of the factors analyzed in this chapter or because it is "another industry." This is difficult to answer on theoretical grounds, but it is possible, by reestimating the regression equations with castings excluded, to test empirically whether or not the inclusion of castings biases the results presented above. This was done, and the results were essentially the same. The main effect was to lower the significance of NF and, in the process, cause the values of R^2 to fall somewhat. All of the previously significant variables retained their signs and their orders of magnitude. The conclusion is that including or excluding castings does not significantly affect the economic implications of the results, though it does have some effect on their statistical quality.

In summary, the estimated versions of the cross-sectional model support price discrimination and short-run adjustment as explanations for downstream integration. They do this by establishing that several of the observable implications of these theories are upheld by the data. On the other hand, the cross-sectional model does not support the market-development explanation for downstream integration.

Time-Series Test. Fifteen years (1965–1979) of data are available on the U.S. primary producers' share of total wrought products shipments, but unfortunately, only one of the variables that the theory suggests could explain the changes over time was measurable, namely, the number of primary producers. Time-series equivalents of the relevant variables used in the cross-sectional model could not be estimated or proxied reasonably on an annual basis over the relatively brief fifteen-year period, hence the model is a very restricted one, and probably biased through misspecification, but at least the effect of the number of primary producers on integration can be tested, an effect that could not be tested in the cross-sectional model.

The general version of the time-series model is

$$VI\%_t = f(NPP_{t-i}, CU_t),$$

where $VI\%_t$ is the percentage of gross wrought products shipments in year t made by the U.S. primary producers, NPP_{t-i} is the number of U.S. primary producers in year $t - i$, and CU_t is the percentage of capacity utilization of U.S. smelters in year t. It was predicted earlier on the basis of Carlton's model that $VI\%$ and NPP should be related positively, because as the number of primary producers increases, the reliability of a primary spot-market declines; however no significant effect could be found because, according to Williamson's theory, contracts become more efficient as the number of traders increases, so contracting, not integration, could be what increases with *NPP*.

The capacity-utilization variable is included in the equation to account for any cyclical influences, and of course it should have a positive sign. This is so because, if supply-side rationing occurs during periods of excess demand (when capacity utilization is high), the integrated producers will tend *not* to be rationed, and the independent fabricators will tend to be rationed. The integrated producers should therefore increase their share of the fabrications market. Conversely, when there is excess supply, the independents are more likely to cut prices, and not being supply-constrained, they should increase their share of the market.

In Carlton's and Williamson's models it is only the number of producers that is relevant, because the models assume the producers are of equal size. Nevertheless, one can imagine that their relative sizes would also be relevant. To allow for this possibility, two variables measuring concentration were also tested as alternatives to *NPP*, the annual three-firm concentration ration ($C3_{t-i}$) and the annual Herfindahl (H_{t-i}). They were both calculated on the basis of producer capacities, using conventional definitions. Because $C3$ and H are by definition both negative functions of *NPP*, they should be related negatively to *VI%*.

Six estimated versions of the model are presented in Table 5.9, with *NPP*, *C3*, and *H* each included both singly and with *CU*. The equations are linear and fitted the data best when the concentration variables were lagged by two years. The results are statistically sound, with high values of $\bar{R}^2$ and insignificant or inconclusive serial correlation in the estimated-error terms. The concentration variables are highly significant, positively signed, and give similar results. However, the capacity-utilization variable does not have the expected sign, and it has modest significance. Several other activity variables were also tried, but they too were insignificant.

While the results on the concentration variables do support Carlton's short-run adjustment theory of downstream integration and are not inconsistent with Williamson's theory, they

Table 5.9 Regression equations for the integrated U.S. producers' share of wrought-products shipments over time (dependent variable in all cases is $VI\%_t$, $t = 1965$ through 1979).

Constant	$NPP(-2)$	$C3(-2)$	$H(-2)$	CU	R^{-2}	Durbin-Watson statistic
45.2[a] (13.1)	2.68[a] (7.89)	—	—	—	.814	1.32
60.2[a] (4.81)	2.26[a] (4.74)	—	—	−11.2[b] (−1.24)	.821	1.47
118[a] (29.7)	—	−0.527[a] (−10.6)	—	—	.888	1.82
114[a] (23.6)	—	−0.481[a] (−6.45)	—	−6.32 (−0.848)	.885	1.88
99.8[a] (37.8)	—	—	−131[a] (−10.6)	—	.887	2.32
104[a] (20.7)	—	—	−119[a] (−6.47)	−6.63 (−0.897)	.886	2.30

Note: R^2 values adjusted for degrees of freedom; t-statistics in parentheses. See Appendix E for full definitions of variables.
a. 99% signifcant in a one-tail test.
b. 85% significant in a one-tail test.

should be treated with caution. The observation period is short, relative to the slow trend in the dependent variable, and it is doubtful that the clear-cut relationship captured in the equations would have arisen could the observation period have been extended back to the 1950s. As was noted earlier, concentration and vertical integration both *declined* during that period. About the most that can be concluded is that the time-series model is consistent with the short-run adjustment explanation for downstream integration.

Product Differentiation and Integration

The vast majority of aluminum is sold on an arm's-length basis as producer goods to the manufacturers of final products and the producers of services. The buyers are firms, such as construction companies, transport equipment producers, appliance manufacturers, and power authorities, rather than final consumers. For all the usual reasons found in studies of industrial marketing, such buyers are not susceptible to brand differentiation. After account is taken for quality and terms of sale, price is the predominant marketing variable. The ultimate consumer products and services in which aluminum is involved are sometimes different from each other in the minds of consumers, such as canned soft drinks, refrigerators, and airplane trips, but any gains from differentiation accrue to the manufacturers and marketers of the products and services and not to the input suppliers. The aluminum producers cannot, and do not, enter these consumer businesses to secure the differentiation rents, because they typically lack the necessary production skills and have no advantage over other potential entrants in scaling the product-differentiation barriers to entry, which (by definition) must exist for the differentiation rents to exist.

There are, however, several consumer-product businesses in which the aluminum producers are active, and my argument is that they are involved in these businesses as a means of internalizing the rents from product differentiation. The major product line included in this category is household foil; to a lesser extent kitchen utensils and possibly some home-handyman building products are also included. The aluminum producers originally developed these product lines for end-use market development reasons, but this does not explain why the producers became and continue to be major manufacturers of the lines rather than leave the manufacturing to specialists. Recall that, at least in the period following World War II, the aluminum producers encouraged specialist fabricators and manufacturers to commercialize most new end-product applications once they had been developed in the aluminum producers' research and development divisions.

There are two major reasons why the aluminum producers entered the manufacturing of consumer foils and kitchen utensils. First, the manufacture of these products is compatible with the producers' traditional production and technical skills. Foil is simply very thin sheet aluminum, and pots and pans are just sheet that has been shaped, so their production is no more than a simple extension of sheet fabrication. Aluminum producers therefore have a production advantage over independent foil and kitchen utensil manufacturers. There are probably even some flow-process economies in physically combining sheet production and foil production.

Second, consumer foils and kitchen utensils have intrinsic characteristics that allow them to be differentiated in the minds of consumers. In the United States consumer foils and aluminum kitchen utensils were first introduced by Alcoa, and as Corey's study revealed, Alcoa could differentiate aluminum wraps and utensils from those made of traditional materials because their aluminum composition distinguished them. According to Corey, "If the features of the end product can be clearly identified with the material from which it is made and if these features are important to the consumer . . . promotion by the materials producer may be useful in creating *primary* demand for the product."[33] But, of much greater, lasting importance is the proposition that consumer foils and utensils are also amenable to differentiation by *branding;* competing aluminum-foil and utensils producers can differentiate their product offerings from each other's, and hence the potential exists for differential profit margins across aluminum-foil and utensils manufacturers.

Consumer foil is certainly the major case in point, and competition between different brands put out by the aluminum producers has been the dominant force behind the determination of the structure of the U.S. aluminum-foil industry. The most interesting feature of the resultant structure is the extent to which the aluminum producers are integrated into the manufacture of foil.

Before pursuing the case of foil in depth, brief mention should be made of cooking utensils and home-handyman products. The cooking-utensils market for aluminum is small and grows slowly; currently it absorbs about 1.5 percent of wrought products shipments and has not grown for a decade. Alcoa has for many years marketed branded utensils and cutlery, usually under its Wear-Ever label, but its share of the market does not appear to be large. Reynolds markets a number of lines of branded building products, such as Do-It-Yourself Aluminum and Climate Guard, but it appears that volumes are small. In any case, the application of the theory of product differentiation (presented below) to both cooking utensils and home-handyman products indicates that attempts to differentiate these products in the eyes of consumers are unlikely to be very successful. That is, retail-price premiums based on image advertising are unlikely to be large. Combined with the small size of these markets, this indicates that the manufacture of branded utensils and home-handyman products is not a significant motivation for downstream integration by fabricators. The fact that Alcoa and Reynolds are the only primary producers that have ever bothered significantly with these lines support this conclusion.

The Foil Industry

The market for consumer foil is also a small market. Shipments of household and institutional foil represent only about 2.5 percent of wrought products shipments, and only the shipments to households are amenable to product differentiation. However, here the primary producers dominate the market, so their reason for adopting this dominating strategy needs to be explained. Although the explanation directly accounts for only a small fraction of the overall degree of downstream integration undertaken by the primary producers, it is worthy of analysis for two other reasons. First, an explanation for integration into consumer foil is also an indirect explanation for integration into foil generally, because it was the consumer market that the primary producers were after when they integrated into foil. Most of them failed in that market and withdrew from it but have remained in institutional and industrial foil, probably to utilize the fixed assets and accumulated experience they amassed during the fight for the consumer-foil segment. Today, the total foil market represents a significant 8 percent of wrought products shipments, and the primary producers have integrated into it more than they have into any other fabricated products except for plate. The second reason why the small consumer foil market is worth analyzing is that, by exception, it helps explain why the primary producers have not chosen to integrate into a number of the other final products based on aluminum. The exceptional feature of foil is that it can very profitably be differentiated to the advantage of the manufacturer. Most other predominantly aluminum products cannot.

To explain the producers' downstream integration into foil, some historical background will be useful. Aluminum foil was first produced some time before World War I, but it was not until 1941 that Alcoa launched its first consumer-foil product, branded as Wear-Ever. The development was typical of Alcoa's efforts to expand the market for aluminum through new-product development and consumer education, and the brand name was consistent with Corey's argument that branding can be useful in developing primary demand by differentiating a new product from entrenched products (in this case, waxed paper, which was not very durable). Alcoa's monopoly meant that primary demand equaled Alcoa's demand, but this identity soon dissolved when in 1946 Reynolds and Kaiser become large integrated producers, thanks to their allocations of governmental wartime capacity. Almost immediately, in 1947, Reynolds began marketing Reynolds Wrap, and a twenty-year era of interbrand warfare had begun. The prize for the victor was a large portion of the potential rents from product differentiation.

Reynold's ultimate victory is now well recognized, but it is interesting to speculate whether or not the outcome was predictable back in 1947. The Reynolds Metals Company was formed in 1928, but effectively it began around 1920, when its predecessor, the United States Foil Company, was formed.[34] U.S. Foil was a joint venture between the R. J. Reynolds Tobacco Company and the British-American Tobacco Company, created to produce tin and lead foil for cigarette packaging. R. J. Reynolds's nephew, R. S. Reynolds, was behind the formation of U.S. Foil; he became its first president, and he took over control of the company about 1925. In 1926 the company switched from tin and lead foil to aluminum foil, and in 1928 its name was changed to the Reynolds Metals Company.

The historical account is important for several reasons. First, R. S. Reynolds's association with the R. J. Reynolds Tobacco Company exposed the founder of the aluminum company to a consumer product industry during a dynamic period in that industry's history. R. S. Reynolds joined his uncle's tobacco business as a young man in 1903, at a time when Reynolds Tobacco was a small producer of noncigarette tobacco products and was formally under the control of the famous tobacco trust.[35] After the dissolution of the trust in 1911, the industry underwent a marketing revolution when Reynolds Tobacco introduced Camel cigarettes in 1913. Camel represented a new concept in product, packaging, and promotion and began an era of product differentiation through heavy advertising; its share of the market exploded from less than 1 percent in 1913 to 42 percent in 1925. The young R. S. Reynolds apparently played an important role in the development of Camel before he left his uncle's firm in 1912. Furthermore, his continued association with the firm and the family no doubt kept him in contact with marketing developments for many more years.

R. S. Reynolds's connection with Reynolds Tobacco was also of more tangible significance, because the cigarette producer was probably a secure outlet for aluminum foil. It appears that during the late 1920s and 1930s Reynolds Metals grew to become the nation's dominant producer of aluminum foil, constrained only by the volume of aluminum that Alcoa allocated to the foil producer (less than 1 percent of its national output in the late 1930s). Although Reynolds had diversified into some other aluminum fabrications, foil was its major product-line.

Reynolds's immediate entry into consumer-foil production following its acquisition of primary capacity in 1946 may indicate that Alcoa, its previous monopolist supplier, had somehow prevented its earlier entry, but in any case, Reynolds had two major advantages over Alcoa (and later Kaiser) as a consumer-foil producer and marketer. First, it had twenty years of accumulated experience in aluminum-foil production and merchandising, and that experience would have helped lower its unit costs. Second, and probably of greater importance, was R. S. Reynolds's exposure to consumer-marketing techniques at Reynolds Tobacco, and specifically, the marketing of what I call a convenience good. Alcoa, and particularly Kaiser, had very limited experience in the marketing of such goods. In the language of business policy, there was considerable synergy between consumer foil and Reynolds's existing product lines and skills. The synergies were recognized at the time: "The Reynoldses are . . . good salesmen and merchants. Probably it's an inheritance from their long experience in the foil business where they were in constant association with all the hot-shot merchandizers in the food, soft-drink, and cigarette fields. They have long looked unbeatable in foil." [36] R. S. Reynolds himself was still at the helm (as chairman) when the company entered consumer foil, and while his personal involvement began to decline, his four sons were assuming responsibility, and "so strikingly in his image, physically and mentally, are the blocks off the old chip [sic] that the transition is almost imperceptible." [37]

It is therefore not at all surprising that Reynolds entered consumer foil, and it is no more surprising that the company forthrightly informed its competitors that "we selected Reynolds Wrap to be our champion." [38] Reynolds Wrap sales grew by about 20 percent per year, and by 1955 it had 85 percent of the market. Alcoa and Kaiser did not react at first, but apparently not because they recognized Reynolds's competitive advantages, because in the mid-1950s they both made determined entries. In 1956 Alcoa replaced its slow-selling Wear-Ever foil with Alcoa Wrap, backed with the threat that "we are never content to be second." [39] Then, in 1957, Kaiser joined the fray with Kaiser Foil. As the brand names suggest, interbrand rivalry was the order of the day. During the late 1950s, Alcoa spent about $1.5 million per year on network television and printed media advertising, and by 1959 it had won almost 20 percent of the market.

Kaiser had similar success in increasing its market share riding in on its sponsorship of the American Broadcasting Company's television show "Maverick." But regrettably, even "Maverick" was not enough to help Kaiser, because Reynolds's horse had already bolted away. Certainly Reynolds's share had fallen to 60 percent, but its advertising budgets were lower in both relative and absolute terms.

The intense competition among brands continued into the 1960s, but rather than further document the details of the firms' conduct, it is more important to explain why the firms so desperately wanted to secure as big a share as possible of this relatively small downstream market. The easiest reason to see is that by the early 1960s consumer foil was moving from the growth phase to the mature phase of its product life cycle (PLC).[40] Data on consumer foil sales are not published, but total foil shipments in the United States grew by an average annual rate of 15.5 percent during 1953–1960, 8.5 percent during 1961–1970, and 6.6 percent during 1971–1978. The decline in the growth rate of consumer foil shipments was probably even more marked. Both theory and evidence indicate that entry and market-share growth are much easier during a product's high-growth phase than during its mature phase, and it was probably Alcoa's and Kaiser's recognition of this that produced their aggressive marketing strategies in the late 1950s and early 1960s.

The PLC explains the timing of the drive by Alcoa and Kaiser to diminish Reynolds's domination of the consumer foil market, but the intensity of their drive was in recognition of the years of product differentiation rents that would be on offer during foil's mature phase. The value of the rents to the individual firm would be the product of market size, market share, and unit rents (appropriately discounted to net present value). Market share would play a dual role, because net unit rents would likely increase with market share, owing to the economies of scale available in national consumer product advertising.[41] But the vital parameter in the calculations of net present value was the unit rent: why were differentiation rents available on foil, and were they large enough to be worth fighting for?

Consumer foil is a classic example of what has become known as a "convenience," or "pull," good, a product that has intrinsic characteristics that make it amenable to differentiation in the minds of consumers via branding and advertising. Pull goods have a long tradition in marketing, but recently Michael Porter gave them theoretical respectability in studies in economics.[42] Briefly, Porter argues that consumers choose between brands by maximizing expected utility in a world of uncertainty and incomplete information. The acquisition and analysis of information relevant to a choice between available brands of a product reduces uncertainty and allows a more objective decision to be made, but such information is also costly. Strictly speaking, the consumer will expend resources on information acquisition and analysis only up to that point where the expected gains from a more informed choice equal the expected costs. This tradeoff varies across products and depends on numerous factors, such as the availability of information, the costs of acquiring it, and the importance of the purchase involved.

In the case of what Porter calls convenience goods, the tradeoff typically amounts to the consumers' relying heavily upon manufacturers' advertising messages for information. Interbrand choice in convenience goods is relatively unobjective, and this gives the manufacturers the opportunity to supply subjective information to convey the brand's "image" via the mass media at low message-per-dollar cost. This of course amounts to brand differentiation via advertising. Furthermore, to the extent that any manufacturer can successfully lower the cross-price elasticity of demand for his brand, and hence can price it above cost and earn differentiation rents, his rents are not eroded by the retailer, because the retailer has minimal impact upon the consumer's interbrand choice. In simple terms, the successful manufacturer's advertising will "pull" his brand through the retail sector. If consumer foil is a convenience good, then its manufacturers have the opportunity to earn differentiation rents.

Porter's analysis yields the following list of characteristics for convenience goods: (1) relatively small unit-price; (2) purchased repeatedly; (3) probable gains from making price and quality comparisons small relative to the consumer's appraisal of search costs, and hence mass-media advertising is common; and (4) will usually be purchased from convenience retail outlets. Convenience retail outlets are in turn characterized by little or no sales assistance in the form of salesperson interaction and high locational density of outlets. Consumer foil, and the stores through which it is sold, fit these characteristics extremely well.

Support for this assessment is provided by the data contained in a paper by Robert Blattberg and Subrata Sen, which develops "a new segmentation strategy desired to provide better information to the marketing decision maker." [43] They illustrate their ideas with detailed data on the consumer foil purchasing histories of a *Chicago Tribune* panel of consumers in the Greater Chicago area. The original data consisted of the consumer foil purchases, described by brand, store, package size, and price, for the panel members between 1962 and 1965. The data Blattberg and Sen summarize in their paper related to the 50 heaviest buyers of foil from the panel. Brand and stores names were disguised, but they were coded and classified by type, and Reynolds Wrap's code number was very easy to identify. Complete purchase histories were provided for only 9 of the 50 heavy buyers, but they are claimed to be representative of the members of the eight market segments that Blattberg and Sen identified. In total, their paper provides complete summaries of 279 purchases (31 for each of the 9 representative panel members). All of the quantitative data summarized below relate to these 9 members, with aggregates or averages being weighted across the market segments by the number of panel members (out of the 50) classified in each segment.

Using the Chicago panel's data to test the characteristics of consumer foil against those Porter lists for convenience goods convincingly indicates that consumer foil is indeed a convenience good. The weighted average unit purchase price was 48¢; the most common actual prices were 85¢ for the "economy size" (a 75-foot roll) and 29¢ for the "regular size" (a 25-foot roll). On any scale of unit prices for consumer products, these are "relatively small unit prices." On purchase repetition, there were 58 panel members who had a record of 31 or more purchases over the five years, an average of at least 6 purchases per year. There were 310 members who had 5 or more purchases, but unfortunately, the total number of consumers on the panel was not disclosed. In any case, it is clear that the heavy users of foil purchased it repeatedly.

The best practical guide to the classification of a good as a convenience good, in Porter's opinion, is the type of retail outlet in which it is sold. The weighted averages of data from the panel produce the following distribution of individual purchases: major supermarket chains, 42.7 percent; independent food chains, 44.6 percent; major drugstore chains, 9.4 percent; and other stores, 3.3 percent. Probably all of the chain stores, responsible for almost 97 percent of sales, were self-service, and almost by definition they would have been densely distributed.

Blattberg and Sen's data and analysis also provide compelling evidence not only that consumer foil is a convenience good, but that brand differentiation can be successful and can create price premiums. Table 5.10 summarizes their analysis of market segmentation, which defined segments according to each consumer's purchasing behavior — patterns of brand and store loyalty, proneness to "deals" (bargains), and preferences in package sizes — and categorized consumers into the segments using a form of discriminant analysis. Sixty-six percent of the panel members fell into segments characterized by considerable or exclusive loyalty to one brand. On a weighted-average basis, these consumers paid a price premium of 12.8 percent per foot of foil (after correction for the average quantity discount available on economy-sized packages). At the extreme, the highly brand loyal segment (dedicated Reynolds Wrap buyers) paid an average premium of almost 40 percent over the bargain-oriented segment. Further evidence of the success of the branded foils is provided by comparing average transactions prices and market shares by brand. Reynolds Wrap had a 70-percent market share and a price premium of about 15 percent above private label brands.

The other two national brands, probably Alcoa Wrap and Kaiser Foil, did not fare well. Although the data from the panel cannot be accurately extrapolated to cover the national market, it seems that Alcoa's and Kaiser's market shares were probably no more than 10 percent each, and their price premiums were small. This must have been true at least for Kaiser, because in 1967 it withdrew from the consumer foil market. "Kaiser tried to enter the aluminum foil market, but it came a cropper. Last year it converted those operations to making industrial foil. 'Foil

Table 5.10 Characteristics of consumer-foil market segments.

Market segment	Number of members (total = 50)	Average price paid[a]	
		25-foot roll	75-foot roll
Non-Price-Sensitive			
1. *Highly brand loyal:* almost exclusive loyalty to Reynolds Wrap	9	35¢	85¢
2. *Brand loyal:* some switching among the national brands, but considerable loyalty to favorite brand	8	31¢	80¢
3. *National-brand loyal:* strong loyalty toward national brands, but brand switching common	5	30¢	76¢
4. *Last-purchase loyal:* strong loyalty to a particular brand over several successive purchases, sequences broken by a brand switch (usually because of a bargain)	2	—[b]	78¢
5. *Dual-product loyal:* strong brand loyalty to two foil types, heavy-duty and regular-duty, of same brand	1	—[b]	77¢
Price-Sensitive			
6. *Bargain oriented:* no brand loyalty, stocks up on bargains, shops at different stores for bargains	8	21¢	64¢
7. *National-brand bargain-oriented:* strong loyalty to national brands, but shops at different stores for national-brand bargains	10	26¢	—[b]
8. *Low-priced store affected:* strong loyalty to a particular store and its (low-priced) private label	7	30¢	70¢

Source: R. C. Blattberg and S. K. Sen, "Market Segmentation Using Models of Multidimensional Purchasing Behavior," *Journal of Marketing* 38 (October 1974), 17–28.
  a. Average prices paid by the representative consumers.
  b. Representative consumer in this segment did not purchase any packages of this size.

just cost too much to promote,' Ready [then Kaiser's president] says."[44] Notice, however, that Kaiser stayed in industrial foil (and seemingly, even expanded in it). Eventually, in 1974 Alcoa succumbed as well and ceased production of consumer foils. However, it continued to supply institutional customers, and, like Kaiser, it continued to produce industrial foils, possibly because they wished to utilize the specific and durable assets involved in foil production such as plant, accumulated know-how, and distribution channels.[45] Another possible reason is that the highly concentrated structure of the foil industry (a four-firm concentration of 80 percent) was allowing pricing above marginal cost.

The nationally advertised brand market now belongs exclusively to Reynolds, and presumably it is highly profitable. Apart from Reynolds Wrap, Reynolds now also markets several other specialized consumer foil products, such as Fanci-foil, Redi-Pans, Flex-Can, and Brown-in-Bag. It is worth noting that private label brands probably hold the remaining 30 to 40 percent of the market, with Anaconda Aluminum as a major supplier. Apparently, Anaconda secured this market through aggressive pricing while the majors were concentrating upon the branded segment, an observation that does not seem consistent with the hypothesis that high concentration in foil leads to oligopolistic pricing.

Several solid conclusions can be drawn from this analysis of the U.S. consumer foil industry. First, consumer foil is a convenience good, and it has been differentiated successfully to produce price premiums for preferred brands. Second, the differentiation rents represented by the price premiums seem to be quite large on a per-unit basis. Third, Reynolds has established itself as the sole recipient of the rents. The reasons for Reynolds's ascendancy include (1) the company's previous experience in convenience-good marketing and foil production and merchandising, (2) the nine years in which Alcoa and Kaiser allowed Reynolds Wrap to become an entrenched brand during the product's high-growth phase, (3) the small absolute size of the mature market relative to the economies of scale that occur in national-brand consumer-product marketing, and (4) Reynolds's belief in its ability to succeed in foil and the assurance to its competitors that it would be "eternally" committed to foil.

Fourth, the downstream integration of producers of primary aluminum into foil production was motivated originally by user education, but subsequently by the producers' desire to internalize the rents from product differentiation on consumer foil. Operating economies motivated their simultaneous production of industrial foil, and when some companies withdrew from consumer foil, they retained industrial foil in order to utilize specific and durable assets and, possibly, because a high concentration of firms in foil production fostered tacit collusion on their pricing of industrial foil.

Conclusions

This chapter has investigated the vertical integration of primary smelting and fabrication in the U.S. aluminum industry since World War II. The data indicate that the overall degree of integration has generally been high but that it has followed two distinct trends, first declining until the early 1960s and then increasing slowly since then. The data also indicate that the degree of integration varies substantially across fabricated-product types, being very high for sheet, plate, foil, and aluminum cable steel-reinforced and bare cable, intermediate for powder, forgings and impacts, and rolled and continuous-cast rod and bar, lower for insulated and covered wire and cable, bare wire, extrusions and welded tube, and extremely low for castings. The purpose of the chapter has been to try to explain these observations.

Four major explanations exist for the firms' downstream integration. First, primary metal producers are sometimes forced to produce the fabrications required for newly developed aluminum products. The small size of new-product markets, the risk aversion of the producers of entrenched products, and their vested interests in the durable assets specific to the old products can make the growth of new-product markets slow and dubious. The historical record shows convincingly that during the first decade or two after World War II this problem, combined with the large number of new applications of aluminum pioneered by the aluminum producers, forced them to integrate heavily into fabricating for reasons pertaining to end-use market development. To the rather significant extent that this occurred, it seems fair to conclude that society gained, but the evidence also indicates that the rate of new-product development in the aluminum industry has dropped markedly since the mid-1960s, and today there are few products that require a firm's integration forward to sustain them. Market development is no longer an important explanation for downstream integration.

A second reason for integration across the primary market, however, is that it can be advantageous to the primary producers if it allows them to price discriminate across end-use markets according to long-run elasticities of demand. This theory implies that if such price discrimination occurs one would expect to observe high degrees of integration into fabrications having elastic demands. The Charles River Associates' econometric model indicates that demand elasticities do differ across end markets, and the evidence from regression equations indicates that integration across various types of fabricated products is consistent with the existence of price discrimination. Support exists for the proposition that aluminum users with elastic demands could well be receiving metal at lower prices than users with inelastic demands. If this is so, the welfare implications are unclear. Distributional effects would exist, but they are difficult to evaluate from the total society's point of view, while the effects of price discrimination on allocative efficiency are ambiguous. The policy implication is that if price discrimination occurs, the best solution is to remove the underlying market power and all forms of noncompetitive pricing. U.S. antitrust policy toward the aluminum industry has generally been in this direction for many years, and the steady decline in the concentration of firms engaged in primary smelting is encouraging.

The third and major reason for continued high integration across the primary market is that, from the point of view of the firms involved, it improves short-run adjustment following exogenous shifts in final demand. Prices on the primary market do not usually adjust sufficiently to clear the market, partly because of the inelasticities of short-run supply and demand and partly because stable prices are in the interests of the primary-producing oligopolists. As a result, nonprice rationing procedures are used, and integration offers an escape from quantity rationing and allows the close coordination and information processing that minimize transactions costs and improve decision making with respect to scheduling, shipments, inventories, and so on. Plenty of evidence indicates that rationing occurs in the primary aluminum market, and by using Carlton's model of a market that does not clear reliably through price, a number of links between the degree of integration across the market and the structural characteristics of the market were identified. These links were tested over time and across fabricated-product types, and it was found that downstream integration patterns in the U.S. aluminum industry are consistent with integration's being used as a type of substitute institutional arrangement in lieu of efficient price coordination.

According to Carlton's model this sort of arrangement is not socially desirable. If this is correct, then one worrisome implication is that the problem will get worse as the number of primary producers increases, but working in the opposite direction is the likelihood that prices should become more flexible as producer concentration decreases. It is difficult to assess which effect will be the strongest, but the recent evidence suggests that integration is increasing as producer concentration declines. On a positive note, the theory and evidence show that integration declines as the number of fabricators and minimum efficient scales in fabrication decline. Continual market growth ensures that the potential number of efficient-scale fabricators will increase, assuming that no dramatic technological changes occur to affect returns to scale.

The fourth explanation for downstream integration is that it allows the aluminum producers to internalize the product-differentiation rents available on certain aluminum consumer products. The most important product line involved is consumer foil, although the effect may also apply, to some extent, to kitchen utensils and home-handyman products. Consumer foil is a convenience good, and hence manufacturers' brands can be differentiated in the minds of consumers via brand advertising and promotion in the mass media with the result that the most successfully differentiated brands earn price premiums. There is strong evidence that Reynolds has achieved this position with its brand Reynolds Wrap: it holds a major share of the market and it retails with a significant price premium. Reynolds won this position after a long battle with Alcoa and Kaiser, and it has an obvious incentive to remain integrated through to final-product manufacture and marketing. Alcoa and Kaiser have withdrawn from the consumer foil market but continue to produce institutional and industrial foils, probably as a means of utilizing some of the specific and durable assets accumulated during the fight for the differentiation rents on consumer foil. These factors explain foil's special characteristics, but it was also found that integration into foil is consistent with the price discrimination and short-run adjustment explanations for downstream integration.

The product differentiation of Reynolds Wrap is probably not in society's interest, because it commands a price premium but is not a superior product in a functional sense. This could be argued away by pointing out that as long as its image cuts the costs of information acquisition and transactions, it is effectively a superior product. But, the main problem is that Reynolds has been able to drive out the competition and exclude entry via brand differentiation so that it can now charge something like a monopoly price (adjusted for the private-label segment). Note, however, that these antisocial effects are not a result of vertical integration. They result from the convenience-good nature of consumer foil and would probably have been exploited by a marketing-oriented independent if Reynolds had not identified the opportunity.

6 Conclusion

The purpose of this book was to investigate the vertical organization of the international aluminum industry. It describes how the industry's vertically connected stages of production are coordinated, coordination coming through an intricate combination of arm's-length markets, long-term contracts, joint-venture organizations and vertical integration. And most important, it explains *why* the observed combination occurs. In this final chapter the major results are summarized, some forecasts on future trends are suggested, and conclusions are drawn regarding the industry's performance and the need and role for public policy to improve it. Aside from these normative implications from a societal point of view there are also normative implications for individual aluminum firms regarding the vertical structure decision, probably the most important strategic decision that they make.

The major descriptive finding of the study is that vertical integration by the individual firm has always been, and continues to be, the predominant institutional arrangement for the coordination of economic activity from bauxite mining to metal fabrication. After fabrication, arm's-length markets predominate. Beginning with the coordination of mining and refining, it was found that during the late 1970s about 80 percent, by volume, of bauxite transactions were through intracorporate transfers. An additional 10 percent consisted of quasi-intracorporate transfers, involving arm's-length sales by a miner to his joint-venture refinery partners. Strictly arm's-length sales between independent miners and refiners, usually in fulfillment of long-term sales contracts, constituted the residual 10 percent. Rarely do miners and refiners plan to trade regularly on the bauxite spot market, a very thin market that only serves the purposes of agents having short-term or unexpected surpluses and deficits.

This apportionment of bauxite transactions across the various institutional mechanisms has not changed much for many years, and it is unlikely to change much in the future. The only exception to this generalization is that the quasi-intracorporate, or vertical-link, joint-venture transactions are a relatively recent phenomenon, arising in the late 1960s when one major arm's-length bauxite supplier, Comalco of Australia, organized two refining joint ventures as captive outlets. It is unlikely that many more, if any, of these sorts of arrangements will occur. The conclusion is that the vast majority of bauxite will continue to flow from mine to refinery without an effective change in ownership, that is, via vertical integration, and that the arm's-length bauxite market will remain relatively thin. This conclusion has important implications for the intending entrant and for the unintegrated going firm.

Why is it that miners and refiners prefer to integrate these two stages of production, or in the language of economics, what causes the failure of the bauxite market? The basic explanation is that, without integration, the majority of bauxite transactions would occur on bilateral-monopoly or small-numbers, bilateral-oligopoly markets. As already elaborated, such markets experience a number of major difficulties in a stochastic world: principally, they are very expensive to operate in terms of transactions costs, and they expose their traders to substantial financial risks emanating from opportunistic exploitation by trading partners. These difficulties cause the spot market to fail almost completely, and they are apparently so severe that even long-term contracts are usually inadequate. The problem with long-term contracts is that, in an uncertain world, they are always incomplete. Their revision and fine-tuning again incur heavy transactions costs, and they do not provide sufficient insurance against exploitation, given the specific and long-lived nature of the assets that the miner or refiner puts at risk.

The only other option is to internalize bauxite transactions, that is, to integrate vertically. The advantage of this arrangement over arm's-length transactions is that it harmonizes interests at the two stages of production by removing opportunism. The firm's internal incentive and control mechanisms can force the mining division and the refining division to cooperate for the good of the corporation, and this cuts transactions costs drastically and ensures an outcome that approximates joint profit-maximization. Even within the firm, vertical coordination is no simple task, as implied by the fact that the internal organization designs of the major integrated firms include a functional line connected directly to the chief executive's office, the most sophisticated and intricate design available for functional management.

The bilateral-monopoly nature of bauxite-exchange relationships results from several largely immutable technical and structural factors. First, bauxite is a heterogeneous commodity, and the ore in any deposit has unique chemical and physical properties. The efficient processing of a given bauxite usually requires a tailor-made refinery with specially designed technologies for chemical processing, materials handling, and waste disposal. Once a mine and its associated infrastructure is developed, and its appropriately designed refinery is constructed, the two plants are locked together to the economic extent of their technical complementarity. The evidence indicates that, in economic terms, the complementarity is often strong, meaning that within a wide range of bauxite transaction prices the mine and refinery are wedded together economically.

A second set of factors locking mines and refineries together includes the wide geographical spread of the world's major bauxite deposits, the vast distances between the deposits and primary smelters, the low value of bauxite at the mine's front door, relative to freight rates, and the over 50-percent reduction in material volume during refining. The last three factors encourage the back-to-back location of mines and refineries to minimize transport costs. The wide geographical spread of deposits, plus the fact that most large, modern mines are located in isolated and otherwise undeveloped areas, means that back-to-back plants are cemented together even more securely. Even if there are other refineries that can efficiently process a miner's output, an adjacent refinery has a major advantage over them, because refiners care about delivered bauxite prices while miners care about exmine prices. Of course the effect is symmetrical for the refiner when he seeks alternative sources of supply. The role transport costs play in inducing pairing is increasing as the widely separated bauxite-source countries, including Australia, Guinea, and Brazil, become more dominant as bauxite suppliers and as the relative price of transport rises along with relative energy prices.

Aside from technical complementarity and transport costs, a small-numbers trading situation on the bauxite market is brought about by the structure of the mining and refining industries. Both mining and refining, even without the effect of vertical integration, have substantial to very high barriers to entry, and hence they are fairly concentrated industry-wide. Concentration promotes mutual dependence-recognition and collusion, and if these occur in both mining and refining then a bilateral oligopoly results.

This industry-wide concentration not only reinforces the bilateral-monopoly relationships caused by bauxite's heterogeneity and transport costs, relationships that become effective after pairs of plants become operational, but it also jeopardizes the efficiency of what can be called the market for bauxite-deposit information. A firm planning a new refinery has a choice of bauxite-supply sources that is unconstrained, because, as yet, the refinery's technology and location are undetermined. The firm realizes that once its refinery is built it will be locked-in with a particular supplier, and hence it wants to select a supplier whose deposit has good long-run supply and price prospects. The evaluation of potential suppliers obviously requires extensive information about them and their bodies of ore, information that can be distorted through their opportunistic behavior. Williamson calls this sort of behavior strategic misrepresentation, caused here by information impactedness and the small-numbers structure of the bauxite-deposit supply industry. One way for refiners to improve the reliability and accuracy of their information is to

integrate upstream into exploration and mining-lease ownership, a first step toward operational upstream integration. Again
internal control mechanisms work to keep the exploration division "honest" in its dealings with the rest of the firm. By integrating upstream, the firm improves its refinery investment
decision.

The institutional arrangements and explanations for the coordination of refining and smelting are similar to those occurring
between mining and refining. During the late 1970s about 85
percent of alumina transactions, by volume, were intracorporate transfers, with most of the remainder being arm's-length
sales in fulfillment of long-term contracts. Here again the spot
market is thin.

One group of incentives for integration across the alumina
market is qualitatively the same as that for bauxite, namely,
small-numbers bargaining problems and financial risks resulting
from commodity heterogeneity, transport costs, and the technical and spatial specificity of plants that they cause. But these
forces are not so strong in alumina as they are in bauxite, and the
evidence indicates that they are weakening slowly over time.
Aluminas are becoming less heterogeneous, because the use of
sandy alumina increasingly dominates that of floury alumina,
because aluminas can be substituted for each other without too
marked an effect on smelter efficiency, and because conversion
of refineries to produce a different type of alumina is considerably less expensive than their conversion to take different bauxites. Furthermore, transport-cost effects are much less important
in the alumina industry because alumina is a relatively valuable
commodity, because its volume is reduced by less than half
during smelting, and because smelter location depends more
upon the availability and price of power.

But the integration of refining and smelting has also been
encouraged by industry structure factors. Minimum efficient
scales of operation in refining have always been large, relative to
total market size, ensuring high concentration at this stage of
production. In the past, the same applied to smelting, and hence,
without integration the alumina market would have been a
bilateral oligopoly, a market structure to be avoided if possible.
Effective collusion on each side of such a market produces a

trading environment that is expensive in transactions costs and is financially risky because of exogenously induced alterations in the bilateral power balance. On the other hand, if collusion across such a market is weak, the problems of successive monopoly can arise. In such a case, each stage of production treats input prices as fixed, and then prices its output as a conventional monopolist would, behavior that injects two monopolistic wedges into price and output determination and produces an overall outcome that is privately (and socially) inferior to joint-profit maximization. Integration across the two stages of production removes successive monopoly distortions, reduces transactions costs and financial risks, or both, and it produces an outcome that improves the overall industry's profitability.

At the same time, integration serves to raise barriers to entry into the industry. With thin intermediate product markets, an entrant must enter with complete integration, which raises capital requirements and often economies-of-scale barriers to entry. The alternative, which in this instance is entry into smelting without having in-house alumina, subjects the entrant to the alumina pricing or rationing policies of the integrated firms. For these reasons, most new entrants attempt to secure in-house alumina supplies, often via joint ventures at the refining stage. Mirror-image logic applies to the specialist bauxite miner who has to rely upon integrated refiners as customers: for him the integrated refiners behave as monopsonists. Refining has always been the stage of production most closely controlled by the aluminum majors.

In the last decade or so there has been significant entry of primary producers without in-house alumina, usually in industrializing countries where the state has fostered entry. The majors have been unable to prevent such entry, but it has worked to their advantage by making the primary-aluminum industry a considerably less concentrated industry than refining. The majors' response has been to consolidate their dominance in refining with the presumed intention of extracting their rents through the open-market alumina price. Alcoa has led this strategic change, and it now has an alumina capacity about twice that of its smelting capacity. It sells its excess alumina under long-term contracts to a large number of small, unintegrated primary producers, and it is no surprise that its profitability has been high. The success of Alcoa's strategy, the continual entry of unintegrated primary producers, and the previously mentioned weakening of refinery-smelter technical linkages all suggest that the integration of refining and smelting will continue its downward trend. Accordingly, the arm's-length alumina market will slowly thicken, though the terms of trade on this market will continue to be dominated by the refining majors for some time. The only way in which seller market-power on this market will decline is if new miner-refiners enter the industry.

One method available to aluminum firms for overcoming economies of scale and vertical integration barriers to entry in the upstream stages of production is to participate in joint ventures with other producers. For example, a bauxite-alumina joint venture between several primary producers allows the simultaneous achievement of upstream integration and efficient-scale raw material costs. This is one of the explanations behind the rapid increase in the use of joint-venture organizations in the aluminum industry that began in the mid-1960s. At that time about 15 percent of bauxite, alumina, and primary capacity was in jointly owned organizations, but by the end of the 1970s this had increased to 66 percent in bauxite, 51 percent in alumina, and 35 percent in primary.

This quite dramatic increase in the role of joint ventures is also due to a number of other factors. An important one is that in the last twenty years the industry has grown much more rapidly in countries outside the established industrial regions of North America and Europe than it has within these regions. The governments of new "aluminum nations" often insist on local participation in projects, seemingly as a means of monitoring and protecting local interests, and by so doing they enforce the formation of joint ventures. Local participation can also be advantageous to foreign firms because the local participant can supply to the joint venture specialized local knowledge on customs, laws, and so on, information that is difficult and risky to buy on an arm's-length information market. Such information can be supplied and synthesized more efficiently within the relatively cooperative atmosphere of a joint venture, where the local supplier of the information has an incentive to perform honestly and reliably because his payment comes as future profits.

There is also some evidence that the internationalization of the industry has promoted joint-venture formation via the desire of firms for internal diversification as a risk-reducing mechanism. Investment in foreign countries, particularly the so-called Third World countries, is often perceived by the American and European multinationals as more risky than domestic investment. Because wholly owned investments in the upstream aluminum industry come in very large chunks, it is difficult for an individual firm to arrange an internationally diversified portfolio of operations, but joint ventures can make this possible by reducing the absolute sizes of separate investments. Firms concerned about their total risk, rather than just their systematic risk, may therefore be led toward joint ventures, though the evidence suggests that this line of causation is not a major explanation for the boom in joint ventures.

✓Another possible finance-based explanation for joint ventures is that where large and risky projects are involved, the capital markets prefer the projects be developed as joint ventures. One reason for this is that a joint venture allows the partners to avoid making major alterations in their closely monitored financial policies, in particular, in leverage and dividends, and hence they avoid sending negative signals to the capital markets concerned about their financial security. The capital markets may also have a preference for joint ventures because, since joint ventures are separate and formal institutions, outside investors can monitor and police their internal financial management more precisely and guard against wealth transfers from outside investors (particularly bondholders) to insiders (the operational partners). This helps explain why joint ventures in aluminum are often highly leveraged, a financing arrangement now generally referred to as project financing. The advantageous effect of each of these factors is, in the final analysis, to reduce a project's cost of capital.

The important general point about joint ventures is that they represent a formal institution through which a continuous series of transactions between otherwise independent parties can be made efficiently. In project financing, for example, the series of transactions involved are cash flows between outside investors and the joint venturers, and the joint-venture organization reduces what are known as agency costs. But the general point goes much further than this to include many of the interfirm transactions that occur in the upstream aluminum industry, particularly those transactions not mediated by a thick arm's-length market and where, therefore, the traders have to haggle on bilateral monopoly markets. Where the assets involved indicate a long-run relationship, the traders face the prospect of many years of expensive and risky bargaining. Here the advantages of a joint venture as a vehicle for the continuous transactions relationship are that it provides the organizational machinery to cut bargaining costs and, if the partners jointly own expensive fixed assets through the joint venture, bargaining risks are also cut, because each partner's stake in the assets is contingent upon survival of the bilateral relationship. In short, joint ventures help achieve the benefits of collective action in situations in which the market system fails.

This argument is applied easily where joint ventures replace intermediate-product markets, for example, when a bauxite miner combines with a primary producer to form a refining joint venture. Here there is no escape from the zero-sum game of setting a transfer price after the joint profit-maximizing throughput rate has been decided upon, but because the refining joint venture requires cooperation for its survival, it provides a counterbalance to the natural conflict in the transfer price. Similarly, foreign-local joint ventures foster cooperation in a situation that has powerful elements of conflict. The evidence is strong that joint ventures also play an important role as vehicles for the exchange of technical and management know-how. The firms possessing these intangible assets and the firms wishing to hire their services have difficulty transacting the services on an arm's-length basis because of contractual incompleteness and the risks of strategic misrepresentation, but when they are exchanged implicitly within a joint venture, transactions costs and risks are reduced. The reason is that, once again, joint investment in specific and durable assets provides a strong incentive for cooperation that counteracts the natural conflict in arm's-length trades.

There is another set of interfirm relationships that joint ventures can also help organize to the advantage of the participants —the management of oligopolistic rivalry. The number and pattern of partnerships between the aluminum firms with moderate to great mutual interdependence indicate clearly the potential for explicit communication, and it would be surprising if the firms did not use joint-venture management committee meetings to discuss industry-wide policies on pricing, capacity utilization, capacity expansion, and so on. In this way joint ventures presumably play a role in helping the aluminum oligopolists approach the collectively optimal set of policies, though my evidence in support of this claim is purely circumstantial.

The final pair of vertically connected stages of production that this book examined was smelting and fabrication, although the empirical analysis was restricted to the U.S. industry. Once again vertical integration was found to be the major mechanism responsible for interstage coordination, an arrangement that (if anything) is becoming even more entrenched. The most important reason for continued high degrees of integration across the primary market is that, from the point of view of the firms involved, it improves short-run adjustment following exogenous shifts in final demand. Prices on the primary market usually do not adjust sufficiently to clear the market, partly because of the inelasticities of short-run supply and demand and partly because stable prices improve the ability of the primary-producing oligopolists to collude in setting the average price level. As a result, nonprice rationing procedures are employed, and integration offers an alternative to quantity rationing and allows the close coordination and information processing that minimize transactions costs and improve the management of production scheduling, shipments, inventories, and so on.

A second reason for integration across the primary market is that it can be advantageous to the primary producers by allowing them to discriminate in prices across end-use markets according to their long-run elasticities of demand. There is sound evidence that end-use elasticities do differ, and there is modest evidence that downstream integration patterns indicate that the primary producers are taking advantage of the differences.

There is also evidence that smelting-fabrication integration is highest in those fabricating industries that can support only a relatively small number of efficiently scaled plants. The primary producers integrate forward into these industries, in which market power can arise, as a means of preventing bilateral oligopoly bargaining problems or successive-monopoly distortions problems. Fabricators in industries with relatively large minimum efficient scales of operation, such as sheet and plate, also prefer to be integrated to ensure a reliable supply of primary to maintain throughput for their capital-intensive plants. Forward integration into fabrication may also be encouraged for those fabrications that are sold to powerful buyers as a way to counter the bargaining power of the buyers. The aluminum industry does better when the powerful primary producers, rather than a group of competitive fabricators, are the ones that confront powerful end-use buyers.

The aluminum firms tend not to integrate beyond fabrication into end-product manufacturing but sell their fabricated products at arm's length to a multitude of final-product manufacturers; however, there is one notable exception to this generalization—the aluminum foil industry dominated by the primary producers. The production of foil is technically compatible with sheet production, but the main reason why the primary producers internalize its production and marketing is that such a strategy allows them to capture the product differentiation rents that branded consumer foils provide. Consumer foil is a convenience good, and hence manufacturers' brands can be differentiated in the minds of consumers via brand advertising and promotion, with the result that the most successfully differentiated brands earn price premiums. There is strong evidence that Reynolds has achieved this position in the United States with its brand Reynolds Wrap: it holds a major share of the market and it retails with a significant price premium.

Although the emphasis of the study has been upon *why* the aluminum industry is arranged vertically as it is, some welfare and policy implications were also discussed. As noted in the introduction, public-policy economists have been suspicious for many years that vertical integration is of dubious social worth, mainly because of its ability to create or bolster market power. They have also become suspicious of joint-venture organizations. The general conclusion produced by this study is that both vertical integration and joint ventures have mixed effects upon welfare, and that the net effect of any specific case of integration or joint-venture formation depends upon how the various issues involved are evaluated. However, it is worth stressing for the benefit of "free-market" economists that vertical integration and joint ventures in the aluminum industry certainly do have some advantages over the alternative market-based coordination mechanisms.

One relatively strong result is that vertical integration aimed at internalizing bilateral monopoly relationships should, on its own, be encouraged. In the aluminum industry, the major case in point is the integration of bauxite mining and alumina refining. There bilateral monopolies arise largely because of basic technical factors, and they cannot be removed by public policies aimed at restructuring the two separate industries. The integration of mining and refining is advantageous for several reasons. First, it substantially reduces transactions costs, and this simply means a reduction in overall operating costs, a definite private advantage and at least a potential social advantage. Second, integration encourages the back-to-back location of mines and refineries, and this also cuts overall costs by reducing transport costs. Third, integration improves operating efficiency by matching feedstocks with refineries and improving scheduling. Finally, the removal of bilateral monopolies encourages joint-profit maximization, which is beneficial because it is then possible for the socially optimal throughput rate to be achieved.

These arguments favoring mining-refining integration lose much of their force when applied to refining-smelting integration. Sandy alumina is becoming the predominant alumina type, and it is a relatively homogeneous commodity. The failure of the alumina market in the past resulted principally from structural factors, namely, high industry-wide concentration on both sides of the market, and this is being eroded slowly through the entry of new firms. The arm's-length alumina market is thickening, a trend to be encouraged when possible. The best way of achieving this would be to foster the entry of new miner-refiners. This would have the effect of removing the main source of market power in the aluminum industry.

It is in this context that joint-venture organizations can play a major beneficial role. There is no doubt that joint ventures in the upstream stages of production have facilitated the entry of new firms by enabling them to share in plants that are technically efficient in terms of scale and technology for processing. The opportunities joint ventures offer for collusive behavior to occur certainly work against the beneficial effects of new entry, but my assessment is that the net effect of joint ventures has been positive. The fact is that joint ventures in mining, refining, and smelting have decreased the share of the industry directly controlled by the majors and have helped twenty new firms become established as viable competitors. Such a decline in concentration must, in the long run, work against oligopolistic collusion. The temptation for a small firm to cheat on a group agreement is very strong, even if it is tied up in joint ventures.

In any case, collusion in an industry like aluminum is not all bad. One of the socially least desirable features of the upstream aluminum industry is that it regularly suffers from waves of over and under capacity. Final demand is sensitive to the overall rate of economic activity, while capacity comes in large chunks, with lead-times of several years. Everybody loses through the misallocation of resources associated with the resulting over and under capacity, and it would appear that improved upstream cooperation, through joint ventures, for example, could improve the matching of capacity with demand. Of course, the aluminum oligopolists would prefer to have that capacity that is equated with the monopoly output rate, which of course is not the optimal rate for resource allocation.

Many joint ventures in the aluminum industry also serve the worthwhile purpose of providing a formal institution through which the multinational aluminum firms and host countries can manage their economic relationships. The industry has now spread to include many of the world's small and less-developed nations, a process that usually has involved the multinational aluminum firms, particularly the six majors. As a result, considerable trading occurs between these nations and the multinationals. In essence, the nations sell a package that includes access to bauxite deposits, power sources, and final markets, while the multinationals sell a package that includes technical know-how and experience, access to aluminum's intermediate-product "markets," and possibly improved access to international capital markets. Such transactions often involve specific and durable investments of various types, such as mines, refineries, and ports, so once a transactional relationship has been established, the host country and the multinational become bilateral monopolists of a sort. The "packages" they trade do not have world-market prices, so continual bargaining and haggling, or what is more popularly referred to as the conflict of interest between national sovereignty and multinational enterprise, occurs. The underlying conflict is unavoidable, but the advantages of managing it through a joint venture are significant. A joint venture has an indefinite life that is matched with the longevity of the assets involved, and, if the parties share the original investment and receive their benefits over time as successive and successful transactions are executed, they have a strong incentive to maintain the joint venture's existence. But, of greater importance is that the joint venture provides the organizational machinery and information to cut transactions costs.

As far as the social welfare effects of the integration of smelting and fabrication are concerned, pursuasive arguments in its favor are hard to find. The major purpose of integration is to support a system of nonprice rationing and stable prices, and the merits of this allocative system are dubious to say the least. On the negative side, integration encourages price collusion among the producers of primary, it jeopardizes the viability of going independents, and it raises barriers to entry for potentially independent, new smelting and fabrication firms. On the positive side, the primary producers argue that price stability is advantageous because it promotes the use of aluminum by manufacturers who dislike unstable input prices. This argument is probably accurate in a descriptive sense, but it is not at all clear that overall resource allocation is improved accordingly. On a practical level, aluminum prices tend to be more stable than the prices of substitute products such as copper, timber, steel, and plastic, so if there are allocative effects associated with the relative stabilities of substitute input prices, a case could be made that aluminum prices should be less stable than they are, to remove the "stability bias" in favor of aluminum. Besides, neoclassical welfare economics posits that resources are allocated optimally via a free price-system reflecting marginal production costs, and this is not what occurs in the primary aluminum industry. Without integration, the price of primary would certainly become more dynamic.

It can also be argued that smelting-fabrication integration is socially advantgeous because it improves the flows of information back upstream from final markets, and hence allows more efficient scheduling, inventory management, and so on. There is certainly some truth to this argument under the present regime of integration and nonprice rationing, but it would lose its credence in a world of freely fluctuating primary aluminum prices. The daily prices determined on a thick arm's-length primary market would represent most of the information required for short-term operational planning. On an international scale, the arm's-length primary market, and even more particularly the primary spot market, are growing both absolutely and relatively, so probably by the end of the 1980s these markets will handle a sufficient volume of primary transactions to generate "the market price of primary." In addition to the spot market, since 1978 firms have also been able to trade on the London Metals Exchange (LME) forward market, which can also help operational management. Like the spot market, the forward market will improve as an allocative mechanism as the grip of the primary producers further loosens. It is not surprising that the aluminum majors were opposed to the formation of the LME forward market.

Any role that primary-fabrications integration plays in allowing the primary producers to price discriminate across end-use sectors is also of doubtful worth from society's point of view, but public-policy makers would probably be wasting their effort in directly attempting to prevent such practices. On purely pragmatic grounds, price discrimination would be very difficult to identify, prove, and legislate against, while on theoretical grounds its removal would probably not add many social benefits. If the primary producers do price discriminate across end-use sectors, then they must be colluding successfully, and if this is so, then they could also operate a number of other less-than-perfectly-competitive pricing policies, such as a uniform monopoly price. Whether price discrimination is inferior to other such policies is difficult to assess from society's point of view, so even if public policy could remove price discrimination, society might not be any better off. What is clear is that allocative efficiency would be maximized if all primary were transacted at minimum average cost, and the best way of achieving this would be to encourage further declines in the concentration of firms producing primary.

Downstream from fabrication, most aluminum products are traded on arm's-length producer-goods markets, and there appears to be no reason to alter this organization through public policy. There is a problem with the consumer foil market that derives from the nature of the product as a convenience good, namely, the earning of product differentiation rents from image advertising. Consumers do pay a premium for successful brands that is not based on the product's superior technical quality, a premium protected by product differentiation barriers to entry and mobility. But there is nothing unique about consumer foil in this respect, because countless other convenience goods have similar price premiums, and they too seem immune to the effects of public policy. In any case, it has to be stressed that even though the differentiation rents on consumer foil are earned by forward-integrated primary producers, the rents would probably not disappear if disintegration were enforced. Certainly, disintegration would prevent the primary producers from earning the rents, at least directly, but the rents would still be available to an independent consumer foil producer, because disintegration would not affect the intrinsic differentiability of the product. Furthermore, if, in the United States, Reynolds was forced to dispose of its consumer foil interests, it would receive the capitalized value of the rents on Reynolds Wrap from the acquiring independent.

Taking all of the welfare implications together, the overall recommendation is that no major public-policy initiatives are required to improve the aluminum industry's performance. It has been argued that its performance would improve with a further decline in primary-producer concentration and with an increase in the number of integrated miner-refiners. These claims rest on the proposition that decreases in concentration on

both sides of the alumina and primary markets would remove the
need for integration and increase competition. Public policy
toward the aluminum industry, at least in the United States, has
for many years been directed at decreased concentration, hence
I believe that no new initiatives are required.

However this goal should not be pursued at the expense of
technical efficiency; the independent entry of inexperienced
firms with less-than-efficient-scaled plants should be avoided.
The high-cost positions that occur in small or poorly designed
and operated plants do nothing to improve the industry's price
levels. In the past, entry of this type has occurred, including the
entries of U.S. producers Harvey Aluminum, Revere Copper
and Brass, Olin Mathieson, and Conalco. The private performances of these firms have suffered from technical inefficiency,
and they have not been capable of price competition with the
majors because of their high-cost positions. Reduced concentration and increased technical efficiency can be achieved simultaneously, however, through joint ventures that include at least
one experienced firm. The best case of this in the United States is
Alumax, a firm that entered the industry in the late 1960s by
partnering the experienced major PUK in two large and apparently efficient smelters. Alumax now has the established outlets
and technical experience to go it alone, as demonstrated by the
commencement of an independent smelter in South Carolina.

A final issue worth commenting upon is the applicability of the
results of this study to other industries. I am convinced that many
of the explanations for vertical structure in aluminum apply in
very similar ways to other natural resource based industries. I
have applied the list of motives for vertical integration produced
by this study to several other mining industries, namely copper,
lead, zinc, and tin, and it performs strongly in predicting degrees
of integration. My approach of examining each pair of vertically
connected stages of production in turn is also useful, not least of
all because it forces an analysis to be systematic. The work in
Chapter 4 on joint ventures should also apply to other natural
resource industries where, casual observation indicates, joint
ventures are also of increasing importance, but care should be
taken not to assume that the case of aluminum applies simply to
that of other industries. A general finding of this book is that

vertical integration and joint ventures result from a complex combination of factors rather than a single predominant factor, and this helps explain why vertical integration and joint ventures have not been treated thoroughly in research on economics or management. The implication is that the analysis of vertical integration and joint ventures, from whatever point of view, must be undertaken using a case-by-case approach.

The Data Base

The major quantitative data used in the study were plant capacity data. The beginning-of-year capacities for approximately 250 bauxite mines, alumina refineries, and primary smelters were approximated for the twenty-five-year period 1955–1979, implying over six thousand observations. Obviously the data cannot be listed here, but it is important that sources, methods, and assumptions be detailed, because the data are not generally available.

Capacity

A plant's capacity was taken to be its yearly output of finished product in metric tons if operated at its technically optimal rate (that is, minimum average cost). This measure is well defined and easily available for smelters. Refineries have wider ranges of efficient operation, and the data are not so readily available, but the data collected on refineries should be accurate within approximately 5 percent. Bauxite mines do not have a unique capacity, but usually they are operated over a range of output rates that vary by about 20 percent. Data were generally difficult to obtain, but the rule of thumb adopted was that a mine's capacity was equal to its production during the industry's most recent high capacity utilization period.

The resulting estimated capacities for mines and refineries were converted to equivalents of primary aluminum. This was simple for refineries—a conversion factor of 1.95 tons of alumina to one ton of primary was used. Obtaining conversion factors for mines was a problem, because they differ significantly over mines and even over time within one mine. Conversion factors for large, modern mines were found in companies' annual reports and in journals such as the *Engineering and Mining Journal*, but for some old, small mines it was usually assumed that 4.5 to 5.5 tons of bauxite produced one ton of primary.

Sources

The major sources for capacity data and conversion factors were:

  Company annual reports and the U.S. Security and Exchange Commission's 10-K forms

  American Bureau of Metal Statistics, *Non-Ferrous Metal Data* (New York: American Bureau of Metal Statistics), 1960–1980

  U.S. Bureau of Mines, *Minerals Yearbook* (Washington, D.C.: U.S. Bureau of Mines), 1956–1980

  Engineering and Mining Journal (1960–1980)

  Metal Bulletin, *Integration in Aluminum* (London: Metal Bulletin, 1969)

  Metal Bulletin, *World Aluminium Survey* (London: Metal Bulletin, 1977)

  Mining Journal (1960–1980)

  W. R. Skinner, *Mining Year-Book* (London: Mining Journal), 1960–1980

  Comalco, *Aluminium Industry Facts* (1977, 1979)

Ownership of Plants

The ownership of plants was also determined from the above sources. Based upon ownership, the capacity of each plant in each year was allocated across what were defined as "basic aluminum firms." While formally there are hundreds of separate firms involved in the upstream aluminum industry, the number of effectively independent firms is considerably less. The idea was to identify the corporate groups involved in the industry that were firms in the economic and business sense. Thus a basic aluminum firm consists of all of the plants, and shares of joint-venture plants, controlled by a centralized management responsible for group strategy.

The practical application of the idea is probably best indicated by characterizing the firms that were *not* categorized as "basic aluminum firms."

1. Corporate groups or financial institutions with a minority holding in one or several scattered aluminum operations, that appeared to regard their holdings as just investments, were not "basic aluminum firms." Examples include Nippon Steel, with a 5 percent holding in Alumax of the United States; Hanna Mining, with a 30 percent holding in Alcominas of Brazil; and the Australian Mutual Provident Society, with a 12.1 percent holding in Gove Alumina of Australia.

2. State-owned firms with a minority holding in local operations and/or without a management input beyond guarding the local interest were not "basic aluminum firms." In most cases, state firms were excluded because they had minimal impact upon the supply of raw material and disposal of output. For example, the Jamaican government was not classified as a basic aluminum firm, even though it now holds 7% of Jamalcan (93% Alcan), 6% of Jamalco (94% Alcoa), 51% of Kaiser Jamalco Bauxite (49% Kaiser), and 51% of Jamaica Reynolds Bauxite Partners (49% Reynolds). On the other hand, Aluminium Bahrain was classified as a basic aluminum firm, even though Kaiser holds a 17% interest. The Bahrainian state holds 78%, and the smelter buys its alumina and disposes of its primary seemingly independently of the Kaiser network.

3. Joint-venture firms owned at least in part by one or more firms that were themselves classified as basic aluminum firms were generally not classified as basic aluminum firms. Examples include Alumina Partners of Jamaica and Queensland Alumina, Limited. However, several firms of this type were classified as basic aluminum firms because they clearly have a separate corporate identity, that is, they have their own strategic manage-

ment and claim to compete independently of their parent companies. The important cases include Comalco, Alumax, British Aluminium, and Hindustan Aluminium.

Following these guidelines, the corporate groups classified as basic aluminum firms for at least some of the time between 1955 and 1979 can be listed as follows:

Alcan Aluminium Limited
Aluminum Company of America (Alcoa)
Alumax, Incorporated
Aluminium Corporation of India
Aluminium Delfzijl NV
Anaconda Company
Schweizerische Aluminium AG (Alusuisse)
Bauxites Eliconos
Bauxites Parnasse Mining Company
British Aluminium Company Limited
Companhia Brasileira de Aluminio (CBA)
Companhia Vale do Rio Doce (CVRD)
Comalco Limited
Corporation Venezolana de Guayana (CVG)
Eleusis Bauxite Mines, Incorporated
Gebrueder Giulina GmbH
Gove Alumina Limited
Harvey Aluminum, Incorporated
Hindustan Aluminium Company
Kaiser Aluminum and Chemical Corporation
Martin Marietta Corporation
Metallgesellschaft AG
Mitsubishi Light Metal Industries Limited
Mitsui Aluminium Company Limited
Montecantini Edison S.p.A.
National Southwire Aluminum
Noranda Mines Limited
Norsk Hydro AS
Olin Mathieson Chemical Corporation
Pechiney Ugine Kuhlmann (PUK)
Phelps Dodge Corporation
Ramunia Bauxite Mining Company

Revere Copper and Brass, Incorporated
Reynolds Metals Company
Riotinto Zinc Corporation
Royal Dutch Shell
Showa Denko KK
Sumitomo Aluminium Smelting Company
Usine d'Aluminium Martigny SA

The states and state-owned groups treated as "basic aluminum firms" can be listed as follows:

Argentina: Aluminio Argentinos
Austria: Vereinigte Metallwerke Ranshofen-Berndorf
Bahrain: Aluminium Bahrain
Guinea: Office des Bauxites de Kindia
Guyana: Guyana Mining Enterprise and Guyana Bauxite
India: Bharat Aluminium
Indonesia: Aneka Tambang Mining
Iran: Iranian Aluminium
Italy: Ente Partecipazioni Finanziamento Industria Manifat-
    turiera (EFIM)
Norway: Det Norsk Nitrid Aluminium
Taiwan: Taiwan Aluminium
Turkey: Etibank and Aluminium Tesisleri
West Germany: Vereinigte Aluminium-Werke (VAW)

The capacity of each plant was allocated in each year across one or more of the firms in the list. The following guidelines determined the allocation:

1. The capacity of a plant *wholly* owned by a basic aluminum firm was allocated entirely to that firm.

2. The capacity of a plant *partially* owned by a basic aluminum firm was allocated entirely to the basic firm. Examples of firms with such plants include: Indian Aluminium Company, 55% Alcan and 45% Indian interests, allocated entirely to Alcan; Aluminium of Korea, Limited, 50% PUK and 50% Korea Hyundai Heavy Industries, allocated entirely to PUK; and Mosal Aluminium, 45% Alcoa and 55% Elkem-Spigerverket, allocated entirely to Alcoa.

3. The capacity of a plant *fully* owned by a *group* of basic

aluminum firms was distributed among the basic firms according to their equity shares. Examples include: Alumina Partners of Jamaica, 36.5% Kaiser, 36.5% Reynolds, and 27% Anaconda, allocated to these three firms in the proportions 36.5:36.5:27; and Queensland Alumina, Limited, 30.3% Comalco, 28.3% Kaiser, 21.4% Alcan, and 20% PUK, allocated to these four firms in the proportions 30.3:28.3:21.4:20.

4. The capacity of a plant *partially* owned by a group of basic aluminum firms was allocated across the basic firms according to *their* equity shares. An example is: Cie des Bauxites de Guinea, 49% government of Guinea and 51% Halco Mining (in turn 27% Alcan, 27% Alcoa, 20% Martin Marietta, 10% PUK, 10% VAW, and 6% Montedison), allocated to the latter six firms in the proportions 27:27:20:10:10:6.

Joint-Venture Firms

The procedures described above for distributing plant capacities among basic aluminum firms had the effect of dissolving joint-venture firms and allocating their capacities to the basic aluminum firms that owned them. The only joint-venture firms that survived dissolution were the strategically independent firms Comalco, Alumax, British Aluminium, and Hindustan Aluminium. However, in Chapter 4, where joint ventures are analyzed, all joint-venture firms were reconstituted. Any firm or plant not wholly owned by a basic aluminum firm was classified as a joint venture. All of these firms are listed and described in Appendix D.

Regression Models of Interfirm Differences in Upstream Integration

Three ordinary least-squares regression models were estimated in an attempt to explain why some firms are not completely integrated across mining, refining, and smelting and why some firms have imbalanced integration. The models are summarized in Table B.1 and the variables' definitions are as follows:

Dependent Variables

$VINT_i$ = number of stages of production out of three (mining, refining, and smelting) in which firm i was active at the start of 1979;

$BABAL_i = 1 - BC_i/AC_i$ if $AC_i > BC_i$; and $1 - AC_i/BC_i$ otherwise; and

$APBAL_i = 1 - AC_i/PC_i$ if $PC_i > AC_i$; and $1 - PC_i/AC_i$ otherwise; where

BC_i = firm i's bauxite capacity in primary equivalent tons at the start of 1979;

AC_i = firm i's alumina capacity in primary equivalent tons at the start of 1979;

PC_i = firm i's primary capacity at the start of 1979; and

i = index of basic aluminum firms.

By construction $BABAL$ and $APBAL$ range between zero (for a

Table B.1 Regression equations of interfirm differences in upstream integration.

Dependent variable	Constant	AGE	STATE	SPEC	BNATION	JAPAN	DA	DP	R^2
VINT	1.70 (7.72)[a]	1.33 (2.64)[a]	−0.303 (−1.11)	—	—	—	—	—	0.15
BABAL	0.392 (2.01)[b]	−0.0417 (−0.155)	0.0273 (0.172)	−0.128 (−0.635)	0.442 (2.29)[b]	0.424 (1.75)[b]	0.218 (1.23)	—	0.14
APBAL	0.520 (3.74)[a]	−0.493 (−2.27)[b]	0.207 (1.58)[c]	−0.0587 (−0.389)	—	—	—	0.235 (1.92)[b]	0.27

Note: R^2 values adjusted for degrees of freedom; t-statistics in parentheses.
a. 99% significant in one-tail test.
b. 95% significant in one-tail test.
c. 90% significant in one-tail test.

firm with perfectly balanced integration) and one (for a specialist firm).

Explanatory Variables

AGE_i = number of years firm i had been active in one or more of mining, refining, and smelting as at 1979;

$STATE_i$ = 1 if firm i is state owned, and 0 otherwise;

$SPEC_i$ = the estimated proportion of firm i's 1978 sales from aluminum products;

$BNATION_i$ = 1 if firm i is based in a major bauxite-source country, and 0 otherwise;

$JAPAN_i$ = 1 if firm i is based in Japan, and 0 otherwise;

DA_i = 1 if $AC_i > BC_i$, and 0 otherwise; and

DP_i = 1 if $PC_i > AC_i$, and 0 otherwise.

$BABAL$ and $APBAL$ do not measure the direction of a firm's imbalance. For example, if $BABAL_j$ equals 0.5 then firm j could either have twice as much bauxite capacity as alumina capacity, or vice versa. DA and DP are dummy variables included in the second and third models, respectively, to distinguish the direction of imbalance. The positive coefficient on DA in the second model indicates that firms with more alumina than bauxite capacity are relatively more imbalanced than are firms with more bauxite than alumina capacity. Similarly, the positive coefficient on DP in the third model indicates that firms with more primary than alumina capacity are relatively more imbalanced than are firms with more alumina than primary capacity. These results imply that if tapered integration is necessary, it is better to have it in an upstream than a downstream direction.

The Sample

The sample includes forty-five of the fifty-two basic aluminum firms listed in Appendix A. The seven firms not included had exited from the aluminum industry by 1979, or insufficient data were available on their operations.

Internal Organization Structures of Alcoa, Alcan, and Reynolds

This appendix describes the internal organization structures of the Aluminum Company of America (Alcoa), Alcan Aluminium, Limited, and the Reynolds Metals Company, using the diagrams in Figures C.1–C.5. The descriptions are based largely on the limited information available in annual reports and 10-K Forms of the U.S. Securities and Exchange Commission information that typically amounts only to lists of senior officers and descriptive titles of their positions. Further information on Alcoa was found in A. D. Chandler, *Strategy and Structure* (Cambridge, Mass.: Massachusetts Institute of Technology Press, 1961), while for Alcan, I. A. Litvak and C. J. Maule, *Alcan Aluminium, Limited: A Case Study*, Royal Commission on Corporate Concentration, Study no. 13 (Ottawa: Minister of Supply and Services, 1977), was valuable. The following descriptions for Alcoa and Alcan are probably quite accurate, relative to how the companies are actually managed, but I have less confidence in the information on Reynolds.

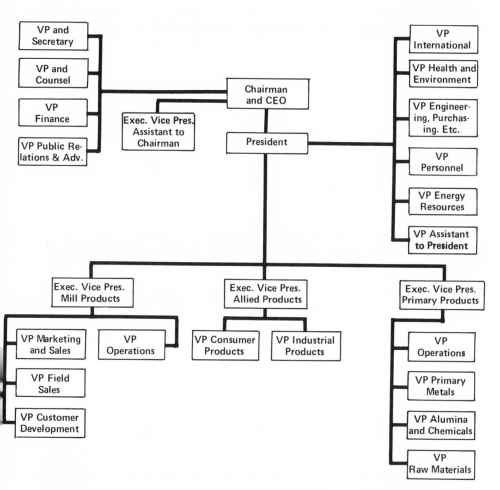

Figure C.1 Alcoa's organizational structure, 1978. *Source:* Aluminum Company of America, *Annual Report,* 1977; and Chandler, *Strategy and Structure* (Cambridge, Mass.: Massachusetts Institute of Technology Press, 1962), pp. 337–340.

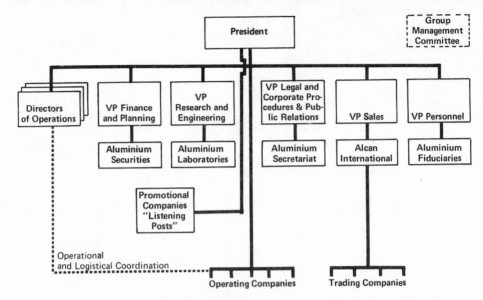

Figure C.2 Alcan's organizational structure before 1968. *Source:* I. A. Litvak and C. J. Maule, *Alcan Aluminium Limited: A Case Study,* Royal Commission on Corporate Concentration Study no. 13 (Ottawa: Minister of Supply and Services, 1977), p. 108.

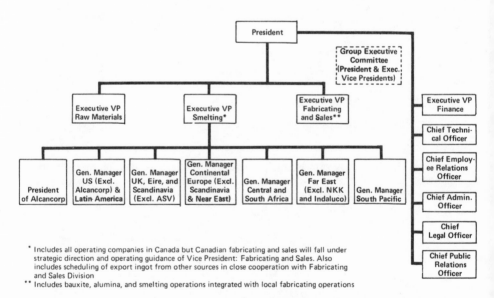

Figure C.3 Alcan's organizational structure, 1968–1973. *Source:* I. A. Litvak and C. J. Maule, *Alcan Aluminium Limited: A Case Study,* Royal Commission on Corporate Concentration, Study no. 13 (Ottawa: Minister of Supply and Services, 1977), p. 111.

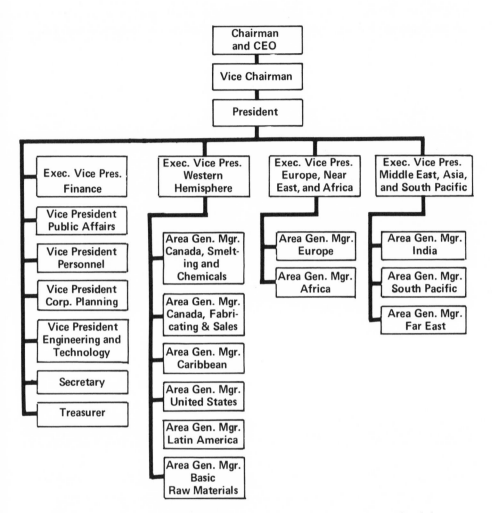

Figure C.4   Alcan's organizational structure, 1978. *Source:* Alcan Aluminium Limited, *Annual Reports,* 1975, p. 4; 1976, p. 6; and 1977, pp. 2, 11.

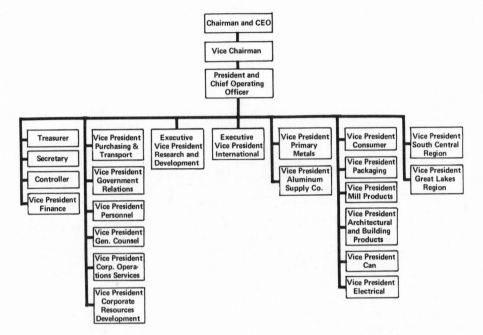

Figure C.5 Reynolds's organizational structure, 1978. *Source:* Reynolds Metals Company, *Annual Report,* 1977; and the U.S. Securities and Exchange Commission's 10-K form, 1976.

Description of Joint-Venture Firms in Aluminum

This appendix describes the essential features of sixty-four joint ventures that have existed at some time between 1955 and 1979. In most cases they still exist. Only joint ventures that produce bauxite and/or alumina and/or primary are included. The list includes the vast majority of all joint ventures that have existed over the relevant period.

The descriptions include the names of the joint-venture firms; the location of their plants; their start-up dates (and termination dates if relevant); their bauxite (B), alumina (A), and primary (P) capacities (in thousands of tons of primary equivalent); if they are involved in fabrication (Fab.); and their ownership structures.

The data come from a wide variety of sources, but particularly company annual reports and the industry periodicals listed in Appendix A.

APPENDIX D

Joint-venture firm, location, start-up year (and termination year if relevant)	Capacity of wholly owned or controlled operations, 1979 or at termination (thousands of tons)		Partners and equity shares, 1979 or at termination (in percentages)		Other information
Alcan Australia, Ltd. Australia 1969	B = A = P = Fab.	0 0 45	Alcan Australian Institutions	70.5% 29.5	Strategically controlled by Alcan
Alcoa of Australia, Ltd. Australia 1963	B = 1,760 A = 1,760 P = 100 Fab.		Alcoa Western Mining Corp. Broken Hill South Broken Hill North Other	51.0 20.0 16.0 12.0 1.0	Strategically controlled by Alcoa
Aluminio Sarda, S.p.A. (Alsar) Italy 1973	B = A = P = Fab.	0 0 125	Mineraria Carbonifera Sarda Alumetal	68.0 32.0	
Alumetal, S.p.A. Italy 1973	B = A = P = Fab.	5 103 105	EFIM (state) Montedison	94.0 6.0	Created when Italian government took over Montedison's ailing aluminum business
Alumina Partners of Jamaica (Alpart) Jamaica 1969	B = A = P =	606 606 0	Kaiser Reynolds Anaconda	36.5 36.5 27.0	
Alumax, Inc. United States 1973	B = A = P = Fab.	0 0 0	Amax Mitsui Nippon Steel	50.0 45.0 5.0	Formed when Mitsui purchased 50% of Amax's Aluminum Division. Now independent of parents in operating and strategy
Alumino de Galicia SA (Alugasa) Spain 1961	B = A = P = Fab.	0 0 90	PUK Local interests	68.0 32.0	Strategically controlled by PUK
Aluminio del Caroni SA (Alcasa) Venezuela 1967	B = A = P = Fab.	0 0 120	Reynolds Corp. Venezolana de Guayana (CVG)	50.0 50.0	
Aluminio Espanol SA Spain 1979	B = A = P =	0 400 180	Endasa Banks Alugasa	55.0 25.0 20.0	Refinery on-stream in 1980
Aluminio SA de CV Mexico 1963	B = A = P = Fab.	0 0 45	State Alcoa	56.0 44.0	Originally wholly owned by Alcoa

Joint-venture firm, location, start-up year (and termination year if relevant)	Capacity of wholly owned or controlled operations, 1979 or at termination (thousands of tons)		Partners and equity shares, 1979 or at termination (in percentages)		Other information
Aluminium Bahrain (Alba) Bahrain 1971	B = A = P = Fab.	0 0 120	State Kaiser Breton Investments	77.9 17.0 5.1	
Aluminium Corp. of South Africa (Alusaf) South Africa 1971	B = A = P = Fab.	0 0 78	South African Industrial Corp. Alusuisse	78.0 22.0	
Aluminium de Greece SA Greece 1966	B = A = P = Fab.	0 250 143	PUK State and local private	73.0 27.0	
Aluminium of Korea, Ltd. (Koralu) South Korea 1969	B = A = P = Fab.	0 0 35	Korea Hyundai Heavy Industries PUK	50.0 50.0	
Aluminium Oxide Stade GmbH West Germany 1973	B = A = P =	0 308 0	Reynolds VAW	50.0 50.0	
Anglesey Aluminium, Ltd. United Kingdom 1971	B = A = P =	0 0 112	Kaiser Riotinto Zinc	66.7 33.3	Originally RTZ 47%, Kaiser 34%, and British Insulated Callender's Cables, Ltd. 19%
Alnor Aluminium Co. A/S Norway 1967–1974	B = A = P =	0 0 132	Norsk Hydro A/S Harvey (then Martin Marietta)	51.0 49.0	100% Norsk Hydro since 1974
A/S Ardal og Sunndal Verk Norway 1965	B = A = P = Fab.	0 0 330	State Alcan	75.0 25.0	100% state 1947–1964; 50%–50% 1965–1974
Aughinish Alumina, Ltd. Ireland 1982	B = A = P =	0 410 0	Alcan Billiton (Shell) Anaconda	40.0 35.0 25.0	Currently under construction
British Aluminium Co., Ltd. (Balco) United Kingdom 1958–1978	B = A = P = Fab.	0 103 141	Tube Investments Reynolds	52.0 48.0	Now TI 58%; public institutions 42%
Canadian British Aluminium Canada 1957–1968	B = A = P =	0 0 104	Balco Reynolds Tube Investments	54.0 30.0 6.0	100% Reynolds since 1968
Cia Brasileira de Aluminio (CBA) Brazil 1955	B = A = P = Fab.	120 82 60	Industria Votorantim State	80.0 20.0	

Joint-venture firm, location, start-up year (and termination year if relevant)	Capacity of wholly owned or controlled operations, 1979 or at termination (thousands of tons)		Partners and equity shares, 1979 or at termination (in percentages)		Other information
Cia Mineira de Aluminio (Alcominas) Brazil 1970	B = A = P =	65 70 60 Fab.	Alcoa Hanna Mining Brazilian Interests	50.0 30.0 20.0	
Cie des Bauxites de Guinée Guinea 1973	B = A = P =	1,920 0 0	Halco Mining State	51.0 49.0	Halco Mining is Alcan 27%; Alcoa 27%; Martin Marietta 20%; PUK 10%; VAW 10%; Montedison 6%
Comalco, Ltd. Australia 1961	B = A = P =	2,800 0 112 Fab.	Kaiser Conzinc Riotinto of Australia Public	45.0 45.0 10.0	Largely independent of parents in operational and strategic senses; own corporate image
Consolidated Aluminum Corp. (Conalco) United States 1971	B = A = P =	0 0 163 Fab.	Alusuisse Phelps Dodge	60.0 40.0	Formed in 1971 merger of Alusuisse's U.S. operations and Phelps Dodge's operations
Delphi Bauxites Sa Greece Pre-1955	B = A = P =	60 0 0	VAW PUK	50.0 50.0	
Det Norsk Nitrid Aluminium (DNN) Norway pre-1955–1975	B = A = P =	0 0 24	Alcan Balco	50.0 50.0	33.3% PUK to 1957; now 100% state
Dubai Aluminium Co. (Dubal) Dubai 1979	B = A = P =	0 0 135	State Alusmelter Holdings	80.0 20.0	Alusmelter Holdings is: Alcan 40%; National Southwire Corp. 40%; 20% unallocated as yet
Eastalco Aluminum Co. United States 1976	B = A = P =	0 0 160	PUK Alumax	50.0 50.0	Was 100% PUK until capacity doubled in 1976
Empresa Nacional del Aluminio (Endasa) Spain 1969	B = A = P =	0 0 126 Fab.	State Alcan Other	50.0 25.0 25.0	Was originally (from 1949) a PUK-state joint venture
Eurallumina S.p.A. Italy 1972	B = A = P =	0 370 0	Alsar Alumetal Comalco Metallgesellschaft	41.7 20.8 20.0 17.5	

Joint-venture firm, location, start-up year (and termination year if relevant)	Capacity of wholly owned or controlled operations, 1979 or at termination (thousands of tons)		Partners and equity shares, 1979 or at termination (in percentages)		Other information
Friguia Consortium	B =	360	Frialco Co.	51.0	Frialco Co. is:
Guinea	A =	360	State	49.0	Noranda 38.5%;
1973	P =	0			PUK 36.5%;
					Alusuisse 10%;
					Balco 10%; VAW
					5%; was 100%
					Frialco 1960-1973
Ghana Bauxite Co., Ltd.	B =	88	State	55.0	Was 100% Balco to
Ghana	A =	0	Balco	45.0	1972
1972	P =	0			
Gladstone Aluminium	B =	0	Comalco	30.0	Currently under
Australia	A =	0	Kaiser	20.0	construction
1982	P =	206	Sumitomo Group	21.5	
			Kobe Steel	9.5	
			Mitsubishi Corp.	9.5	
			Yoshida Kogyo	9.5	
Gove joint venture	B =	1,042	Alusuisse	70.0	Gove Alumina is:
Australia	A =	564	Gove Alumina	30.0	CSR Limited 51%;
1971	P =	0			Peko-Wallsend
					12.6%; Australian
					Mutual Provident
					Society 12.1%;
					Mutual Life &
					Citizens' Society
					9.1%; Bank of New
					South Wales 5%;
					Commercial Banking
					Company of Sydney
					5%; and Elders
					IXL 5%
Granges Aluminium	B =	0	Grangesberg AB	79.0	Was 50% Alcan to
Sweden	A =	0	Alcan	21.0	1950
1943	P =	83			
Hamburg Aluminiumwerk GmbH	B =	0	Reynolds	33.3	Was 100% Reynolds
West Germany	A =	0	VAW	33.3	1974–1975
1976	P =	100	VM-RB	33.3	
Hindustan Aluminium Corp., Ltd.	B =	40	Birla family	73.0	
(Hindalco)	A =	95	Kaiser	27.0	
India					
1963					
Howmet Aluminum Corp.	B =	0	PUK	69.0	PUK built up share
United States	A =	0	Local interests	31.0	from 40% in 1962
1962–1975	P =	198			to 100% in 1975
Indian Aluminium Co., Ltd. (Indal)	B =	80	Alcan	55.0	Began as 67% Alcan
India	A =	113	Local interests	45.0	
1943	P =	118			

APPENDIX D

Joint-venture firm, location, start-up year (and termination year if relevant)	Capacity of wholly owned or controlled operations, 1979 or at termination (thousands of tons)		Partners and equity shares, 1979 or at termination (in percentages)		Other information
Industria Venezolana de Alumina (Venalum) Venezuela 1978	B = A = P =	0 0 70	CVG Japanese interests	80.0 20.0	
Intalco Aluminum Corp. United States 1966	B = A = P =	0 0 236	PUK Alumax	50.0 50.0	
Iranian Aluminium Co. (Iralco) Iran 1972	B = A = P =	0 0 45	State Reynolds Pakistan government	82.5 12.5 5.0	
Jamaica Reynolds Bauxite Partners Jamaica 1978	B = A = P =	625 0 0	State Reynolds	51.0 49.0	Was 100% Reynolds
Jamalcan Jamaica 1978	B = A = P =	581 563 0	Alcan State	93.0 7.0	Was 100% Alcan
Jamalco Jamaica 1978	B = A = P =	436 280 0	Alcoa State	94.0 6.0	Was 100% Alcoa
Kaiser Jamalco Bauxite Jamaica 1978	B = A = P =	1,279 0 0	State Kaiser	51.0 49.0	Was 100% Kaiser
Kaiser-Preussag Aluminium GmbH & Co. West Germany 1971	B = A = P =	0 0 72	Kaiser Preussag	50.0 50.0	
Leichtmetallgesellschaft GmbH West Germany 1972–1976	B = A = P = Fab.	0 0 113	Alusuisse Metallgesellschaft	50.0 50.0	Now 98% Alusuisse
Madras Aluminium Co., Ltd. India 1966	B = A = P = Fab.	0 25 25	Public Alumetal	73.0 27.0	
Mineracao Rio do Norte SA (MRN) Brazil 1979	B = A = P =	700 0 0	Companhia Vale do Rio Doce (CVRD) Alcan CBA Ardal og Sunndal Norsk Hydro Empresa Reynolds Billiton	46.0 19.0 10.0 5.0 5.0 5.0 5.0 5.0	Will be greatly expanded in the future

Joint-venture firm, location, start-up year (and termination year if relevant)	Capacity of wholly owned or controlled operations, 1979 or at termination (thousands of tons)		Partners and equity shares, 1979 or at termination (in percentages)		Other information
Mitsui Alumina Co., Ltd.	B =	0	Mitsui	90.0	CSR controls Gove
Japan	A =	205	CSR Limited	10.0	Alumina
1973	P =	0			
Mosal Aluminium	B =	0	Elkem-Spigerverket	55.0	Was 50% to 50% to
Norway	A =	0	Alcoa	45.0	1978
1958	P =	177			
National Southwire Aluminum Co.	B =	0	National Steel	50.0	Southwire is 20%
United States	A =	0	Southwire	50.0	owned by National
1969	P =	163			Steel
New Zealand Aluminium Smelters,	B =	0	Comalco	50.0	
Ltd. (NZAS)	A =	0	Showa Denko	25.0	
New Zealand	P =	150	Sumitomo	25.0	
1972					
Nippon Light Metal Co., Ltd.	B =	0	Alcan	50.0	Was 100% locally
Japan	A =	450	Local interests	50.0	owned from 1939
1952	P =	370			
	Fab.				
Ormet Corp.	B =	0	Conalco	66.0	Was 50% Revere,
United States	A =	280	Revere	34.0	50% Olin Mathieson
1958	P =	236			to 1973
Pechiney Nederland NV	B =	0	PUK	90.0	
Netherlands	A =	0	Hunter Douglas	10.0	
1971	P =	170			
Queensland Alumina, Ltd.	B =	0	Comalco	30.3	
Australia	A =	1,230	Kaiser	28.3	
1967	P =	0	Alcan	21.4	
			PUK	20.0	
Societa Alluminio Veneto per	B =	0	Alusuisse	50.0	Was 100% Alusuisse
Azioni (SAVA)	A =	0	EFIM (state)	50.0	from 1928
Italy	P =	30			
1973					
Sor-Norge Aluminium A/S	B =	0	Alusuisse	74.8	
Norway	A =	0	Norsk Hydro	19.5	
1965	P =	70	Compadec	5.2	
South East Asian Bauxites, Ltd.	B =	160	Alcan	70.0	
Malaysia	A =	0	Local interests	30.0	
1956	P =	0			
Union des Bauxites de France	B =	38	Balco	88.0	
France	A =	0	PUK	12.0	
pre-1955	P =	0			
Volta Aluminium Co., Ltd.	B =	0	Kaiser	90.0	
Ghana	A =	0	Reynolds	10.0	
1967	P =	200			

Variables and Data Used in the Primary–Fabricated
Products Regression Models of Chapter 5

The definitions of the variables used in the regression models of
Chapter 5 are as follows:

$$VI\%_i = \frac{1}{8} \sum_{t=1969}^{1976} \left(\frac{\text{gross shipments of product } i \text{ by integrated producers in year } t}{\text{gross shipments of product } i \text{ by all producers in year } t} \right) \cdot 10^2$$

$$VI\%_t = \left(\frac{\text{gross shipments of all wrought products by integrated producers in year } t}{\text{gross shipments of all wrought products by all producers in year } t} \right) \cdot 10^2$$

$$NF_i = \left(\begin{array}{l} \text{number of plants in the U.S.} \\ \text{in 1969 producing product } i \end{array} \right) \cdot 10^{-2}$$

$$Nm_i = \left\{ \begin{array}{l} 1 \text{ for aluminum cable steel-reinforced and} \\ \quad \text{bare cable, powder, and castings} \\ 0 \text{ for other products} \end{array} \right.$$

$ELAS_i$ = the absolute value of the long run elasticity of demand
for product i

MES_i = (gross shipments of product i in 1969 in tons $\div NF_i$) $\cdot$
10^{-5}

$ELAS \cdot MES_i = ELAS_i \cdot MES_i$

$$G_i = \frac{1}{14} \sum_{t=1960}^{1973} \left(\frac{\text{gross shipments of product } i \text{ in year } t}{\text{gross shipments of product } i \text{ in year } t-1} \right) \cdot 10^2$$

$$VAR_i = \sum_{t=1960}^{1973} \left(\frac{\text{gross shipments of product } i \text{ in year } t}{\text{gross shipments of product } i \text{ in year } t-1} \right)^2 \cdot 10^{-3}$$

NPP_i = number of basic aluminum firms producing primary aluminum in the U.S. in year t

$C3_t$ = U.S. primary-smelting capacity of Alcoa, Reynolds, and Kaiser at the start of year t as a percentage of total U.S. capacity at the start of year t

$H_t = \sum_j S_{jt}$ where S_{jt} = the fractional share of the jth firm in U.S. primary-smelting capacity at the start of year t

CU_t = (U.S. primary aluminum production in year t) ÷ (U.S. primary aluminum capacity at the start of year t)

Data on the cross-sectional variables are given in Table E.1. The data on $VI\%_i$, $VI\%_i$, MES_i, G_i and VAR_i come from the U.S.

Table E.1. Data on the cross-sectional variables.

Product (i)	$VI\%_i$	NF_i	NM_i	$ELAS_i$	MES_i	G_i	VAR_i
Sheet	82.8	.61	0	1.80	.305	10.9	.2727
Plate	90.0	.12	0	2.01	.305	3.42	.0906
Foil	83.1	.26	0	1.82	.0977	8.50	.1329
Extrusions	46.0	2.08	0	1.84	.0417	7.11	.2022
Welded tube	45.5	.24	0	0.791	.0189	11.9	.6434
Powder	68.9	.21	1	0.50	.0596	20.0	.4168
Forgings and impacts	72.3	.67	0	1.70	.0114	8.86	2.4228
Rolled and continuous-cast rod and bar	74.2	.31	0	1.24	.0452	9.61	1.3064
Bare wire	52.1	.83	0	1.34	.0055	5.42	.2386
Aluminium cable steel-reinforced and bare cable	86.7	.39	1	0.383	.0558	7.47	.3096
Insulated and covered wire and cable	56.7	.77	0	0.383	.0147	14.7	.3985
Castings	5.0	28.0	1	1.33	.0028	3.43	.1041

Department of Commerce, "Aluminum Ingot and Mill Products," *Current Industrial Reports,* various issues, 1965–1979.

The data on NF_i, NPP_t, $C3$, H_t and CU_t come from the Aluminum Association. *Aluminum Statistical Review,* various years, 1965–1979.

The data on $ELAS_i$ come from Table 5.5.

Notes

1. Introduction

1. R. H. Coase, "Industrial Organization: A Proposal for Research," in V. R. Fuchs, ed., *Policy Issues and Research Opportunities in Industrial Organization* (New York: National Bureau of Economic Research, 1972), pp. 60, 64.

2. Coase, "Industrial Organization," p. 60.

3. Harvey Aluminum, Inc., *Annual Report*, 1962, p. 2. Harvey has subsequently been acquired by the Martin Marietta Corporation.

4. *Staff Report of the Council on Wage and Price Stability into Aluminum Prices, 1974–75* (Washington, D.C.: Executive Office of the President, 1976), p. ii.

5. Ibid., p. 227.

6. *Australian Financial Review,* November 6, 1978, p. 1.

7. *Australian Financial Review,* October 25, 1978, p. 20 (verbatim text of the Minister's statement).

8. Ibid., p. 21.

9. The $20 million figure comes from an investigation of the costs of some Caribbean bauxite mining projects in the early 1960s, as reported in the "Project Surveys" published in the January issues of the *Engineering and Mining Journal* over the period.

10. Charles River Associates, *An Economic Analysis of the Aluminum Industry* (Cambridge, Mass., 1971), pp. 2.12–2.14. Since the increases in royalties and so forth, variable costs in Caribbean mines have been estimated at 95 percent of average costs; see "The World Aluminum Industry," Intercollegiate Case Clearing House, Case no. 375–351 (Boston: Intercollegiate Case Clearing House, 1975), p. 6.

11. From data given by R. B. McKern, *Multinational Enterprise and Natural Resources* (Sydney: McGraw-Hill, 1976), pp. 219–220.

12. From R. W. Hoppe, "Sangaredi—an African Plateau of Bauxite," *Engineering and Mining Journal,* August 1977, pp. 83–90.

13. "1978 Survey of Mine and Plant Expansion," *Engineering and Mining Journal,* January 1978, p. 68.

14. United Nations, Economic and Social Council, *Pre-Investment Data for the Aluminum Industry* (ST/CID/9), Studies in Economics of Industry, vol. 2 (New York: United Nations, 1966), p. 10. These figures are based on data from U.S. plants in the mid-1960s. The proportions probably have not changed much. The residual 6 percent was described as "miscellaneous costs."

15. From surveys of mine and plant expansion published in the January issues of the *Engineering and Mining Journal,* 1969–1975.

16. McKern, *Multinational Enterprise,* pp. 221–224, for the Gove and Queensland Alumina projects; *Engineering and Mining Journal* annual surveys for the Alpart project; and Revere Copper and Brass, Inc., *Annual Report,* 1975, p. 12.

17. United Nations, *Pre-Investment Data,* p. 18, and personal communication with executives of Alumax, Inc.

18. Ibid.

19. Ibid., p. 13.

20. Ibid., p. 12.

21. *Report of the Council on Wage and Price Stability into Aluminum Prices, 1974–75,* pp. 27–30.

22. U.S. Bureau of the Census, *1972 Census of Manufactures: Industry Series: Non-ferrous Metal Mills and Miscellaneous Primary Metal Products,* MC72(2)–33D (Washington, D.C.: Government Printing Office, 1975).

2. Upstream Vertical Integration

1. G. J. Stigler, "The Division of Labor Is Limited by the Extent of the Market," *Journal of Political Economy* 59 (June 1951), 185–193.

2. Ibid., p. 190.

3. Ibid., p. 188.

4. This conclusion is accurate across a wide variety of assumptions about the structure of the industry and the production functions involved. For a synthesis of the quite extensive literature on the welfare implications of this type of integration, see F. R. Warren-Boulton, *Vertical Control of Markets* (Cambridge, Mass.: Ballinger, 1978). Warren-Boulton also explains that backward integration is not the only possible solution to the unprofitability of bauxite mining. Discriminatory price behavior by the downstream producer on its input markets is theoretically possible.

5. D. H. Wallace, *Market Control in the Aluminum Industry* (Cambridge, Mass.: Harvard University Press, 1937), esp. chaps. 1–9.

6. G. A. Baudart, "Aluminium and Integration," in *Integration in Aluminium* (London: Metal Bulletin Ltd., 1969), p. 37. Baudart, at the time of writing, was an executive in Pechiney Ugine Kuhlmann (PUK).

7. For a more detailed account of these events, see M. J. Peck, *Competition in the Aluminum Industry: 1945–1958* (Cambridge, Mass.: Harvard University Press, 1961), pp. 8–14.

8. Ibid., p. 21.

9. M. R. Rayner, *Marketing Australian Bauxite* (Melbourne: Comalco Ltd., 1975), p. 4.

10. National Steel Corporation, *Annual Report,* 1969, p. 16; 1973, p. 15.

11. Amax, Inc., *Annual Report,* 1964, p. 4.

12. Anaconda Co., *Annual Report,* 1968, p. 3.

13. Stigler, "The Division of Labor," p. 190.

14. T. S. Greening, "Oil Wells, Pipelines, Refineries and Gas Stations: A Study of Vertical Integration" (Ph.D. diss., Harvard University, 1976), p. 157.

15. From an interview with A. G. Powell, General Manager, Swiss Aluminium Australia, Ltd., November, 1978.

16. E. A. Kirke, "Alumina From Darling Range Bauxite" (Paper presented to the Australian Institute of Mining and Metals Conference, Perth, Western Australia, May 1973), p. 562. Kirke was Alcoa of Australia's technical manager at their Kwinana refinery at the time of writing.

17. D. Wood, planning manager, Smelting Division, Comalco Ltd., during an interview in January, 1979.

18. Quoted during my interview with A. G. Powell of Swiss Aluminium Australia.

19. Reynolds Metals Co., *Form 10-K,* U.S. Securities and Exchange Commission, 1976, p. 5.

20. J. W. Moberly, "World Alumina Production Capacity," mimeographed (Menlo Park, Cal.: Stanford Research Institute International, 1978).

21. Ibid.

22. Interview with G. C. O'Farrell, general manager, and F. Ainsworth, secretary-financial manager, of Gove Alumina Ltd., November 1978.

23. Showa Denko K.K., *Showa Denko* (Tokyo: Showa Denko, 1975), p. 20.

24. Kirke, "Alumina From Darling Range Bauxite," p. 560.

25. F. M. Scherer, *Industrial Market Structure and Economic Performance* (Chicago: Rand McNally, 1971), p. 242.

26. W. Fellner, *Competition among the Few* (New York: Augustus M. Kelly, 1965), pp. 245–246.

27. For a detailed analysis producing this result, and the outcomes under several other, similar vertical market structures, see Warren-Boulton, *Vertical Control of Markets,* chap. 4.

28. O. E. Williamson, "The Vertical Integration of Production: Market Failure Considerations," *American Economic Review* 61 (May

1971), 112–123; and "Transaction-Cost Economics: The Governance of Contractual Relations," *Journal of Law and Economics* 22 (October 1979), 233–261.

29. K. J. Arrow, "Vertical Integration and Communication," *Bell Journal of Economics* 6 (Spring 1975), 173–182.

30. Comalco Ltd., *Weipa: Developing an Aluminium Industry* (Melbourne: Comalco, 1977), p. 6.

31. O. E. Williamson, *Markets and Hierarchies: Analysis and Antitrust Implications* (New York: Free Press, 1975), pp. 31–32.

32. The words in quotation marks are those of Joe S. Bain in his seminal work *Barriers to New Competition: Their Character and Consequences in Manufacturing Industries* (Cambridge, Mass.: Harvard University Press, 1956). Comparison of my data on aluminum with Bain's quantitative data and classification scheme seemed to put bauxite mining toward the top of Bain's classification. This was made even more approximate by the fact that Bain's work relates to domestic industries, while I regard the bauxite industry as international.

33. Peck, *Competition in Aluminum*, pp. 166–173, and H. M. Mann, "Seller Concentration, Barriers to Entry, and Rates of Return in Thirty Industries, 1950–1960," *Review of Economics and Statistics* 48 (August 1966), 296–307.

34. This has been shown quite generally in J. M. Vernon and D. A. Graham, "Profitability of Monopolization by Vertical Integration," *Journal of Political Economy* 79 (July/August 1971), 924–925. The precise nature and size of the profits are examined under particular circumstances by R. Schmalensee, "A Note on the Theory of Vertical Integration," *Journal of Political Economy* 81 (March/April 1973), 442–449; and by F. R. Warren-Boulton, "Vertical Control with Variable Proportions," *Journal of Political Economy* 82 (July/August 1974), 783–802.

35. Support for this description of the situation is found in Rayner, *Marketing Australian Bauxite*, pp. 3–4.

36. See Fellner, *Competition among the Few*, pp. 142–191.

37. My hunch here is supported by H. H. Newman, "Strategic Groups and the Structure-Performance Relationship" (Ph.D. diss., Harvard University, 1973). Newman argues that diversification leads firms in a given industry to have multiple and sometimes conflicting goals, which complicates the task of tacit coordination.

38. G. J. Stigler, "A Theory of Oligopoly," *Journal of Political Economy* 72 (February 1964), 44–61; and A. M. Spence, "Tacit Coordination of Industry Activity: Policing Non-Competitive Outcomes," Harvard Institute of Economic Research Discussion Paper no. 465 (Cambridge, Mass.: Harvard Institute of Economic Research, 1976).

39. Alusuisse, *Annual Report*, 1971, pp. 5–6.

40. See *Staff Report of the Council on Wage and Price Stability into Aluminum Prices, 1974–75* (Washington, D.C.: Executive Office of the President, 1976), pp. 107–159, 209–220.

41. J. R. Green, "Vertical Integration and Assurance of Markets," Harvard Institute of Economic Research Discussion Paper no. 383, 1974.

42. Rayner, *Marketing Australian Bauxite,* p. 3.

3. Upstream Long-term Sales Contracts

1. O. E. Williamson, "The Vertical Integration of Production: Market Failure Considerations," *American Economic Review* 61 (May 1971), 115–116.

2. J. E. Meade, *The Controlled Economy* (London: George Allen and Unwin, 1971), p. 183.

3. H. A. Simon, *Models of Man* (New York: John Wiley and Sons, 1957), p. 198. Emphasis in the original.

4. See O. E. Williamson, *Markets and Hierarchies: Analysis and Antitrust Implications* (New York: Free Press, 1975), esp. pp. 90–95.

5. Stanford Research Institute, *World Minerals Availability, 1975–2000: Aluminum, Copper, and Fluorspar* (Menlo Park, Cal.: Stanford Research Institute, 1976), p. 30.

6. Ibid., pp. 24 and 25 for 1975 data; Charles River Associates, *An Economic Analysis of the Aluminum Industry* (Cambridge, Mass.: Charles River Associates, 1971), p. 2.12, for 1970 data.

7. The factual details of this case study come from the following: "Anaconda Suit Asks That Reynolds Metals Meet Alumina Accord," *Wall Street Journal,* July 10, 1975; "Anaconda, Reynolds Settle 1975 Lawsuit over Alumina Dispute," *Wall Street Journal,* January 4, 1977; "Anaconda Files Suit against Reynolds in Contract Dispute," *American Metal Market,* July 11, 1975; "Pre-Trial Meeting Set in Anaconda Suit on Reynolds Alumina Deliveries," *American Metal Market,* May 5, 1976; "Reynolds, Anaconda Said in Accord on Conditions of 1972 Alumina Pact," *American Metal Market,* November 24, 1976; "Pact Settlement Gives Anaconda $4-Million," *American Metal Market,* January 5, 1977; and "Alumina Price Wrangle," *Metal Bulletin,* July 18, 1977.

8. T. C. Schelling, *The Strategy of Conflict* (Cambridge, Mass.: Harvard University Press, 1963), p. 187.

9. *American Metal Market,* January 5, 1977.

10. Atlantic Richfield Co., *Form 10-K,* U.S. Securities and Exchange Commission, 1976, p. A-22. It is not known who the supplying party to this contract is, but it could be Alcoa or Kaiser.

11. Williamson, *Markets and Hierarchies,* esp. pp. 41–54, 95–192, 117–154; and *Corporate Control and Business Behavior* (Englewood Cliffs, N.J.: Prentice Hall, 1970); K. J. Arrow, *The Limits of Organization*

(New York: Norton, 1974). See also the group of papers published under the heading "Economics of Internal Organization" in the *Bell Journal of Economics* 6 (Spring 1975).

12. J. K. Galbraith, *Economics and the Public Purpose* (Boston: Houghton Mifflin, 1973), pp. 122–133.

13. S. Macaulay, "Non-Contractual Relations in Business: A Preliminary Study," *American Sociological Review* 55 (February 1963), 58.

14. Williamson, *Markets and Hierarchies*, p. 10.

15. Comalco Ltd., *Annual Report*, 1974, p. 17.

16. Comalco Ltd., *Annual Report*, 1976, p. 6. The reader may have noted an apparent inconsistency between the *decline* in 1976 bauxite sales to Japan reported in this quotation and the 15.4 percent *increase* in 1976 bauxite shipments to Japan presented in the preceding table. Both data come from Comalco's annual reports, so the differences can be accounted for if sales are defined as price × quantity, and shipments as merely quantity, and possibly, in a bookkeeping sense, if sales and shipments are identified at different points in the production-loading-shipping sequence.

17. Comalco Ltd., *Annual Reports:* 1972, pp. 2, 3; 1973, p. 5; 1974, p. 5; 1975, p. 8; 1976, pp. 3, 6; and 1977, pp. 8, 13.

18. Ibid., 1975, p. 8.

19. See J. A. Stuckey, "Vertical Integration and Joint Ventures in the International Aluminum Industry" (Ph.D. diss., Harvard University, 1981), p. 195, for details.

20. See, for example, "Top Aluminum Trio Turn on Ad Pressures as Rivalry in Wrap Market Intensifies," *Advertising Week,* June 26, 1959, pp. 11–12. On price leadership see "Price Leadership: Aluminium's Stately Dance," *The Economist,* December 26, 1959, p. 1261; and for one pricing saga, see the *Engineering and Mining Journal,* January 1964, p. 21; February, p. 23; April, p. 23; June, p. 25; and July, p. 25.

21. For colorful descriptions of the battle, see "Battle for British Aluminium," *The Economist,* December 6, 1958, p. 913; and "How Reynolds Won the Battle," *Business Week,* January 17, 1959, p. 59. Alcoa may have had the last laugh, however, because British Aluminium turned out to be a continual drain on Reynold's financial performance, to the point where in early 1979 Reynolds sold its interest in the company.

22. For comprehensive discussions of Alcoa's problems in the late 1950s and early 1960s, see G. Bookman, "Alcoa Strikes Back," *Fortune,* November 1962, pp. 112, 114, 160; "Alcoa: Ordeal by Competition," *Forbes,* September 1, 1965, pp. 18–22; and J. Thackray, "Alcoa's Arduous Profits," *Management Today,* November 1969, pp. 89–91.

23. Bookman, "Alcoa Strikes Back," pp. 114, 116.

24. Bookman, "Alcoa Strikes Back," p. 160.

25. This summary of the causes of internal organization failure

comes from Williamson, *Markets and Hierarchies,* chap. 7; and Arrow, *Limits of Organization.*

26. A. D. Chandler, Jr., *Strategy and Structure* (Cambridge, Mass.: Massachusetts Institute of Technology Press, 1962); and O. E. Williamson, *Corporate Control and Business Behavior.*

27. J. M. Stopford and L. T. Wells, Jr., *Managing the Multinational Enterprise* (New York: Basic Books, 1972), p. 10.

28. Ibid., part I.

29. H. O. Armour and D. J. Teece, "Organizational Structure and Economic Performance: A Test of the Multidivisional Hypothesis," *Bell Journal of Economics* 9 (Spring 1978), 106–122.

30. Stopford and Wells, *Managing the Multinational Enterprise,* p. 60.

31. Chandler, *Strategy and Structure,* pp. 326–327, 337–340.

32. Readers with an interest in mathematical programming will see exciting prospects in the formalization of this constrained optimization problem. Their appetites will be further whetted by reading A. C. Hax, "Integration of Strategic and Tactical Planning in the Aluminum Industry," Massachusetts Institute of Technology, Operations Research Center, Technical Report no. 86 (Cambridge, Mass.: Massachusetts Institute of Technology, 1973). Hax builds a pair of interactive linear programming models, one modeling the long-run strategic issues associated with resource planning, the other oriented toward the tactical problems of short-range resource utilization. The models were built to assist management in a large integrated firm (almost certainly Kaiser). The Kaiser network at the time was less complicated than Alcoa's, but even so, the Hax model is excellent evidence of the complexity of the organizational task in an integrated aluminum firm.

33. R. Hill, "Can Alcan Fabricate a Healthier Future?" *International Management,* February 1972, pp. 40–42; and *The Economist,* September 6, 1969, pp. 48–49.

34. I. A. Litvak and C. J. Maule, *Alcan Aluminium Limited: A Case Study,* Royal Commission on Corporate Concentration, Study no. 13 (Ottawa: Minister of Supply and Services Canada, 1977), p. 119.

35. Ibid.

36. Alcan Aluminium, Ltd., *Annual Report,* 1977, p. 14.

37. Chandler, *Strategy and Structure,* p. 380.

4. Upstream Joint Ventures

1. J. F. Brodley, "The Legal Status of Joint Ventures under the Antitrust Laws: A Summary Assessment," *Antitrust Bulletin* 21 (Summer 1976), 453–483.

2. Olin Mathieson Chemical Corporation, *Annual Report,* 1956, p. 11.

3. James Beizer, "Alumina's Joint Venture is Set," *Iron Age*, August 4, 1966, p. 27.

4. "Amax-Mitsui (A)," Intercollegiate Case Clearing House, Case no. 9-375-350 (Boston: Intercollegiate Case Clearing House, 1975), p. 6.

5. D. J. Hibberd, "The Organizing of Consortia for Major Projects" (Paper presented to the Commonwealth Public Service Board Second Division Seminar, Canberra, September 1970), p. 3.

6. K. J. Arrow, *Limits of Organization* (New York: W. W. Norton, 1974), p. 33.

7. For a discussion of research and development economies of scale in mature industries see D. C. Mueller and J. E. Tilton, "Research and Development Costs as a Barrier to Entry," *Canadian Journal of Economics* 4 (November 1969), pp. 570–579.

8. J. Cook, "Staying on Top," *Forbes*, July 1, 1977, pp. 54–55.

9. J. H. Stopford and L. T. Wells, *Managing the Multinational Enterprise* (New York: Basic Books, 1972), pp. 102–103.

10. W. G. Friedmann and J. P. Beguin, *Joint International Business Ventures in Developing Countries* (New York: Columbia University Press, 1971), p. 382. See pp. 388–389 and 410–411 for details on the information summarized in the following paragraphs.

11. See R. J. M. Wyllie, "OBK, Guinea's National Bauxite Company, Operates 2,500,000-ton Mine and Railroad," *World Mining*, April 1976, pp. 72–75.

12. The information on Dubal comes from "Arab World's Second Aluminum Smelter to Start up in October," *Engineering and Mining Journal*, May 1979, pp. 39, 42.

13. P. R. Dixon, "Joint Ventures: What Is Their Impact on Competition?" *Antitrust Bulletin* 6 (May-June 1962), 399.

14. D. J. Hibberd, "The Organizing of Consortia for Major Projects," pp. 1–2.

15. J. Hirshleifer, "On the Theory of Optimal Investment Decision," *Journal of Political Economy* 66 (August 1958), 329–352.

16. For one of a number of rigorous proofs of risk independence, see S. C. Myers, "Procedures for Capital Budgeting under Uncertainty," *Industrial Management Review* 9 (Spring 1968), 1–20. For a nontechnical but clear exposition of the principle and its implications, see J. L. Treynor and F. Black, "Corporate Investment Decisions," in S. C. Myers, ed., *Modern Developments in Financial Management* (Hinsdalle, Ill.: Dryden Press, 1976), pp. 310–327.

17. For quite sophisticated alternative evaluation procedures, see J. L. Treynor, F. Black, A. A. Robichek, and S. C. Myers, "Conceptual Problems in the Use of Risk-Adjusted Discount Rates," *Journal of Finance* 21 (December 1966), 727–730. For a more pragmatic, though theoretically more naive, approach see J. F. Weston, "Investment De-

cisions Using the Capital Asset Pricing Model," *Financial Management* 2 (Spring 1973), 23–33.

18. On capital structure, see F. F. Modigliani and M. H. Miller, "The Cost of Capital, Corporation Finance, and the Theory of Investment," *American Economic Review* 48 (June 1958), 261–279; and on dividend policy, see their "Dividend Policy, Growth and the Valuation of Shares," *Journal of Business* 34 (October 1961), 411–433. In support of the conclusion on the relevance of capital structure, see the following articles: A. H. Chen and E. H. Kim, "Theories of Corporate Debt Policy: A Synthesis," *Journal of Finance* 34 (May 1979), 371–384, and the comment by E. S. Schwartz, 386–387; M. H. Miller, "Debt and Taxes," *Journal of Finance* 32 (May 1977), 261–276; and J. H. Scott, "Bankruptcy, Secured Debt, and Optimal Capital Structure," *Journal of Finance* 32 (March 1977), 1–19. On dividend policy, see F. Black, "The Dividend Puzzle," chap. 4 in S. C. Myers, ed., *Modern Developments in Financial Management;* and F. Black and M. Scholes, "The Effects of Dividend Yield and Dividend Policy on Common Stock Prices and Returns," *Journal of Financial Economics* 1 (May 1974), 1–22.

19. S. C. Myers, "Interactions of Corporate Financing and Investment Decisions — Implications for Capital Budgeting," *Journal of Finance* 29 (March 1974), 1–25.

20. For a summary of studies of agency costs, see T. E. Copeland and J. F. Weston, *Financial Theory and Corporate Policy* (Reading, Mass.: Addison-Wesley, 1979), chap. 12.

21. See L. Wynant, "Essential Elements of Project Financing," *Harvard Business Review* 58 (May-June 1980), 165–173.

22. Comalco, Limited, *Aluminium Smelting in New Zealand: Summary of Negotiations with Government since 1959* (Melbourne: Comalco, 1977), p. 9. This was the major source for my discussion of Comalco's projects.

23. Hibberd, "The Organizing of Consortia for Major Projects," pp. 1–2.

24. M. A. Mawby to K. J. Holyoake, 14 February 1966, quoted in Comalco, Limited, *Aluminium Smelting in New Zealand,* p. 14.

25. During the 1975 to 1977 slump in the industry, worldwide alumina capacity utilization averaged just over 80 percent, while QAL averaged over 100 percent of rated capacity.

26. Hibberd, "The Organizing of Consortia for Major Projects," p. 9.

27. A. M. Spence, "Tacit Co-ordination and Imperfect Information," *Canadian Journal of Economics* 13 (August 1978), 490–505.

28. A. Phillips, "A Theory of Interfirm Organization," *Quarterly Journal of Economics* 75 (November 1960), 607.

29. See H. H. Newman, "Strategic Groups and the Structure-Per-

formance Relationship," *Review of Economics and Statistics* 60 (August 1978), 417–427; R. E. Caves and M. E. Porter, "From Entry Barriers to Mobility Barriers: Conjectural Decisions and Contrived Deterrence to New Competition," *Quarterly Journal of Economics* 92 (May 1977), 421–441; and M. E. Porter, "The Structure within Industries and Companies' Performance," *Review of Economics and Statistics* 61 (May 1979), 214–227.

30. For example, see J. Pfeffer and P. Nowak, "Patterns of Joint Venture Activity: Implications for Antitrust Policy," *Antitrust Bulletin* 21 (Summer 1976), 315–339; and W. J. Mead, "The Competitive Significance of Joint Ventures," *Antitrust Bulletin* 12 (Fall 1967), 818–849.

31. M. J. Peck, *Competition in the Aluminum Industry: 1945–1958* (Cambridge, Mass.: Harvard University Press, 1961), chap. 10.

32. See, for example, Stopford and Wells, *Managing the Multinational Enterprise,* chaps. 11 and 12.

33. An "operation" is defined as being either a jointly owned firm, a wholly owned subsidiary in a nonhome country, or all of the plants in the home country.

34. Paraphrased from an interview with an executive who asked that this opinion remain anonymous.

35. K. J. Arrow, *The Limits of Organization.*

5. Downstream Vertical Integration

1. E. R. Corey, *The Development of Markets for New Materials: A Study of Building New End-Product Markets for Aluminum, Fibrous Glass, and the Plastics* (Boston: Division of Research, Harvard Business School, 1956), p. 234.

2. M. J. Peck, *Competition in the Aluminum Industry* (Cambridge, Mass.: Harvard University Press, 1961), p. 124. For the 1970s estimate, the volume of metal flowing from mill-products fabrication into manufacturing *within* the integrated firms was estimated as: U.S. primary and secondary production of metal + metal imports – net ingot shipments – [net U.S. producer mill-products shipments – (net ingot shipments – ingot exports – castings shipments)]. The assumptions are: (1) all ingot exports are arm's length rather than intracorporate, and (2) all metal used by independent fabricators goes into either castings or mill products. The ten-year average should remove any bias owing to differential inventory changes across the various stages of production. The definitions and data come from the Aluminum Association, *Aluminum Statistical Review 1977* (Washington, D.C.: The Aluminum Association, 1978).

3. M. E. Porter and A. M. Spence, "Vertical Integration and Differentiated Inputs," Harvard Institute of Economic Research, Discussion Paper no. 576, September 1977.

4. Peck, *Competition in Aluminum*, p. 123.

5. D. H. Wallace, *Market Control in the Aluminum Industry* (Cambridge, Mass.: Harvard University Press, 1937).

6. This point is brought out by F. R. Warren-Boulton, *Vertical Control of Markets: Business and Labor Practices* (Cambridge, Mass.: Ballinger, 1978), p. 66.

7. Wallace, *Market Control in Aluminum*, p. 217.

8. M. K. Perry, "Price Discrimination and Forward Integration: Alcoa Re-examined," Bell Laboratories Economics Discussion Paper no. 80, 1977.

9. Warren-Boulton, *Vertical Control of Markets*, pp. 73–74.

10. R. H. Bork, "Vertical Integration and the Sherman Act: The Legal History of an Economic Misconception," *University of Chicago Law Review* 18 (Autumn 1951), 198.

11. A good guide to the number, and specificity in application, of alloys is provided in Metals Week, *Aluminum: Profile of an Industry* (New York: Metals Week, 1969), pp. 52–59, 65.

12. M. K. Perry, "Price Discrimination and Forward Integration," *Bell Journal of Economics* 9 (Spring 1978), 209–217.

13. Unless otherwise indicated, all data on shipments come from the Aluminum Association, *Aluminum Statistical Review*, for various years.

14. The Charles River Associates have published several different versions of their econometric model of the aluminum industry; the version used here comes from their publication *Cartelization in the World Aluminum–Bauxite Market: Economic Analysis and Policy Implications* (Cambridge, Mass.: Charles River Associates, 1976).

15. Rank-order correlations are made using Spearman's rank-difference correlation coefficient. See J. P. Guilford and B. Fruchter, *Fundamental Statistics in Psychology and Education* (New York: McGraw-Hill, 1973), pp. 283–285.

16. The average was taken over the period 1969–1976 to remove short-term variations. The year 1969 is the first year for which the data are published, while 1976 was chosen so that there were sufficient observations to even out short-term variations and so that the data period would compare with the period over which the elasticities were estimated. In any case, trends in the integration percentages since 1969 have been slight.

17. Other versions of the CRA model produced comparable results. For example, estimates of the own-price short-run elasticity in other versions have been -0.558 and -0.066, and while somewhat higher than the -0.0146 estimate, they are still clearly inelastic.

18. *Staff Report of the Council on Wage and Price Stability into Aluminum Prices, 1974–75* (Washington, D.C.: Executive Office of the President, 1976), p. i.

19. Ibid., pp. 114–115.

20. Peck, *Competition in Aluminum,* pp. 29–34.

21. M. Spence, "Tacit Co-ordination and Imperfect Information," *Canadian Journal of Economics* 11 (August 1978), 490–505.

22. M. Spence, "Stable Prices, Fluctuating Demand, and Inventory Adjustments in Oligopolistic Industries," Harvard Institute of Economic Research Discussion Paper no. 463, March 1976.

23. The initial version of D. W. Carlton's work appears in "Market Behavior under Uncertainty" (Ph.D diss., Massachusetts Institute of Technology, 1975), but much of the material has been published in three papers: "Uncertainty, Production Lags, and Pricing," *American Economic Review* 67 (February 1977), 244–249; "Market Behavior with Demand Uncertainty and Price Inflexibility," *American Economic Review* 68 (September 1978), 571–584; and "Vertical Integration in Competitive Markets under Uncertainty," *Journal of Industrial Economics* 28 (March 1979), 189–190. For the other contributions, see J. R. Green, "Vertical Integration and Assurance of Markets," Harvard Institute of Economic Research Discussion Paper no. 383, October 1974; and I. Bernhardt, "Vertical Integration and Demand Variability," *Journal of Industrial Economics* 26 (March 1977), 213–229.

24. Much of the information on Alcan's history that follows comes from I. A. Litvak and C. J. Maule, *Alcan Aluminum, Limited: A Case Study,* Royal Commission on Corporate Concentration Study no. 13 (Ottawa: Minister of Supply and Services, 1977).

25. U.S., Congress, House, Select Committee on Small Business, Subcommittee No. 3, *Hearings, Aluminum Industry,* 84th Cong., 1st Sess., 1955, p. 144.

26. Peck, *Competition in Aluminum,* chap. 7, provides a detailed account of the independents' complaints regarding primary rationing between 1950 and 1956.

27. N. V. Davis, "Alcan Now Stronger, Sounder after Decade of Growth, Change," *The Compass* (June 1967), p. 4. *The Compass* is an Alcan publication.

28. Alcan Aluminium, Limited, *Annual Report,* 1958.

29. N. V. Davis, in a speech made to the Cleveland Society of Security Analysts, Cleveland, Ohio, May 5, 1971.

30. "Defensive Standoff," *Forbes,* February 15, 1969, p. 59.

31. U.S., Congress, House, Select Committee on Small Business, Subcommittee No. 3, *Hearings, Aluminum Industry,* 85th Cong., 1st and 2nd Sess., 1958, p. 325.

32. Noranda Mines, Ltd., "President's Address," Annual Meeting, 1966, pp. 8–9.

33. Corey, *The Development of Markets for New Materials,* p. 241. Emphasis mine.

34. The historical information on Reynolds comes from the lengthy and informative article "Look at the Reynolds Boys Now," *Fortune,* August 1953, p. 106.

35. The information on the U.S. tobacco industry summarized here comes from the excellent account in R. B. Tennant, *The American Cigarette Industry* (New Haven, Conn.: Yale University Press, 1950), esp. part 2.

36. "Reynolds Boys," p. 178.

37. Ibid., p. 109.

38. "Top Aluminum Trio Turn on Ad Pressures as Rivalry in Wrap Market Intensifies," *Advertising Week,* June 26, 1959, p. 11.

39. Ibid.

40. For a review of the PLC concept, see T. Levitt, "Exploit the Product Life Cycle," *Harvard Business Review* 43 (November-December, 1965), 81–94.

41. See M. E. Porter, "Interbrand Choice, Media Mix, and Market Performance," *American Economic Review* 66 (May 1976), 398–406; and W. S. Comanor and T. A. Wilson, "The Effect of Advertising on Competition: A Survey," *Journal of Economic Literature* 17 (June 1979), 467–470.

42. M. E. Porter, *Interbrand Choice, Strategy, and Bilateral Market Power* (Cambridge, Mass.: Harvard University Press, 1976), chaps. 2–6.

43. R. C. Blattberg and S. K. Sen, "Market Segmentation Using Models of Multidimensional Purchasing Behaviour," *Journal of Marketing* 38 (October 1974), 17–28.

44. "Out-Kaisering the Kaiser," *Forbes,* September 15, 1968, p. 25.

45. The opportunity to deploy specific and durable assets in industrial foil lowered the barriers to exit from consumer foil. See R. E. Caves and M. E. Porter, "Barriers to Exit," in R. T. Masson and P. D. Qualls, eds., *Essays in Industrial Organization in Honor of Joe S. Bain* (Cambridge, Mass.: Ballinger, 1976), chap 3.

Index